On the Edge of the Holocaust

From artist Manuel Kantor's book of anti-Nazi cartoons, *De Munich a Nuremberg*, published in Buenos Aires in 1946. The cartoon first appeared on June 20, 1938, in the newspaper *El Diario*, with the title "Racial Superiority." The text reads: "Berlin, 18– On the order of the Gestapo the pitiless campaign against the Jews has been extended to Germany as a whole. An eyewitness from Frankfurt stated that members of respected old families are dragged out of bed at dawn and brought to the police station. According to information every night 65 trucks full of Jews arrive at the Buchenwald concentration camp near Weimar."

On the Edge of the Holocaust

The Shoah in Latin American Literature and Culture

Edna Aizenberg

Brandeis University Press · Waltham, Massachusetts

BRANDEIS UNIVERSITY PRESS
An imprint of University Press of New England
www.upne.com

Manufactured in the United States of America
Typeset in Skolar by Passumpsic Publishing

COVER ILLUSTRATION: Diego Rivera, *Nazi Kultur*, from the mural series Portrait of America, New Workers' School, New York, 1933.
Additional information on this illustration can be found on the last printed page of this book.

Library of Congress Cataloging-in-Publication Data
available upon request

5 4 3 2 1

. . . un hombre lapidado, incendiado
y ahogado en cámaras letales,
un hombre que se obstina a ser inmortal
y que ahora ha vuelto a su batalla . . .

. . . A man stoned, burned
And suffocated in lethal chambers,
A man stubbornly immortal
Now returned to his battle . . .

JORGE LUIS BORGES, "Israel"

. . . .

Los que hemos sobrevivido en las afueras del holocausto, hemos estado muriendo día a día . . .

Those of us who have survived on the edge of the holocaust, have been dying day by day.

GABRIELA MISTRAL

Contents

Preface

Didn't All the Nazis Go to Argentina?

Didn't all the Nazis go to Argentina? The question inevitably pops up, like a knee-jerk reaction, whenever I mention Latin America and the Holocaust. Didn't all the Nazis go to Argentina, or Brazil, or Chile, or Paraguay?

The answer is, of course, some of the big Nazis, and more than a few little ones, did go to South America. These hierarchs of the National Socialist German Workers' Party (NSDAP), the biggest of them Adolf Eichmann, one of the major organizers of the Holocaust, arranged their escape to a future Fourth Reich on Latin American soil as the Third Reich was expiring and Adolf Hitler was swallowing poison in his underground Berlin bunker (or did he? Perhaps he escaped to Patagonia). Aided and abetted by sympathetic Vatican officials, the International Red Cross, the SS flight network known as Odessa, and dictators of the fascist ilk such as Paraguay's Alfredo Stroessner and Argentina's Juan Domingo Perón, Nazis were taken in by republics that wanted so-called Nazi gold, German know-how, and a "whitening" of their mestizo populations.

Stories of the hunted Hitler men, disguised under pseudonyms and handwoven ponchos, squirreled away in jungle hideouts and nondescript suburbs, and of buried Nazi bullion financing all manner of devious plots have circulated for decades, occasionally in scholarly fashion, more often embroidered and exaggerated, shutting out any other narratives about Latin America and the Shoah.[1] Now, some seventy years after the end of the Second World War, when accurate facts are more important than ever, it is time to tell the story of Latin American intellectuals and diplomats who refused to kowtow to Hitlerism—sometimes, dramatically, as the secret police were waiting or the bombs were falling—and who "represented" the Holocaust in written and visual culture.

In telling their story I don't aim for encyclopedic or handbook-like coverage, or for the conferring of sainthood. Rather, I travel back to the time of the Shoah, labeled by Jorge Luis Borges "the time of the wolf, the time of the sword," in order to show how five prominent Latin American authors, Borges, Clarice Lispector, Alberto Gerchunoff, João Guimãraes Rosa, and Gabriela Mistral, *wrote the disaster*, to paraphrase the influential French literary theorist Maurice Blanchot, combining overt and covert political-diplomatic activism with culture making—literature, journalism, and art. Leaving aside the frequent separation between Spanish- and Portuguese-language letters, I try to show how these authors' imaginings early on challenge prevailing truths about Latin American literature from that period, and question misconceptions about Latin Americans and writing on the Shoah. While I focus on these major culture makers, the import of my meditations goes beyond the five writers to reveal a whole new way of interpreting the Shoah in Latin American thought and culture, until now eclipsed by an emphasis on the United States, Europe, and Israel.

The English-speaking world knows almost nothing about the implications of the anti-Nazi work of these world-class authors: Borges, a leading light of twentieth-century fiction, whom I have placed first in the book in order to introduce its themes and conundrums; Lispector, my second author, a major innovator of Brazilian-Portuguese letters, who shared with Borges the "fantasist who ignored reality" label; Gerchunoff, patriarch of Judeo-Argentine writing, whose combat prose was among the earliest to denounce the Shoah in Latin America; and finally, the duo of diplomats who fought Hitler in situ, Guimarães Rosa—together with Lispector the towering figure of twentieth-century Brazilian literature, and consul in Hamburg under the Nazis—and the Chilean Mistral, first winner of the Nobel Prize for Literature after the hecatomb of the Second World War, and consul in Nice and Petrópolis, Brazil, when anti-Nazism wasn't the fashion. The English-speaking world knows almost nothing about how they all defied Hitler and confronted dilemmas of the literary craft—the "barbarism" of poetry after Auschwitz, in Theodor Adorno's dictum—not only *after* but even *during* Auschwitz. As a significant complement to my reading of what they wrote, I incorporate Latin American anti-Nazi visual art in the form of caustic drawings and powerful cartoons.

The Shoah, Reality and Unreality

My book fills a huge gap in Holocaust Studies, where Latin America has scarcely wiggled through, but it also modifies certain truisms of Latin American Studies, most of all about the nature of regionalism and reality in the area's literature of the Second World War and postwar. The intellectuals I study were creating at the very moment when a strong literary current was turning away from Latin America's long-reigning documentary-regionalist mode and the purported reproduction of social reality, from what Erich Auerbach, the German-Jewish intellectual penning in Turkish exile after fleeing for his life from Nazism, called *mimesis*.[2]

In the shift away from mimesis, fantasy, dreamwork, interior monologue, linguistic novelty, the uncanny, and the ersatz marked much of these authors' innovative work, often feted precisely for turning away from traditional realism, even as the pull of regionalism continued—the pampas, the backlands, the mountains, the pueblos. Given this antimimetic turn, how could they write about the most chillingly real of events with the tools of unreality? It isn't coincidental that Erich Auerbach reviewed the history of mimesis in the Western tradition at exactly this juncture, when the reality of the West as he knew it was under siege, or that he did it from the eastern edge of the Western order. The Latin Americans arguably performed a similar staging of a mimesis-in-crisis at the same time, from the Occident's other edge, its southern outposts. They have not been given enough credit for this staging.

The Shoah presented an unprecedented human and literary challenge, still debated by authors and critics of every nationality and stripe. It may well be that the Latin Americans began to confront this fantasy/reality conundrum during the Hitler moment itself because they didn't fight in the conflict (Brazil was a late exception) and were not occupied by the Nazis and, more significantly, because they possessed what Clarice Lispector called a *lateral* view vis-à-vis Europe, a perceptive distancing, as Borges too argued in his highly influential essay "The Argentine Writer and Tradition," drafted postwar with the shadow of Nazism still hovering. There, he stated that Latin Americans, placed both inside and outside Western culture, tied to it yet feeling different, could irreverently innovate using all European themes—with fortunate consequences. His Holocaust story "Deutsches Requiem," which I analyze in the opening chapter, exemplifies this stance. Borges's perceptive push-me, pull-you posture, close to the conflict yet not part of it, offered the writers the space for creating astonishing hybrid texts.

Because fantasy or no fantasy, the real demanded its due, straining the limits of the made-up. So poets like Gabriela Mistral, who agonized over Europe's self-immolation, questioned how travail and torment could be rendered through the beauty of high art, and stripped away prettifying in favor of plain speaking. And narrators like Alberto Gerchunoff, head of the Argentine journalists' antifascist league, chronicled the creeping Final Solution in the press, giving up the local-colorist Jewish gaucho of his early work for unvarnished reporting and denouncing until such time as the Nazi beast would find its end. João Guimarães Rosa, who as a consul in Nazi Hamburg helped save Jews, developed hybrid modes that oscillated between fact and fiction, and Clarice Lispector, who denounced purity projects even while she was the wife of a Brazilian diplomat in wartime Italy, adopted a path that presented nonrepresentative, traumatic prose.

What ties these writers together literarily is the creation, through the Shoah, of fresh forms of narration, or of journalism, or of poetry, each author coming at the unconventional production from a different vantage point, but ultimately pointing ways toward post-Holocaust literature.

The Shoah requires us to rethink these authors' writing, complicating interpretations of some of their well-known and lesser-known works. Seen through the Holocaust, we may never read them in the same way. I hope my book achieves this purpose.

Indirection is one key to what all these intellectuals did, a reflection not only of the lateral, inside-outside view, but in some cases of censorship and in others of the remaining weight of the local. At the time, to be "Latin American" and not be accused of foreignness or irrelevance still largely required that you write on "national" themes and spaces. Borges and Lispector suffered particularly for not adhering to this "standard." So even if the works I study, in a wide generic range, don't always *declare* the Shoah, if they are set in a Brazilian landscape among rural folk, or they occupy a niche in an author's oeuvre, the Shoah is there, laterally and forcefully. How it is there makes for absorbing reading on the question of "poetry after Auschwitz," and for an engaging decoding of the signs that combine the "Latin American" and the "European."

To paint a fuller picture of what the Latin Americans did and wrote, I extensively use a variety of genres—personal letters, diplomatic dispatches, unpublished diaries, journal essays, and newspaper articles, along with fiction and poetry. Today we view "literature" as a continuum on which fact and fiction tussle, sustaining and challenging each other, and we acknowledge life-writing and the epistolary as legitimate literary genres, part of an authorial legacy. We can't understand Borges's or Lispector's or Gerchunoff's or Guimãraes Rosa's or Mistral's art, *particularly* when it comes to the Shoah, without taking this wider view of the literary craft that has replaced narrow constructions of "literature."

I was privileged to have access to archival material that shakes up all sorts of received ideas about the five authors. I have especially benefited from written and pictorial documentation I found in the Arquivo Clarice Lispector at the Fundaçao Casa Rui Barbosa and the Biblioteca Nacional in Rio de Janeiro; the Biblioteca Nacional and Archivo del Ministerio de Relaciones Exteriores in Santiago, Chile; the Archivo Gerchunoff at the Instituto Emilio Ravignani of the University of Buenos Aires; the CeDInCi (Centro de Documentatción e Investigación de la Cultura de Izquierdas en Argentina, Documentation and Research Center of the Cultures of the Left), the Fundación Espigas, Biblioteca Nacional, and the AMIA–Marc Turkow Center for Research on Argentine Jewry, also in Buenos Aires; the Department of Righteous Among the Nations in Yad Vashem, Jerusalem; the Library of Congress, Washington, D.C.; the Victoria Ocampo Papers, Houghton Library, Harvard University; the Gabriela Mistral Collection, Barnard College; the Kupferberg Holocaust Resource Center and Archives, Queensborough Community College, City University of New York; the Library of the Jewish Theological Seminary of America; the Leo Baeck Institute and YIVO materials at the Center for Jewish History; the Jewish Division of the New York Public Library; and the Annenberg Rare Books and Manuscripts Library at the University of Pennsylvania.

I also have gained from the warm generosity of Professor Georg Otte of the University of Minas Gerais, Brazil, in obtaining João Guimãraes Rosa's unpublished diary, and the special help of Marcela Cavada and Gloria Duhard in Santiago for helping me see the diplomatic face of Gabriela Mistral; also in Santiago, Ana Maria Tapia of the Center for Jewish Studies at the University of Chile for patiently assisting me in obtaining the first published version of Mistral's poem "Al pueblo hebreo" with its original, attractive, Art Deco frame; Eliane Vasconcelos in Rio for shining a light on Guimarães Rosa and Lispector, and Anita Weinstein in Buenos Aires for all things Gerchunoffian and otherwise. Nicholas Watts of the Barclays Group Archives in Manchester, England, helped me with Mistralian material. Dr. Ariel Feldman of the University of Chicago also helped get important sources on Mistral. I would especially like to acknowledge Phyllis Deutsch, editor extraordinaire, who helped give this book its shape and supported this project with unfailing enthusiasm; Jason Warshof was a superb copy editor, tracking down errors in the most hidden corners of the text. Deep thanks to my dear family for their support as I researched and wrote this book. Above all, as for the last fifty years, to my beloved Josh-Isidoro-Shie, a man of many names and many talents. Gracias, mi amor.

It is my intention that this book, in its double thrust in Latin American and Holocaust Studies, counter existing emphases on Borges and Lispector's fantastic escapism, Guimãraes Rosa's uncanny regionalism, Mistral's Americanist maternalism, and Gerchunoff's quaint gauchism, even as it certifies that the challenge of the Shoah was not alien to Latin Americans. The Nazis may have "gone to Argentina," but the anti-Nazis were there, ready to stand against them.

On the Edge of the Holocaust

Seré fusilado por torturador y asesino.
I'll be shot as a torturer and murderer.
. . . "Deutsches Requiem"

1

Jorge Luis Borges "Represents" the Shoah

Borges at the United Nations

On September 20, 2002, Ramsey Clark, a former United States attorney general, addressed a sharply worded letter to the United Nations. In it he condemned his country's imminent invasion of Iraq, and desperately appealed to Secretary-General Kofi Annan to seek peace, not war. Amid its thick discussion of no-fly zones and weapons inspections Clark's politically charged missive contained the following, seemingly unlikely, literary reference to a story written in the 1940s: "Like the Germany described by Jorge Luis Borges in 'Deutsches Requiem,' George Bush has now 'proffered (to the world) violence and faith in the sword,' as Nazi Germany did. And as Borges wrote, it did not matter to faith in the sword that Germany was defeated. 'What matters is that violence . . . now rules.' Two generations of Germans have rejected that faith," Clark asserted. "Their perseverance in the pursuit of peace will earn the respect of succeeding generations everywhere" (Clark 2002). Clark's letter spread over

This illustration accompanied *Escenas de la crueldad nazi* (Scenes of Nazi Cruelty), Borges's Spanish translation of Heinrich Mann's anti-Nazi vignettes. The translation appeared in *Revista Multicolor de los Sábados*, the Saturday magazine of the strongly anti-Nazi Buenos Aires newspaper *Crítica* (May 5, 1934). Borges was a regular contributor to the magazine.

the Web like wildfire and was a central text in the opposition movement to the Iraq war.

A little less than forty years earlier, on November 19, 1964, the Yale critic Paul de Man published an elegantly crafted review of Borges's then newly translated collections *Dreamtigers* and *Labyrinths* in the *New York Review of Books*. Lamenting Borges's neglect in the United States, de Man offered guideposts to this (then) unknown modern master. Borges, he writes, is "often seen as a moralist, in rebellion against the times. But such an approach is misleading." "It is true," de Man goes on, that "Borges writes about villains. . . . But Borges does not consider infamy primarily as a moral theme: the stories in no way suggest an indictment of society or of human nature or of destiny. . . . Instead, infamy functions here as an aesthetic, formal principle." Although always centered in an act of infamy and full of terror, plagiarism, impersonation, and espionage, Borges's fictions "are about the style in which they are written," the celebrated Belgian scholar concludes (Alazraki, *Critical*, 56–57). De Man doesn't mention "Deutsches Requiem," but his silence on this text and the approach he propounded became central traits of academic Borges criticism for decades.

Which was it then, Borges the acute political seer, and "Deutsches Requiem" his politically charged Holocaust story as exemplary for our already troubled twenty-first century; or was it Borges the esthetician of infamy, and "Deutsches Requiem" as a historically and morally irrelevant fiction? In this opening chapter I want to survey the changing fortunes of Borges's tale of Otto Dietrich zur Linde, the condemned Nazi war criminal, subcommandant of the "Tarnowitz" concentration camp, justifying his actions the night before his execution as a torturer and murderer. The fiction appeared in the preeminent Buenos Aires literary journal *Sur* (South) in February 1946 at the time of the Nuremberg Trials, and it is structured as a counterpoint between zur Linde's apologia pro vita sua and the comments of an editor contained in footnotes. These marginalia undercut the Nazi's testimony, providing a contrasting narrative. Zur Linde's Jewish victims are represented by the poet "David Jerusalem," whom the editor says is perhaps a symbol of the many Jewish intellectuals tortured by the Nazi beast.

The narration's place of publication isn't incidental. Edited by the wealthy, influential Franco- and Anglophile woman of letters Victoria Ocampo, *Sur*'s mutating core group included, along with Borges, Adolfo Bioy Casares, Eduardo Mallea, and other important Argentine intellectuals (King 1986). Ocampo, initially "apolitical," later set a strong pro-British, anti-Nazi tone in an Argentina ruled since the 1930s by military juntas that were supposedly neutral but were during World War II not so quietly pro-Axis (Senkman 1991).[1] Together with other antifascist publications—the newspaper *Argentina Libre*, for example—*Sur* stood against ultranationalist periodicals of the ilk of *Crisol* (Crucible), pushing the agenda of the Jewish "menace" and the fascist "revolution."[2]

As a way of surveying the changing fortunes of "Deutsches Requiem," I will give a literary history of the fiction, focusing on zur Linde's journey from not so benign neglect to renown. By tracing how this masterpiece of a story was ignored or misinterpreted by critics until only yesterday, I will set the stage for the rest of my book, with the intent of counteracting the lack of knowledge and slighting of Latin American literature on the Shoah, and of indicating how Borges created new hybrid forms that exemplify how to "do" literature during and after Auschwitz.

My historical-literary journey will also pinpoint ongoing issues in Holocaust writing, such as the problem of representation that Borges presciently discerned and that continues to vex scholars today. The history will additionally relate Latin America's Shoah literature to prominent philosophers—Martin Heidegger, Emmanuel Levinas—on differing sides of the ethics and ideology divide, thinkers recognized by significant audiences but rarely in connection to the southern Americas.

An Argentine in the World

I'd like to start by giving a brief biographical background on how Borges came to compose a narrative of mourning for a Germany perverted by Nazism, the nation- perpetrator of the Shoah that Borges, an admirer of German culture, sorely wanted to be defeated. Borges, born in 1899 in Buenos Aires, the city on the River Plate, was at once deeply rooted in his homeland, with ancestors who fought in Argentina's nineteenth-century independence wars, and an internationalist fluent in several languages, including German. Buenos Aires was often styled Babel for its mixture of peoples and tongues, and Borges himself was "babelic," raised in a bilingual, bireligious home, since his paternal grandmother was English and Protestant; to his family and friends he was known as Georgie.

Georgie's cosmopolitan exposure was reinforced by a high school education in Geneva, Switzerland, where his family lived around the time of the First World War. His closest student buddies were Simon Jichlinski and Maurice Abramowicz, boys of Jewish-Polish origin. Among the standoffish Swiss, Borges remembered, he discovered Jewish ethnicity—he once called Maurice his *frère dans la race*, "race" brother—and what to him were Jewish texts: German books on the Kabbalah, and the poetry of Heinrich Heine and the German Expressionist poets of the conflict period. Spain, where his family went next, provided another *frère dans la race*, his literary mentor, the Hispano-Jewish polymath Rafael Cansinos-Assens, who taught him the ways of Jewishly inspired poetry and activism. The Jewish connection, ethnically more mythic than real, was one Borges would foster throughout his life, writing consistently on the Bible, the Kabbalah, and Judaism and essaying against antisemitism from his beginning days as an author: "Judería" (Jewish quarter) was a 1920 Cansinos-inflected poem describing the horror of a pogrom, and then renamed "Judengasse," German for the same thing, in the tragic year 1943. It was a little-known precursor of "Deutsches Requiem."

When he returned to Buenos Aires after his European sojourn and rediscovered his hometown, the young poet and essayist developed the seeds of his signature style: wedding the local or the fantastic, or the philosophic, to a sideways view of the worldly, a strategy that produces innovative fiction. Borges's babelic technique for entering his material, particularly his hybrid use of other worlds to talk about our own, and his method of bouncing reality off fantasy, and fantasy off reality, threw critics off course for decades. Borges was an escapist-fantasist unconcerned with reality; nothing could be further from the truth.

Borges turned from verse to fiction in the late 1930s. The shift was undoubtedly related to the times, since the form allowed him to express his ideas more fully, and to portray an uncanny global disorder that he was witnessing (see "Tlön, Uqbar, Orbis Tertius"). His most celebrated volumes of stories, *Ficciones* (1944) and *El Aleph* (1949), were published in the World War II era, and many tales allude to the violence and totalitarianism surrounding him. "Deutsches Requiem," the story no one dared to name, was the culmination of a process that began decades earlier.

Not So Benign Neglect

"Deutsches Requiem" was ignored for many years—it was either unmentioned or roundly dismissed. A look at its classic reception shows three possibilities: no reference at all, passing allusion, or brief negative commentary; downplaying and negativity often went hand in hand (see Stabb 1970 or Christ 1969). Jaime Alazraki's compilation, *Critical Essays on Jorge Luis Borges* (1987), which contains de Man's piece cited at the beginning of this chapter and other articles from the sixties and seventies, doesn't have a single reference to the story.

The tendency to overlook "Deutsches Requiem" hasn't completely ended. Harold Bloom's volume on Borges (2002) omits "Deutsches Requiem." Edwin Williamson's biography, *Borges: A Life* (2004), doesn't speak at all about "Deutsches Requiem," but to Williamson's credit he considers other Holocaust-related stories: "Death and the Compass" ("La muerte y la brújula," *Sur*, 1942), where four murders of Jews occur in a Buenos Aires–like city to the rejoicing of nationalist publications, and "The Secret Miracle" ("El milagro secreto," *Sur* 1943), set in Nazi-occupied Prague, where a condemned Jewish writer mentally "outwits" Hitler's killing machine.

French criticism's reverential rush to Borges also reduced the German requiem to nothingness. Michel Foucault famously wrote out of a passage in "The Analytic Language of John Wilkins." Gérard Genette built palimpsests on "Pierre Menard." Jacques Derrida deconstructed by quoting "Pascal's Sphere," and Maurice Blanchot explored the infinite through "The Aleph." Didier Anzieu gave "Deutsches Requiem" the most attention of all his colleagues—one line.

Among important Argentine critics, the situation was not significantly different, as in Ana María Barrenechea's *La expresión de la irrealidad en la obra de Borges* (1957), Gerardo Mario Goloboff's *Leer Borges* (1978), or Sylvia Molloy's *Las letras de Borges* (1979). The most innovative studies made scant allusion to the story. And at worst, Argentine studies blended rapid insinuation with sharp, sometimes convoluted critique, exemplified in Blas Matamoro's study (1971).

Matamoro represented the 1970s leftist and parricidal generation of writers who saw in Borges the paragon of a literature of evasion or misinformation. Thus, in Matamoro's view, Borges's suggestion in "Deutsches Requiem" that (happily) England defeated Hitler only reinforced British imperialism in Argentina [*sic*]—the unspoken subtext being Borges's opposition to General Juan Domingo Perón, who coming out of the wartime military-authoritarian cliques, took power in 1945. Borges, like many intellectuals who had seen the travails of the war, found him to be a dangerous, antisemitic Mussolini clone, soft on fugitive Nazis, and not an adored social reformer together with his charismatic, now iconic wife, Evita.[3]

Bare-mention currents also flowed from the Uruguayan side of the River Plate, such as in the great Borges critic Emir Rodríguez Monegal's book *Borges, hacia una lectura poética* (1976). But to Borges's lifelong commentator goes the credit for being among the first to propose *another* reading of Borges that might begin to give "Deutsches Requiem" other openings. In his essay "Borges y la política" (1977), Rodríguez Monegal puts forth the then radical notion that "la obra política de Borges [es] más abundante e inesperada de lo que se piensa" (Borges's political writing (is) more abundant and unexpected than one might think) (269). He then goes on to discuss "Deutsches Requiem" as an important text, part of Borges's long activism in his anti-Nazi dossier—an exceptional evaluation in the climate of those times. Rodríguez Monegal had no trouble understanding that Borges could produce what is arguably the most important Shoah narrative coming out of the southern Americas.

A few intrepid, mostly North American scholars did take on "Deutsches Requiem" at greater length. They include John Sturrock in *Paper Tigers: The Ideal Fictions of Jorge Luis Borges* (1977), Carter Wheelock in *The Mythmaker: A Study of Motif and Symbol in the Short Stories of Jorge Luis Borges* (1969), and the long U.S.-based Argentine Jaime Alazraki in *Versiones, Inversiones, Reversiones: El espejo como modelo estructural del relato en los cuentos de Borges* (1977). But their analyses frequently followed the downplaying mode, since they adopted variants of de Man's esthetic position that Borges's stories were about the style in which they were written: infamy only for art's (or thought's) sake.

Sturrock says so point-blank in remarks that jump off the page some thirty-plus years later: "'Deutsches Requiem' is pure artifice; it should not be read as some kind of commentary on the rise and fall of Nazi Germany" (104). Shunting aside Borges's own poignant remarks in the epilogue to the volume *El Aleph*, where the story was collected, to the effect that "Deutsches Requiem" was an attempt to understand the self-immolating destiny of Germany, Sturrock unbelievably chides the author. Borges only "makes things worse" with these comments, he complains, what with a story that is already "uncharacteristically somber and portentous," dealing as it does with the death of a Jew in a concentration camp (104; see also Bell-Villada 1999).

After reminding his readers once again that mere "game playing" marks "Deutsches Requiem," Sturrock proceeds to reveal to us what tragic "destiny" Borges is *really* talking about. It is the "supranational tendency of the human mind towards abstraction" (104). However forcibly then, "Deutsches Requiem" still "fits" the eponymous theme of Sturrock's book, *Paper Tigers: The Ideal Fictions of Jorge Luis Borges*. A few years earlier, Carter Wheelock had made just about the identical argument when he opined, "'Deutsches Requiem' is about ways of conceiving reality, not about Nazis and Jews and a Germany gone wrong" (161). Couldn't a Latin American story, ingeniously, be about both?

The possibility that "Deutsches Requiem" might indeed be about philosophy but also, in a new strategy, about philosophy *and* politics—or, better yet, about philosophy as a *political act* and politics as a *philosophical act*—doesn't even enter the horizon of expectation. In 1969 or 1977, Borges could only be a paper tiger, a purveyor of ideal fictions, in short, a mythmaker mired in unreality.

Borges's friend and assiduous commentator Jaime Alazraki shared these views, sustaining even in 1988, in the course of his moving reflection on the master's just extinguished life, "Borges' work is a prodigious artifice, an iridescent language, a self-contained form severed from historical reality" (*Borges and the Kabbalah*, 187). *And yet*: Alazraki opens his analysis with a *contextual* reference—the story originally appeared in the prestigious Buenos Aires journal *Sur* in February 1946, and it gave narrative substance to Borges's essay in the same publication, "Anotación al 23 de agosto de 1944" (A Comment on August 23, 1944), where, reacting to the liberation of Paris, Borges, in one of his strongest condemnations, famously says that "Nazism is uninhabitable . . . men can only die for it, lie for it, kill and bloody for it. No one in the innermost recesses of his being can hope that it triumphs" ("El nazismo . . . es inhabitable; los hombres sólo pueden morir por él, mentir por él, matar y ensangrentar por él. Nadie, en la soledad central de su yo, puede anhelar que triunfe") (*OC*, 728; Alazraki 1977, 91).

With that unusual historically based start, Alazraki gives a reading of the fiction in which structure—versions, reversions, distorted mirrors—serves society (or, more accurately, at least gestures toward it). The perverted looking glass in "Deutsches Requiem" is none other than Otto's genocidal Nazi philosophy and practice, itself a deformed simulacrum of the very thing it sets out to destroy—the biblically rooted Western order. Borges's narration, far from being "a self-contained form severed from historical reality," confronts "el nazismo, con todos los horrores del holocausto . . . la tragedia europea . . . la masacre judía" (Nazism, with all the horrors of the Holocaust . . . the European tragedy . . . the massacre of the Jews) (Alazraki 1977, 94).

To my knowledge, this is the first time a critic used (dared to use?) the word Holocaust in connection with "Deutsches Requiem." Over time the connection would take on major importance; but in 1977 it was still off the screen, too out of fashion, too uncomfortable.[4] What Alazraki also put his finger on *avant la lettre*, as French criticism would say in those years, was the difficulty in interpreting Borges's unprecedented story. Okay, Borges *was* saying something about the rise and fall of Nazi Germany, but what exactly was he saying? The story begins strangely with an epigraph from the Book of Job, "Though He slay me, yet will I trust in Him" (13:15), which Otto Dietrich uses to frame his Hitler-drenched apologia pro vita sua. So is Borges implying that Nazism is a more horrific and impenetrable version of Job's travails, ironically and inevitably enmeshed within the "Judaism" it seeks to obliterate (this is Alazraki's basic reading after much struggle with the text)?

Is he saying too that attempts to comprehend the enormity of the Holocaust and Germany's Götterdämmerung within our common paradigms are as unsatisfactory as Job's puny human endeavors to fathom his tribulations (another suggestion Alazraki makes, also a touchstone of post-Holocaust theology)?[5] Alright then, but why couldn't Borges just say it plain and simple, especially since these twists and turns (such a literate Nazi, such links with Judaism) can be interpreted otherwise. Could Borges somehow even have been defending Nazism? The suggestion was floated in 2000 (see Louis, "Besando"). What Borges was doing was complicating the narrative, from his standpoint as a "mere" Argentine (his words).

The Turning Tide

On December 1, 1987, midway between Paul de Man's review and Ramsey Clark's letter, the *New York Times* published a photo of de Man, who had died four years earlier. With it ran the headline "Yale Scholar's Articles Found in a Nazi Paper." In his native Nazi-occupied Belgium, the revered scholar and guru of deconstruction had written close to two hundred articles for *Le Soir*, a major newspaper toeing the Hitler line. The most infamous of them, entitled "The Jews in Contemporary Literature," decried the thankfully mediocre "Semitic interference" in Europe's cultural life, and called for the creation of a Jewish colony isolated from Europe to solve the "Jewish problem" (Lehman 1991, 158, 269–71; Barish 2014, 116–25). While de Man was pondering the merits of such "isolation," the Jews of Antwerp, where he was living, were undergoing exactly this kind of persecution and exclusion, the prelude to the worse yet to come.

De Man placed this pro-Nazi past "under erasure," in deconstructionist parlance, when he came to the United States, where he initiated his brilliant career; it was only revealed by accident after his death, causing an uproar. (The Belgian scholar Ortwin de Graef, then a graduate student, stumbled on it through archival research).[6] Could deconstruction have been a mass cover-up for a reality so ignominious that one did not wish to face up to it? Was this why de Man never wrote about "Deutsches Requiem" and resisted a reality-related reading of Borges? But the tide was turning, and the irritating tale was moving center stage.

Summarily put, the turning tide brought back history with a vengeance, and cover-ups were more difficult to pull off. Both inside and outside Borges's native land there was a rethinking of "reality as a scandal," with the Shoah period critical to the process. In Argentina, the rethinking began to gain momentum after the 1970s and 80s, when the country descended into, then tens of thousands of disappeared, tortured, and murdered later ascended from its dictatorial, fascist-inspired hell. The years of the *desaparecidos* came after a de facto civil war between left and right, both claiming the mantle of Perón, who after he was overthrown spent decades in exile only to return in 1973 and die months later, triggering a period of state terror on a scale never known before.

About a decade earlier, Adolf Eichmann's capture in Buenos Aires in May 1960, and his subsequent trial in Jerusalem (a replay of the Nuremberg Trials for a new generation), was a rumbling, if not yet a full-blown acceptance, of a return to public consciousness of the war era many dared not name.[7] What had been Argentina's accommodating role during and after the Third Reich? (Ronald Newton has done a thorough study on the subject.) How had Argentine intellectuals, including Borges, reacted in their pronouncements and works? How significant was *anti*fascism during the war period? And how did the mid-twentieth-century European "years of lead" correlate with the late twentieth-century *años de plomo* in the River Plate?[8]

In the changing environment, views of Borges moderated. For decades the bête noir of the left because of his opposition to Perón and to the Cuban Revolution (the ultranationalists didn't like him either partially for his prosemitism), he became the sharp prophesier of the brutalities that had transpired, his fictional dystopias, landscapes of fear, and esthetics of ruination turned into all too real disappearances, military torture centers, drugged bodies dropped out of helicopters, and bombing of Jewish buildings (see Aizenberg 2008).

His unquestionably disturbing, and quickly disowned, comments and decisions in favor of the 1970s military were placed in the context of his strong reiteration of long-held positions—the armed forces live in an artificial world of order, blind obedience, arrests; their wars are deadly follies leading nowhere (Vázquez 1984, 237; Sosnowski 2000, 79–80; see also Gelman, 334–35).[9] Borges was no longer irrelevant, as readers began acknowledging that phantoms of the Third Reich haunt the pages of contemporary Argentine literature, often explicitly Borgesian.[10]

The influential Argentine cultural critic Beatriz Sarlo articulates this shift to Borges: "Against all forms of fanaticism," she asserts, "Borges's work offers the ideal of tolerance. This feature has not always been identified with sufficient emphasis, perhaps because we left-wing Latin American intellectuals have been too slow to recognize it in fictions which deal with questions about order in the world" (5).

Borges's finest stories can be read as "political philosophy," Sarlo goes on, weaving questions of societal order and disorder into the fabric of his plots as a means of actively responding to world-historical processes, fascism and racism foremost among them (84). It isn't surprising, then, that Sarlo no longer neglects but instead comments on "Deutsches Requiem" (85–87).

Outside Argentina official discourses also had to own up to the past—from trials of war criminals to investigations about bank cover-ups and Nazi gold—and intellectual discourses had to keep pace. "Admitting the Holocaust," in Lawrence Langer's phrase, inquiring how best to "represent" reality after the instruments of representation had been irrevocably broken, rose to the top of the critical agenda. Thinkers from Maurice Blanchot to Jean-François Lyotard, from Alain Finkielkraut to Emmanuel Levinas, and authors and filmmakers from Elie Wiesel to Claude Lanzmann, William Styron to Steven Spielberg, confronted these challenges, as did an increasing number of literary and cultural commentators, Saul Friedländer, Berel

Lang, and James Young among them. However, Borges, who had "admitted the Holocaust" years before, was not yet admitted into the club.

Philosophy's collaborationist role, personified most by Martin Heidegger, received special scrutiny. But it was a scrutiny long familiar to Borges, since the Freiburg sage's thought had been brought to Argentina (and often lambasted there by Borges and others) starting in the 1930s. The label "Heidegger, filósofo oficial del nazismo" stuck to the venerated existentialist — as Borges called him tongue in cheek — the way it had in Europe; but it had its ups and downs — the Nazi link was hushed up, briefly reawakened postwar, and then resuscitated again at the end of the last century, not incidentally by research of the Chilean Victor Farías, who knew something about fascism from his own country[11] (OC, 1063).

After his embrace of Nazism, Heidegger saw in Hitler — the chief of state filling the newspaper headlines — the embodiment of his own philosophical doctrines, particularly the *Führerprincip* (leadership principle). And he considered his own engagement with National Socialism, including purifying the *Volk*, the political actualization of philosophical "existentials" — historicity, destiny, potentiality for Being-a-Self (Wolin 1991, 3–5).

Against the background of the late twentieth century, the possibility that "Deutsches Requiem" might be about philosophy *and* politics, or about philosophy as a *political act* and politics as a *philosophical act*, entered the horizon of expectation. Critical interest in the story rose, and began to revolve around three crucial areas — ideology and ethics; the problem of representation; and the vexing question of the Nazi-as-speaker, Otto Dietrich zur Linde's star role in the narrative. Latin Americans could be relevant after all.

Ideology and Ethics

From the tried-and-true argument that "Deutsches Requiem" shouldn't be read as "some kind of commentary on the rise and fall of Nazi Germany," opinions, still largely by scholars working on Latin American topics, have veered in the opposite direction.[12] Researchers now see "Deutsches Requiem" as an on-target portrayal of Nazi philosophy and its deathly consequences mouthed by a high-ranking practitioner. Leonardo Senkman, Antonio Gómez López-Quiñones, Beatriz Sarlo, Ann Warner, Erin Graff Zivin, and I have studied the fiction from the perspective of Nazi thought and rhetoric, keeping in mind the chilling pronouncements of the Hitler men themselves, as well as theoretical analyses of the Holocaust, totalitarianism, and post-Nazi ethics.

Especially fascinating is how these scholars have taken to the tale and produced readings that place it squarely within the context of writings by chief theoreticians of fascism and antisemitism, Theodor Adorno, Hannah Arendt, Jürgen Habermas, Max Horkheimer, and Slavoj Žižek. The new investigators frequently cite the work of trauma researcher Dominick La-Capra and of historians George Mosse, Raul Hilberg, Saul Friedländer, Lucy Dawidowicz, and Daniel Goldhagen. Erin Graff Zivin's keen examination of "Deutsches Requiem" uses the lens of Emmanuel Levinas's post-Auschwitz philosophy—the response to Heidegger—with its uncompromising emphasis on the ethical relationship between the same (zur Linde) and the other (Jerusalem).

Borges, with his fluency in German, presciently touched on major keys of Hitler's ideological and verbal arsenal, what Victor Klemperer termed "Lingua Tertii Imperii," and he was to give these keys narrative substance. We can't identify everything Borges heard or read about in the Third Reich's language—the subject needs more research. We do have an idea, however. Here are a few examples of condemnatory essays and articles from *Sur*, and from *El Hogar* (Home), a kind of *Ladies' Home Journal* where Borges had a regular "Foreign Books and Letters" column.

Borges knew about General Erich Ludendorff's antisemitic, anti-Masonic, anti-British, and anti-Goethe ranting (*los folletos iracundos*, "the hysterical pamphlets") and his mystical racist "Aryan" religion (*El Hogar* September 3, 1937; *Textos cautivos*, 165; *Sur* July 1940; *Borges en Sur*, 229). He knew (mightily) about Oswald Spengler's *Der Untergang des Abendlandes* (*The Decline of the West*) and its relation to the biologically mad Germany of 1936, the inheritor, as Borges put it, of the tendency to build grandiose dialectical edifices, always ignorant of reality (*El Hogar* December 25, 1936; *Textos cautivos*, 65–66). Like Nietzsche, Spengler was appropriated for Nazi thinking because of his hatred of democracy, glorification of the "true German" sprit, and advocacy of war as essential to life. Otto Dietrich zur Linde spouts their philosophies murderously.

Borges also knew (indignantly) about Elvira Bauer's best-selling antisemitic children's primer, *Trau keinem Fuchs auf gruener Heid und keinem Jud bei seinem Eid* (Don't Trust a Fox in a Green Meadow or the Oath of a Jew), published by the notorious Jew-baiter Julius Streicher and later entered as evidence of Nazi propaganda at the Nuremberg Trials, which condemned Streicher to death. Borges reviewed the picture book three times, minutely transcribing its racist language and loathsome illustrations, emphasizing the frightful brainwashing effect of text and image on young German

Cover of Elvira Bauer's antisemitic children's book *Trau keinem Fuchs auf gruener Heid und keinem Jud bei seinem Eid* (Don't Trust a Fox in a Green Meadow or the Oath of a Jew; published in Nuremberg, 1936, by Julius Streicher). Borges provides a description of many of the volume's pictures.

minds (*El Hogar* May 28 1937; *Textos cautivos*, 136–37; *Sur* May 1937; *Borges en Sur*, 145–46; *Revista Judaica* May 1937).[13]

At the adult end of Nazi publishing, Borges knew about Doctor Johannes Rohr's version of A. F. C. Vilmar's *Geschichte der Deutschen National-Literatur* (History of German National Literature; Berlin, 1936), which expurgated Jewish and non-Nazi authors, left out Schopenhauer (much quoted by Borges), mutilated Goethe, Lessing, and Nietzsche, and acclaimed the literary labors of Joseph Goebbels, Alfred Rosenberg, and Adolf Hitler (*Sur* October 1938; *Borges en Sur*, 155–57).

As early as 1934, Borges had already translated exiled German author Heinrich Mann's parodies of Hitler-speak under the title "Escenas de la crueldad nazi" (Scenes of Nazi Cruelty) for the *Revista Multicolor de las Sábados*, the illustrated Saturday magazine of the newspaper *Crítica*, edited by Natalio Botana, which had a staunchly anti-Nazi line. Botana, a journalistic innovator, combined sensationalism with high culture, and allowed two young writers, Borges and Ulyses Petit de Murat, to edit the short-lived but significant *Revista Multicolor* (1933–1934). Graphic humor was essential to the style, and Hitler a particularly "beloved" object of caricature. Some of the pictures in this chapter originally accompanied Borges's translation of Mann (see Helft 1999, Efrón and Brenman 2009, and Romero and Tato 2002; my chapter on Gerchunoff in *Books and Bombs in Buenos Aires* develops the topic of drawing and denunciation).

Borges likewise knew—this is an understatement—about a Nietzsche reengineered as a prime source for Nazi ideology, with the concepts of the "will to power," "holy cruelty" (pity is a sin), and the *Übermensch* and *Untermensch*. The Volkish religion of the Reich, with its "nobler values," was to triumph over Christianity (itself an enfeebled Jewish plot) and create a

Illustration accompanying Borges's translation of Heinrich Mann's *Scenes of Nazi Cruelty* (*Revista Multicolor de los Sábados*, May 5, 1934). The text on the upper left side is the Spanish rendering of a Nazi "blood and iron" hymn that reads in English: "Let the only music of our days sound forth on bugles and trumpets. Today we want, man by man, to redden iron with blood, the blood of executioners, and the blood of Frenchmen. Oh, sweet day of vengeance! This is what every German wants; this is, in truth, what matters."

transcendent Nietzschean community that was both "primal and future oriented" (Yablon 2003, 743; Nietzsche, 88). No wonder, then, that Borges wrote sadly at war's outbreak that a local partisan of the Reich is one who "aprueba con fervor que Hitler obre a lo Zarathustra" (fervently approves of Hitler's actions Zarathustra-style). A planetary Nazi victory would spew forth in what especially frightened Borges, a despicable host of "home-grown supermen" (*Uebermenschen caseros*)—a prospect that didn't seem so far-fetched in 1939 (*Sur* October 1939: *Borges en Sur*, 28–30).

Beatriz Sarlo, Antonio Gómez López-Quiñones, and Ann Warner examine the Nietzschean strands in "Deutsches Requiem," as Otto Dietrich zur Linde sets forth the Nietzsche-inspired vindication of Nazism and faith in its ultimate, pitiless triumph: "No en vano escribo esa palabra: la piedad por el hombre superior es el último pecado de Zarathustra." "Lo que importa es que rija la violencia, no las serviles timideces cristianas." (Not in vain do I write this word: for Zarathustra mercy is the superman's ultimate sin. What is important is that violence reign, not servile Christian timidity) (*OC*, 578, 581).

Spengler too receives attention in these critics' work, what with Otto Dietrich's "homage" to the "deeply German" philosopher: "Rendí justicia . . . a la sinceridad del filósofo de la historia, a su espíritu radicalmente alemán (*kerndeutsch*), militar. En 1929 entré en el Partido" (I gave just due . . . to the sincerity of the philosopher of history, to his radically German [*kerndeutsch*], military spirit) (*OC*, 577). Interestingly, the assertion of Nazi Party membership closes the paragraph that begins with the words "Hacia 1927 entraron en mí vida Nietzsche y Spengler" (Around 1927 Nietzsche and Spengler came into my life). For many intellectuals, including Spengler, Nazism (particularly at its outset) was the logical conclusion to philosophical speculations that often, Borges had perceptively noted, did not take into account its sinister real-life implications.

The new "Deutsches Requiem" investigators often cite Hannah Arendt's research on the origins of totalitarianism, focusing on the lack of "common sense" in ideologies such as Nazism, with its fostering of mass think and a loss of individuality, demonizing antisemitism, use of terror and pseudoscience, and future orientation. All of these elements are present in Otto Dietrich's discourse: David Jerusalem, his Jewish victim, isn't a person ("ante mis ojos no era un hombre" [in my eyes he was not a man]) but an ideological construct, a "detested zone"; hence he can be "surgically" tortured in the name of the final Nazi victory (*OC*, 579).

"El nazismo, intrinsicamente, es un hecho moral, un despojarse del viejo hombre, que está viciado, para vestir el nuevo" (Nazism is in essence a moral act, a stripping of the old man, now corrupted, to dress the new) (OC, 578). Strange as it may seem, Otto Dietrich's statement sums it up. Claudia Koonz quotes it in her book *The Nazi Conscience* and, after citing Borges's uncanny subcommandant, goes on to say: "Scholars have analyzed the broad outlines and subtle nuances of Nazi ideology without taking Hitler's promise of a new moral order seriously. In this book, I examine . . . [his] comprehensive ethical revolution" (1, 16). Her interest in Nazi ethics and reading of "Deutsches Requiem" as a precursor text reflects other researchers' concern with this dimension. Antonio Gómez López-Quiñones engages with Lucy Dawidowicz's documentation of the Nazis' care to overcome pity, and Erin Graff Zivin examines "Deutsches Requiem" through Lévinas: How do you turn the face into an Other in order to annihilate it? Otto Dietrich ruminates about David Jerusalem's looks and about the "danger" of confronting him as a "rostro," a human face, not an anonymous zone or cipher.

The Problem of Representation

Theodor Adorno's now canonical dictum that to write poetry after Auschwitz is barbaric hasn't stopped the writing—but how to make words, the material of fiction, commensurate with the crematoria? (Aizenberg 1997)

Borges, held to be a paragon of unreality, seemed ill equipped to represent Auschwitz, where survivor Jean Améry chillingly witnessed reality was as unbearably real as a glance at the watchtowers, a whiff from the gas chambers. But as contemporary criticism more and more spotlighted the problem of Shoah representation, Borges—as with the other writers I'll discuss—didn't appear so unprepared after all. Far from shirking the bind of fictionalizing the Shoah, Borges grappled with it in tales such as "The Secret Miracle" and "Deutsches Requiem," composed in the heat of the events, way before the critical category "Holocaust literature" existed, before many of the theoretical speculations. The lateral lucidity of the periphery was well operational here in a new way.

Borges recognized early on that the reality of Auschwitz demanded a *poetics of saying and unsaying*—on the one hand, mimetic approximation, documentary accumulation; on the other, escape, fantasy, fragmentation, fractured discourse. Borges saw reality and unreality jostling together, telling, and unraveling what is told. Current scholarship on "Deutsches Requiem" identifies this poetics at work; what was previously seen as weakness (incompleteness, patchwork narration, writing in the margins) is now viewed as strength.

Just as Hitler's heresiarchs were publicly and privately allowed to speak their minds, while the world heard, read, and tried to fathom what made them tick, so does "Deutsches Requiem" let Otto Dietrich zur Linde say his piece (Goldensohn 2004). Argentina's newspapers of the time were filled with headline articles on the judgments, the first time the depth of the atrocities was so publicized. The testimonies and self-justification of Hitler's henchmen spilled over the front pages of the important daily *La Nación*, for instance, the rhetoric as rendered into Spanish often sounding like zur Linde's peroration. One example: we hear Rudolf Hess: "Me siento feliz de saber que cumplí con mi deber como alemán, nacionalsocialista y fiel servidor de mi Fuehrer [*sic*]. Volvería, si tuviera la oportunidad, a proceder en la misma forma, aunque supiera que ello me costaría morir en la hoguera" (I feel happy knowing that I fulfilled my duty as a German, a National Socialist, and a faithful servant of my führer. If I had the opportunity, I would do it again, even if it brought me death by fire) (*La Nación* September 1, 1946, 2; on the first newsreels of the concentration camps shown in Buenos Aires, see the chapter on Gerchunoff in Aizenberg, *Books and Bombs in Buenos Aires*).

"Deutsches Requiem" isn't the only story where Borges uses the first-person confessional mode, but Otto Dietrich's testimony wouldn't have happened without Nuremberg. In a grim way the accused invented a truth and justice commission paradigm, a perverse poetics of recounting and omitting that Borges adopts in his fiction.

And a fiction it is. Even if documentary accumulation molds the account, we are reading a fabrication. Here the unsaying comes into play, as a fractured discourse disturbing Otto Dietrich's clockwork orange of an apologia. Gaps, paradoxes, euphemisms, and inconsistencies mark zur Linde's testimony.

And distant from the ideal of the testosterone-laden superman, Otto Dietrich's genealogy censors his most illustrious ancestor, the Hebraist Johannes Forkel, from the list of his forebears; this redacted information is interpolated in the story's the first footnote. The consequences of his leg amputation after an antisemitic *Aktion* were graver (castrating?) than he let on, interjects another footnote. As for the "establishment's disciplinary measures" (*el regimen disciplinario de nuestra casa*) that Otto Dietrich applied to David Jerusalem—they were torture so unspeakable that the text breaks off, with a footnote marking the gap. (Notice the word *casa* for concentration camp, with its connotations of *heimlich*, domestically cozy.) Representing the Shoah can only be a piecemeal task, as Borges tried to project in the heat of Auschwitz, and it would be disingenuous to suppose a melodramatic photographic fullness rather than a lateral approach.

The Nazi as Speaker

The central conundrum of Borges's fiction is that the main speaker is a Nazi —and not any Nazi but a perpetrator about to be executed for his crimes against humanity. How could Borges, whose anti-Nazi credentials were impeccable, have created such a hero and allowed him such articulate free rein? The scholars I've noted have engaged this issue. "'Deutsches Requiem' es un cuento incómodo," says López-Quiñones. "Escribir las memorias de un nazi desde su punto de vista con el fin de comprender sus obras, no deja de resultar temerario ideológicamente" ("Deutsches Requiem" is an uncomfortable story. To write the memoir of a Nazi from his own perspective in order to understand his behavior is, needless to say, ideologically risky) (136).

Vandorpe and Louis are more accusatory, with Louis charging that Borges plays with a justification of Nazism. For Borges, she points the finger in a throwback to the Borges-the-fantasist-escapist trope, fiction was more important than reality, and what counts isn't Borges's pro-Allied posture but his literary writings where his ideology really resides; in a later rewriting, Louis pulled back somewhat from her position (Vandorpe 1995, 93; Louis 2000, 71; Louis 2008, 308).

Most would have been happier if Borges had put an admonition at the story's end, a moral-didactic disclaimer affirming "Nazism is bad and I stand against it." But Borges didn't, although he did provide a tag and an early reading frame in the epilogue to the volume *El Aleph* (1949), where "Deutsches Requiem" was first collected. He declares: "En la última guerra nadie pudo anhelar más que yo que fuera derrotada Alemania; nadie pudo sentir más que yo lo trágico del destino alemán; "'Deutsches Requiem' quiere entender ese destino, que no supieron llorar, ni siquiera sospechar, nuestros 'germanófilos,' que nada saben de Alemania" (In the last war no one wished more than I did for Germany to be defeated; no one felt more than I did Germany's tragic fate. "Deutsches Requiem" tries to understand that fate which our so-called Germanophiles, who know nothing about Germany, couldn't mourn, much less foresee) (*OC*, 629).

We are not obligated to use this frame or any other frame—Borges's anti-Nazi articles or, for that matter, his other stories—although we almost inevitably do. Yet these particular remarks are illuminating, in my opinion. They explain Borges's posture more fully and how it relates to "Deutsches Requiem." Most notably, they explain the story's internal logic, comfortable or uncomfortable as it may be.

Borges passionately wanted Nazi Germany to be defeated (this is the part everyone focuses on); at the same time, he deeply felt the tragedy of

Germany's destiny (the more tricky part). "Deutsches Requiem" wants to understand this destiny *through its own logic*, logic of violence, hatred, and destruction, but logic nonetheless. How did Germany come to destroy itself, as it destroyed millions of people, Jews with special ferocity? What was the attraction of the Nazi system, an attraction that hasn't disappeared? Precisely because Borges admired Germany he tried to comprehend Nazism, an *ethics of cruelty*, on its own terms, possibly the most dangerous yet the most unvarnished, penetrating, and innovative form of doing it. He wrote: "A los alemanes no les ha bastado con ser crueles; han creído necesario construir una teoría previa de la crueldad, una justificación de la crueldad como postulado ético" (It hasn't been enough for the Germans to be cruel; they've felt a need to previously construct a theory of cruelty, a justification of cruelty as an ethical posture) (*Textos recobrados*, 316).

But Borges didn't just leave his story as a presentation of Nazism's logic —he built in the undercutting of the logic. We don't have to believe that truth is on the side of the editor, the main undercutter, but then again, we don't have to believe that it is on the side of the Nazi—the assumption made when we read the story as a straightforward Nazi apologia. The editor does have a crucial advantage, though, the advantage of the margin, where Borges himself was positioned, and where lies are peeled away.

Beneath the reasoning and the verbiage, beneath the euphemisms, hides the reality of the system. In the counterpoint of above and below, upper text and lower text, Borges wove an exposé of Nazism, forcing us to read in the gap between the two, making us work, but then, why not? Some seventy years after Germany's defeat, the war's end, and the "liberation" of the camps, we are still struggling to make sense of what happened.

Works Cited and Consulted

Aizenberg, Edna. *The Aleph Weaver: Biblical, Kabbalistic and Judaic Elements in Borges.* Potomac, MD: Scripta Humanistica, 1984.

———. "Argentine Space, Jewish Memory: Memorials to the Blown Apart and Disappeared in Buenos Aires." *Mortality* 12:2 (2007): 109–23.

———. *Books and Bombs in Buenos Aires: Borges, Gerchunoff, and Argentine-Jewish Writing*. Hanover, NH: Brandeis University Press published by University Press of New England, 2002.

———. *Borges, el tejedor del Aleph y otros ensayos: del hebraísmo al poscolonialismo.* Frankfurt am Main: Madrid: Iberoamericana/Vervuert, 1997.

———. "Borges, Guimarães Rosa, Mistral: intelectuales (y diplomáticos) latinomericanos frente a la Segunda Guerra Mundial y el Holocaust europeo."

In *Jorge Luis Borges: Políticas de la literatura*, edited by Juan Pablo Dabove. Pittsburgh: Instituto Internacional de Literatura Iberoamericana, 2008. 141–53.

———. "Making Monuments in Argentina, a Land Afraid of Its Past." *Chronicle Review*, June 21, 2002.

———. "Mi Buenos Aires herido: Borges and Landscapes of Fear." *Variaciones Borges* 25 (2008): 69–77.

———. "Postmodern or Post-Auschwitz: Borges and the Limits of Representation." *Variaciones Borges* 3 (1997): 141–51.

Alazraki, Jaime. *Borges and the Kabbalah*. Cambridge: Cambridge University Press, 1988.

———. *Critical Essays on Jorge Luis Borges*. Boston: G. K. Hall, 1987.

———. "La escalera de Elías." *Folio* 17 (1987): 9–15.

———. *Versiones, Inversiones, Reversiones: El espejo como modelo estructural del relato en los cuentos de Borges*. Madrid: Gredos, 1977.

Almeida, Ivan. "De Borges a Schopenhauer." *Variaciones Borges* 17 (2004): 103–41.

Anzieu, Didier. "El cuerpo y el código en los cuentos de J. L. Borges." *Jorge Luis Borges*. Introduction by Luis Gusman. Buenos Aires: Freeland, 1978. 33–72.

Arendt, Hannah. *The Origins of Totalitarianism*. New York: Harcourt Brace, 1951.

Barish, Evelyn. *The Double Life of Paul de Man*. New York: W. W. Norton, 2014.

Barrenechea, Ana María. *La expresión de la irrealidad en la obra de Borges*. México: El Colegio de México, 1957.

Bell-Villada, Gene H. *Borges and His Fiction: A Guide to His Mind and Art*. Austin: University of Texas Press, 1981; Rev. ed., 1999.

Bloom, Harold, ed. *Jorge Luis Borges*. New York: Chelsea House, 2002.

———. *The Western Canon: The Books and School of the Ages*. New York: Harcourt Brace, 1994.

Borges, Jorge Luis. *Borges en Sur*. Edited by Sara Luisa del Carril and Mercedes Rubio de Zocchi. Buenos Aires: Emecé, 1999.

———. *Obras Completas*. Buenos Aires: Emecé, 1976.

———. *Textos cautivos*. Edited by Enrique Saceri-Garí and Emir Rodríguez Monegal. Buenos Aires: Tusquets, 1986.

———. *Textos recobrados*, 1931–1955. Edited by Sara Luisa del Carril and Mercedes Rubio de Zocchi. Buenos Aires: Emecé, 2001.

CEANA. Comisión para el esclarecimiento de las actividades del nazismo en la República Argentina. "Informe Final." http://www.bnaibrith.org.ar/PDFs/CEANAINFORMEFINAL.pdf.

Christ, Ronald. *The Narrow Act: Borges' Art of Allusion*. New York: New York University Press, 1969.

Ciamarra, Leonardo Pica. "Filosofia tedesca e nazionalsocialismo: l'utilizzazione nazista di Schopenhauer." *La Sho'ah: Tra interpretazione e memoria*. Edited by Paolo Amodio, Romeo de Maio, and Giuseppe Lissa. Naples: Istituto Italiano per gli Studi Filosofici, 1998. 509–18.

Clark, Ramsey. "Open Letter to the UN Security Council," September 20, 2002. http://www.healingearthresources.com/site/epage/7032_163.htm.
Dawidowicz, Lucy, ed. *A Holocaust Reader*. New York: Behrman House, 1976.
———. *The War against the Jews 1933–1945*. New York: Bantam, 1986.
De Graef, Ortwin. E-mail to author. January 4, 2005.
De Man, Paul. "A Modern Master." In Alazraki, *Critical Essays*. 55–62.
Efrón, Gustavo, and Darío Brenman. "Los medios gráficos argentinos durante el nazismo." *Question: Revista especializada en periodismo y comunicación* 1:11 (2006).
Farías, Victor. *Heidegger and Nazism*. Philadelphia: Temple University Press, 1989.
Faye, Emmanuel. *Heidegger: The Introduction of Nazism into Philosophy in Light of the Unpublished Seminars of 1933–1935*. Translated by Michael B. Smith. Foreword by Tom Rockmore. New Haven: Yale University Press, 2009.
Fló, Juan. *Contra Borges*. Buenos Aires: Galerna, 1978.
Friedlander, Albert H. *Out of the Whirlwind: A Reader of Holocaust Literature*. Revised edition. New York: URJ Press, 1999.
Gelman, Juan. "Borges o el valor." In Lafforgue, 1999. 333–35.
Goldensohn, Leon. *The Nuremberg Interviews*. New York: Knopf, 2004.
Goloboff, Gerardo Mario. *Leer Borges*. Buenos Aires: Huemel, 1978.
González, José Eduardo. *Borges and the Politics of Form*. New York: Garland, 1998.
Graff Zivin, Erin. *The Wandering Signifier*. Durham: Duke University Press, 2008.
Halperin Donghi, Tulio. *La Argentina y la Tormenta del Mundo: Ideas e Ideologías entre 1930 y 1945*. Buenos Aires: Siglo XX, 2003.
Helft, Nicolás. *Revista Multicolor de los Sábados*. Buenos Aires: Fondo Nacional de las Artes, 1999.
Hirsch, Marianne, and Irene Kacandes, eds. *Teaching the Representation of the Holocaust*. New York: Modern Language Association of America, 2004.
King, John. *"Sur": A Study of the Argentine Literary Journal and Its Role in the Development of a Culture, 1931–1970*. Cambridge: Cambridge University Press, 1986.
Klemperer, Victor. *The Language of the Third Reich: LTI; Lingua Tertii Imperii*. Translated by Martin Brady. New Brunswick, NJ: Athlone Press, 2000.
Koonz, Claudia. *The Nazi Conscience*. Cambridge: Belknap Press, 2003.
Kremer, Lillian S., ed. *Holocaust Literature: An Encyclopedia of Writers and Their Work*. 2 vols. New York: Routledge, 2003.
Lafforgue, Martín, ed. *AntiBorges*. Buenos Aires: Vergara, 1999.
Langer, Lawrence. *Admitting the Holocaust*. Oxford: Oxford University Press, 1995.
Lawrence, Ramsey. "Religious Subtext and Narrative Structure in Borges' 'Deutsches Requiem.'" *Variaciones Borges* 10 (2000): 119–38.
Lehman, David. *Signs of the Times: Deconstruction and the Fall of Paul de Man*. New York: Poseidon, 1991.
Louis, Annick. "Besando a Judas: Notas alrededor de 'Deutsches Requiem.'" *Jorge Luis Borges: Intervenciones sobre pensamiento y literatura*. Edited by William Rowe, Claudio Canaparo, and Annick Louis. Buenos Aires: Paidós, 2000. 61–71.

———. *Borges ante el fascismo*. Berne: Peter Lang, 2008.
———. "Borges y el nazismo." *Variaciones Borges* 4 (1997): 117–36.
López-Quiñones, Antonio Gómez. *Borges y el nazismo: "Sur" (1937–1946)*. Granada: Universidad de Granada, 2004.
Matamoro, Blas. *Jorge Luis Borges o el juego trascendente*. Buenos Aires: Peña Lilio Editor, 1971.
Meter, Alejandro. "Deutsches Requiem." In Riggs, 2002. 407–8.
Molloy, Sylvia. *Las letras de Borges*. Buenos Aires: Sudamericana, 1979.
Morgan, Michael L. *Beyond Auschwitz: Post-Holocaust Jewish Thought in America*. Oxford: Oxford University Press, 2001.
Newton, Ronald C. *The "Nazi Menace" in Argentina, 1931–1947*. Stanford, CA: Stanford University Press, 1992.
Nietzsche, Friedrich Wilhelm. *Thus Spoke Zarathustra*. Translated by Walter Kaufmann. New York: Penguin, 1966.
"Púsose término al juicio contra los jerarcas nazis." *La Nación*, September 1, 1946: 2.
Rein, Raanan. *Argentina, Israel, and the Jews: Perón, the Eichmann Capture and After*. Translated by Martha Grenzeback. Bethesda, MD: University of Maryland Press, 2003.
Riggs, Thomas, ed. *Reference Guide to Holocaust Literature*. Introduction by James E. Young. Farmington Hills, MI: St. James Press, 2002.
Rodríguez Monegal, Emir. *Borges, hacia una lectura poética*. Madrid: Guadarrama, 1976.
———. "Borges y la política." *Revista Iberoamericana* 43:100–1 (1977): 269–91.
Romero, Luis Alberto, and María Inés Tato. "La prensa periodística y el regimen nazi." In *Sobre nazis y nazismo en la cultura*. Edited by Ignacio Klich. College Park, MD: Hispamérica, 2002. 157–75.
Sarlo, Beatriz. *Jorge Luis Borges: A Writer on the Edge*. London: Verso, 1993.
Schwarz, Daniel R. *Imagining the Holocaust*. New York: St. Martin's Press, 1999.
Senkman, Leonardo. *Argentina, la Segunda Guerra Mundial, y los Refugiados indeseables, 1933–1945*. Buenos Aires: Grupo Editor Latinoamericano, 1991.
———. "Borges y el mal del nazismo." In Solotorevsky and Fine, 167–80.
Sitman, Rosalie. "Protest from Afar: The Jewish and Republican Presence in Victoria Ocampo's *Sur* in the 1930s and 1940s." In *Rethinking Jewish-Latin Americans*, edited by Jeffrey Lesser and Raanan Rein. Albuquerque: University Press of New Mexico, 2008. 132–60.
Solotorevsky, Myrna, and Ruth Fine, eds. *Borges en Jerusalén*. Madrid: Iberoamericana, 2003. 167–80.
Sosnowski, Saúl. *Borges y la cábala*. Buenos Aires: Hispamérica, 1976.
———. "Memorias de Borges (artificios de la historia)." *Variaciones Borges* 10 (2000): 79–95.
Sosnowski, Saúl, and Leonardo Senkman. "El impacto del aflujo de nazis y colaboracionistas en las letras y otras expresiones culturales argentinas." CEANA, "Informe Final," 671–745.

———. *Fascismo y nazismo en las letras argentinas*. Buenos Aires: Lumiere, 2009.
Spengler, Oswald. *The Decline of the West: Perspectives of World-History*. Translated by Charles Francis Atkinson. 2 vols. New York: A. Knopf, 1926–1928.
Stabb, Martin. *Jorge Luis Borges*. New York: Twayne, 1970; Rev. ed., *Borges Revisited*, 1991.
Stangneth, Bettina. *Eichmann before Jerusalem: The Unexamined Life of a Mass Murderer*. Translated by Ruth Martin. New York: Knopf, 2014.
Stavans, Ilan. "Jorge Luis Borges." In Kremer, vol. 1, 171–76.
Sturrock, John. *Paper Tigers: The Ideal Fictions of Jorge Luis Borges*. Oxford: Clarendon Press, 1977.
Vandorpe, Yasmine-Sigrid. "Ironie et paradoxe dans 'Deutsches Requiem' de Jorge Luis Borges." *Les Lettres romanes* 1995 (hors série): 81–93.
Vázquez, María Esther. *Borges, sus días y su tiempo*. Buenos Aires: Javier Vergara, 1984.
Warner, Ann. "En busca del Borges político en 'Deutsches Requiem.'" Master's thesis, Columbia University, 2001.
Wheelock, Carter. *The Mythmaker: A Study of Motif and Symbol in the Short Stories of Jorge Luis Borges*. Austin: University of Texas Press, 1969.
Williamson, Edwin. *Borges: A Life*. New York, Viking, 2004.
Wolin, Richard, ed. *The Heidegger Controversy: A Critical Reader*. New York: Columbia University Press, 1991.
Yablon, Charles M. "Nietzsche and the Nazis: The Impact of National Socialism on the Philosophy of Nietzsche." *Cardozo Law Review* 24:2 (2003): 739–55.

Tudo real mas visto através de um espelho
Everything was real but seen as through a mirror
• • • *The Besieged City*

2

Clarice Lispector and the Murmur of Catastrophe

Rio: Brazil for Brazilians

Like Borges, whose fictions were not about a Germany gone mad, Clarice Lispector did not write about the Hitler time. One of Brazil's world-class authors, lionized by literary personalities the globe over, Lispector passed in silence over the great catastrophe that surely would have annihilated her if father Pedro hadn't gotten on an immigrant ship, his wife, Marieta, and daughters, Elsa, Tania, and Clarice, in tow, to whisk the family from the steppes to the tropics.

A thumbnail biography of the famous fabulator: Clarice Lispector: sweet Jewish baby born as Haya to Russian- and Yiddish-speaking parents in 1920 in Tchetchelnik, Ukraine; budding student in the Colégio Hebreu-Ídiche-Brasileiro, the Jewish school in Recife, northeastern Brazil, whose name indicates the fulcrum of the learning; polyglot law student in the 1940s at Rio de Janeiro's Facultade Nacional de Direito, and savvy journalist at the Agência Nacional, the government-controlled press office, and the daily *A Noite*, pioneering professions for a woman in those days; young wife accompanying her consul husband, Maury Gurgel Valente, on assignment to Naples, Italy, and Berne, Switzerland, from 1944 to 1949; and, most significant, author of linguistically innovative, introspectively woman-centered novels, the first three gestated in the heat of the European conflagration, *Near to the Wild Heart* (*Perto do coraçao selvagem*, 1943), *The Chandelier* (*O lustre*, 1946), and *The Besieged City* (*A cidade sitiada*, 1949).

Clarice Lispector, so knowledgeable, cosmopolitan, near to the savage hearts and besieged cities she never wrote about.

The Old Continent was self-destructing, its Jews immolated, but Lispector remained quiet, experimenting with a new Portuguese literary idiom and dissecting minutely, her pen a surgeon's scalpel, the daily travails of individual women encased in claustrophobic rooms, dead-end loves, realities not of their own making. Her literature struggled to remake that reality on the blank page (whatever that reality might be), and also to change it in her own life, when she separated from Gurgel Valente in the late 1950s and became a renowned intellectual, no more entirely Clarice Gurgel Valente, as she once acerbically put it.

But where were the signs of the terrible age—the fascist mindset, barbarian assaults, blood, violence, degradation, and corpses? At best, much current thinking goes, she probably alluded to the disaster very, very late, decades after the war, and only in her last novel, *A hora da estrela* (*The Hour of the Star*, 1977), published after her death, a book full of gaps, holes, false starts, whose emaciated survivor-like protagonist, Macabea, thankful for a bun and hot chocolate, is run over by a yellow Mercedes large as an ocean liner, driven by a blond Hans—the Germanic beast, who once marked Jews with a yellow star, murdering the physically helpless, if stubborn and spiritually graced, offspring of the once-military biblical Maccabees. A scrawny fiddler in threadbare clothes, a figure redolent with Jewish suffering, appears on the street corner to play Macabea's pitiful dirge.

Coming at the end of her life, the Shoah-laden underpinnings of this self-conscious post-Holocaust narrative, which haven't been analyzed in full, didn't greatly modify the "Clarice kept aloof" perception of her entire career, as didn't the fine more recent books by Berta Waldman, Nelson Vieira, and Benjamin Moser, and others on her literary Jewishness, inevitably understood as a mystical bent and a sense of foreignness.

Here are the facts: Clarice Lispector *directly* experienced the broad canvas of the Second World War: army transports, injured soldiers, hungry people, bombed-out cities, supposedly neutral bystanders shutting out Satan. Digging her hands into the emotional and physical mud, she left astutely observed *written* testimony every step of the way. The cloistered, closeted, ivory-towered Clarice simply didn't exist. She was a figment of much of the critical imagination until just a few years ago, nurtured by lit-crit theoretical fashions focused on her as the epitome of *écriture feminine*, subversive women's writing, a view propounded by the famed Franco-Jewish critic Hèléne Cixous, who idolized the Brazilian. The war facts and their implications weren't interesting or germane (recall the analogous pooh-poohing of Borges's involvement and testimonies because he too was a "fantasist").

Lispector's skill in hide-and-seek self-fashioning didn't help matters. She obfuscated just about every area of her literature and life — age, ethnicity, language, and religion. Her close friend and colleague Alberto Dines summed it up when he told me, "Clarice nunca foi óbvia, ela sempre preferiu os mistérios" (Personal communication March 27, 2008).

Clarice was never obvious, she always preferred mysteries; her fiction wasn't "about" in a conventional way — an ironclad, sharply defined, frontal story; it was oblique, disjointed, veiled, hesitating between the "real" and the "imagined." Still, the mystery seeker's experience of the conflict begins, along with the textual record, in Brazil itself, even before she left for Naples and Berne as the spouse of an up-and-coming diplomat from a distinguished diplomatic clan. Clarice Gurgel Valente may have held no official appointment, but to live the embassy life, savoring its benefits and enduring its dangers while representing Brazil, she too needed credentials — first and foremost, Brazilian citizenship.

The timing couldn't have been more muddled: 1942, in the middle of the raging war, her adopted homeland since 1930 under the rule of Getúlio Vargas, an authoritarian of fascist leanings who, playing one side against the other throughout the Axis-Allied battle, finally chose to fight with the Allies precisely in 1942. This choice for the democracies, reported on abundantly in the press, including in Lispector's newspaper, *A Noite*, became part of Lispector's story because it determined her sojourn in Europe.

Against this complicated background, a strong nationalist tide in Brazil loudly proclaimed "O Brasil para os brasileiros," "Brazil for Brazilians," a posture solidified in a now-infamous secret memorandum issued in 1937 by Itamaraty, the Brazilian Foreign Office, prohibiting the granting of visas to immigrants of "Semitic origin." The rule could be bent with the right financial massaging or political connections, but it nevertheless stood as official policy, sometimes with life-and-death consequences (see chapter 4, on Guimãraes Rosa).

All was not bad for Jews in Brazil in this period, during which communal life went on always alert to adhere, at least cosmetically, to the "Brazil for Brazilians" campaign — for example the rules that only native-born Brazilians could serve on organizational boards, or that languages other than Portuguese (read here Yiddish and Hebrew) couldn't be taught in communal schools. When I checked old *A Noite* issues in the Library of Congress to get a better sense of the atmosphere that surrounded Lispector, I found front-page headlines such as "O Brasil não tolera traições" (Brazil Doesn't Tolerate Treason), citing the ordinance against foreigners on boards and reiterating the death penalty as the maximum punishment for overseas-inspired sabotaging of "national security." The Brazilian government would only protect those "extracontinental communities" that live and work peacefully without any political agendas (January 22, 1942).

In the words of historian Roney Cytrynowicz, Jews in Brazil, recognizing the largely corporatist, xenophobic, anti-immigrant ideology of Vargas's Estado Novo ("New State") and its call to create a "novo homem brasileiro," a new Brazilian man, sought to behave accordingly and learned how to maneuver and survive in the tricky waters.

Clarice Lispector was one of those Jews. Her skillful negotiation of the authoritarian terrain becomes apparent in a barely known article that she published in the newspaper *Diario o Povo* on January 19, 1941, where she is identified as a staff journalist for the Agência Nacional. The fawning rhetoric in praise of the regime runs thick — in this case paeans to First Lady Darcy Vargas's orphanage, Girls Town, "Cidade das Meninas." But Lispector being Lispector, she manages to reveal her own perspective even in this set propaganda piece: antiwar, antiracist, antixenophobic Brazilianism.

Entitled "Where Happiness Will Be Taught" ("Onde se ensinará a ser feliz"), the essay opens with a subtle *critique* of Father Edward Flanagan's lauded Boys Town, the American model for Vargas's scheme. (Did Lispector see the Oscar-winning film *Boys Town*, starring Spencer Tracy and Mickey Rooney, released in 1938?) She calls the impulse behind the village "um sentimentalismo anacrônico," charming in its "primitiva simplicidade," a city sophisticate's cynical judgment of the children's hamlet utopian kinder-democracy. And yet — what seems counter to "civilization" should be a paradigm for future civilization: without racial and religious prejudice, without hatred — the great hatred born out of inbred individualism, "which at Boys Town dies, humiliated, at the sound of the day's first bell." Father Flanagan's boys will never want war, Lispector concludes. ("Os memmos do padre Flanagan jamais desearaõ a guerra.") Her stance against "preconceitos de raça, de religão, e o odio . . . a guerra," however camouflaged, will appear again and again during the war years.

The thorny sociopolitical context I have just described resounds more personally in two letters Lispector wrote to Getúlio Vargas himself, asking or, really, anxiously begging him to let her become a Brazilian citizen as soon as possible, without the usual yearlong waiting process. (The missives are dated June 3, 1942, and October 23, 1942, the second following the first unanswered one. Lispector got to the president through somebody, *A Noite* editor André Carrazzoni, who knew somebody, Foreign Minister Osvaldo Aranha.) I quote from the first letter, typed on *A Noite* letterhead:

> Quem lhe escreve é uma jornalista, ex-redatora da Agência Nacional (Departamento de Imprensa e Propaganda), atualmente n'*A Noite*, acadêmica da Facultade Nacional de Direito, e casualmente, russa também.
>
> Uma russa de 21 anos de idade e que está no Brasil há 21 anos menos alguns meses. Que no conhece uma sô palavra de russo mas que pensa, fala, escreve e age em português, fazendo disso sua profissão e nisso pousando todos os projectos do seu futuro, próximo ou longínquo. Que não tem pai nem mãe—o primeiro, assim como as irmãs da signatária, brasileiro naturalizado—e que por isso não se sente de modo algúm presa ao país de onde veio, nem sequer por ouvir relatos sobre ele. Que deseja casar-se com brasileiro e ter filhos brasileiros. Que, se fosse obrigada a voltar à Rússia, lá se sentiria irremediavelmente estangeira, sem amigos, sem profissão, sem esperanças.
>
> ....
>
> The one writing to you is a journalist, a former editor for the Agência Nacional (Department of Press and Propaganda) and currently for *A Noite*, a university student at the National Faculty of Law, and, as chance would have it, a Russian as well.
>
> A twenty-one-year-old Russian, who has been in Brazil for twenty-one years, less a few months, and who doesn't know a word of Russian. Who thinks, speaks, writes, and acts in Portuguese, turning it into her profession and depositing in it all her plans for the immediate and long-term future. Who has no father or mother—the former, as well as the signatory's sisters, are all naturalized Brazilians—and who for this reason harbors no feelings for the country from which she came, not even to hear stories about it. Who would like to marry a Brazilian and to bear Brazilian children. Who, if she were forced to return to Russia, would feel like a complete foreigner, bereft of friends, profession, or any hope.

Lispector's letter merits a careful reading because the unsaid and understood play as large a role as the said and stated, anticipating the suggestive indirection of her fiction. (Could an overlooked source of her insinuating and gap-filled prose be censorship, the need to keep quiet while speaking?) Fully aware of the regime's identity politics, and quickly establishing her links with its transmitters—the government news agency, a newspaper that toed the party line—Lispector choreographs these politics through the interplay between the code words *russa* and *brasileira*. "Russian" stands for the undesirable, real and imagined, in Vargas-land: the Bolshevik, Communist Jew ready to violently take over Brazil's government through a supposed "Cohen Plan," or the unassimilated defiler of Rio de Janeiro's most beautiful neighborhoods who had turned Copacabana into a ghetto, "Copacabanovich" (Lesser 96–97, 135).

Russian stands for the "russo-judeu," like the modernist maker of "arte degenerada" Lasar Segall, included in Hitler's infamous 1937 "entartete Kunst" exhibit of Nazi-condemned avant-garde art, and now equally assaulted by certain quarters in his Brazilian country of refuge. Segall wrote a passionate defense of free expression, published in 1943 (see his "Arte e política," quoted in Beccari 1984, 280–81; see also Tucci Carneiro and Lafer 2004). His words bear quoting: "Quando, num momento como este, [reacionários] tentam incentivar preconceitos raciais e étnicos, fomenter ódios, lançar a discórdia e a confusão e sob o pretexto de crítica adotam a terminologia de propaganda das nações do Eixo e aplicam em sentido injurioso a um artista e à sua produção os rótulos 'russo,' 'judeo,' 'arte degenerada,' etc., não pode haver dúdiva quanto aos verdadeiros sentimentos politicos que animan os autores de tais 'críticas de arte' e de onde o vento sopra" (When at a moment like this [reactionaries] try to inflame racial and ethnic prejudice, incite hatred, sow discord, and under the guise of (art) criticism make use of the Axis countries' propagandistic vocabulary, applying the malicious labels "Russian," "Jew," "degenerate art," and so on to an artist's work, there can be no doubt about these "art critics'" true political motives, and the direction from which these winds blow) (Beccari, 280–81; see also Tucci Carneiro and Lafer). Not incidentally, Lispector once remarked that she and her family looked like the immigrants in Segall's paintings, the most famous being *Navío de inmigrantes* (Immigrant Ship), 1939–1941.

"Russo," in short, stood for the Jewish Other who, after decades of a relatively open door in the early twentieth century, could now be kept from entering Brazil or, worse, could be deported once there, most dramatically in the case of Olga Benario, pregnant wife of leftist leader Luís Carlos Prestes, sent back to Europe to be imprisoned, tortured, and ultimately eliminated in Hitler's crematoria.

The specter of being forced to return to Russia isn't just hyperbole in Lispector's letter; it reflects a lurking fear. That is partly why the future novelist distances herself from everything Russian: her birth (almost), her thinking, speaking, writing, and acting, her profession and feelings, her future, even her memory—she doesn't even want to hear tales about the Old Country; a strong statement coming from a storyteller.

Orphaned of father and mother—the links with the Bolshevik USSR—she stands ready to be adopted by a new father- and motherland, to help birth the "novo homen brasileiro" by marrying a native-born, non-Jewish Brazilian (which she was about to do) and by bearing him Brazilian children (which she eventually did). Lispector's letter is a writerly tour de force of "Brazilianness," an apologia pro vita sua couched in the ideological terms required by the regime, from an author supposedly unaware of social issues. The bothersome question, are you Brazilian or foreign, perturbed Lispector her whole career, and she was continually forced to reiterate, "I'm Brazilian, and that's the end of it." Anything Russian or Jewish was kept veiled.

The author eventually received her citizenship papers. And wedding Maury Gurgel Valente in a civil ceremony in 1943, she reinvented herself but also, very little mentioned, protected herself. She was about to move to the European theater of operations, to an Italy still half-controlled by the Nazis, who were busily hunting Jews, then to a postwar Switzerland that had declared "the boat is full" to refugees from Hitler. Switzerland was now suffering from a malaise of neutrality, Gurgel Valente wrote in a message to his superiors, from a shame syndrome at being happy amid so much misery (Lispector 2002, 143). Shielded and privileged, Lispector nevertheless reacted to what she saw in her abundant correspondence and, yes, in her fiction, structuring an intertextual web like Borges, like Guimarães Rosa, like Mistral; an intertextual web that goes beyond fiction even as it impacts on fiction, developing novel forms of narration, and confronting the Second World War and, maybe despite Haya-Clarice herself, the Holocaust.

Naples: Chronicles of the Recent War, August 1944

Maury's posting to Naples wasn't incidental: the southern Italian port served as the headquarters for the Força Expedicionária Brasileira (Brazilian Expeditionary Force), or FEB, the 25,000-man-strong division that fought alongside the Allies in the Italian Campaign. Gurgel Valente was sent, along with other Brazilian diplomats, to establish a mission to support the troops. The FEB has rightly been called the forgotten Allies, but the "Cobras Fumantes" (smoking cobras)—as the division was known—traveling to Europe in U.S. military vessels, and cooperating with the American military command, contributed importantly to the multinational force that dislodged the Germans from the Italian Front.

Journalist Rubem Braga, sent to report on the FEB, and one of Lispector's friends and correspondents in this period, describes a broken and impoverished Italy, victim of Hitler's scorched-earth policies, organized looting, and slave labor; a poor and hungry Naples whose people live, dress, and eat badly; the ancient ruins of great cities with their centuries-old walls, plazas, and statues standing injured beside the new ruins of bombardment and tank warfare; and the courageous fight against the so-called supermen carried out by the allegedly "inferior races"—among them dark-skinned Brazilians whom even self-styled ultranationalist sociologists in Brazil called racially defective, and Jews, many from British Mandatory Palestine, who as excellent soldiers belied Hitler's "Aryan" claims of "Semitic cowardice" (Braga 109–10). Braga later gathered his dispatches into a book entitled *Crônicas da Guerra* (War Chronicles). In a letter to Lispector, he tells her of its imminent publication (*Correspondencias* 210). Braga came to be considered the inventor of the Brazilian newspaper *crônica*—more free-form than a short story, more documentary than fiction.

While Braga was composing his accounts, Lispector was creating her own idiosyncratic *crônicas da guerra* in her numerous letters to her beloved sisters, Tânia and Elisa, and to her personal friends and literary colleagues. Teresa Montero, editor of many of Lispector's published letters, has it right when she says that today we increasingly value an author's correspondence and manuscripts along with "finished" literary creations, because as private documents they reveal stages of a creative process, and lay bare moments of personal and public lived experience (*Minhas queridas*, 15). Nâdia Battella Gotlieb, Lispector's biographer, perceptively characterizes her missives as an amalgam of the epistolary genre and travel literature, the chronicle of daily events and the autobiographical mode (189). They foreshadow the many *crônicas* Lispector later published in the Brazilian press, composing what recent critics have come to appreciate as ingenious writings, akin to the innovative New Journalism.

Unsurprisingly, the writer's wartime letters often move from surface depiction of the lived moment into deeper reflection, with ordinary incidents as protostories leading to penetrating commentary, just as in her developing fiction. One need only read *A cidade sitiada* (1949), the novel resulting from her European years, to see the narrative's cotexts in *vice-consulesa* Clarice Gurgel Valente's wartime letter-diaries.

The novelist's circuitous journey from Rio to Naples took her to places as varied as Lisbon, Liberia, Guinea, Dakar, Algiers, and Casablanca, voyaging on planes of the Air Transport Command (ATC) and staying on Allied bases. As for the last of these, she was sent as a diplomatic courier to the city made mythical by Humphrey Bogart and Ingrid Bergman, and remarked how pretty it was—but nothing like in the film (letter to her sisters from Algiers, 19 August 1944). As in *Casablanca*, itself about the war, Nazis, and refugees, reality and unreality, fact and fiction mingled in this odyssey through cities full of soldiers, hotels taken over by army authorities, and ports loaded with *destróiers*, to use Lispector's spelling. Naples itself was a war zone, the takeoff point for the battlefront (Lispector 2002, 116).

In a letter to her friend and mentor Lúcio Cardoso, Lispector bemoans her trek as exhausting, filled with bouts of anxiety. Her account of a ten-day stay in Lisbon, a small gem of literary reportage, lets us follow the passage from superficial social whirl, humorously recounted, to caustic critique resonant with echoes of the Holocaust.

Talking about the respected personalities and famed writers she met, Clarice tells Lúcio Cardoso, "Generally speaking I was a 'social success.' But later Maury and I stared at each other, pale and exhausted, loathing those people together with their programs of hatred and purity. Everyone is intelligent, good looking, educated, contributes to charity and reads books; but why don't they go to hell?" "De um modo geral eu tenho feito 'sucesso social.' Só que depois eu e Maury ficamos pálidos, exaustos, olhando um para o outro, detestando as populações e com programas de ódio e pureza. . . . Todo o mundo é inteligente, é bonito, é educado, dá esmolas e lê livros; mas por que não vão para um inferno qualquer?" (Lispector 2002, 55).

Battella Gotlieb puts her finger on the essence of Lispector's discomfort, repeated in letters to her sisters, when she says that the encounters in Lisbon lay bare a "concealed identity" that at times explodes (190). Put more bluntly, Clarice the Jew, disturbed by Nazi propaganda in neutral Portugal, who was "passing" in a Europe marked by Hitler's "programs of hatred and purity," felt besieged and, at least verbally, counterattacked. (The comment on German propaganda appears in a letter from Lisbon, written to her sisters on August 7, 1944.)

At the time Portugal was under the iron rule of right-wing dictator Antonio de Salazar, who maintained neutrality but personally favored Hitler. In 1939, Salazar had issued orders to Portuguese consuls not to issue visas to "foreigners of indefinite or contested nationality; the stateless; or Jews expelled from their countries of origin." Those who failed to comply would do so at their own peril, among them the heroic consul in Bordeaux, France, Aristides de Sousa Mendes, who issued transit visas to Jewish victims of

Nazism only to be dismissed from his post and ostracized.[1]

The war diary takes on other ominous shades once in Naples, with Lispector writing to Lúcio Cardoso on March 26, 1945: "I'm working in the American hospital with the Brazilians. I visit all of the wounded men every day, I give them whatever they need, I talk to them, I argue with the administration asking for things, in short, I'm unbelievable. I go there every morning and when I can't go I get annoyed, because the wounded men already expect me as much as I miss them." "Estou trabalhando no hospital americano, com os brasileiros. Visito diariamente todos os doentes, dou o que eles precisam, converso, discuto com a administração pedindo coisas, enfim sou formidável. Vou lá todas as manhãs e quando sou obrigada a faltar fico aborrecida, tanto os doentes já me esperam, tanto eu mesma tenho saudade deles" (70).

If Rio intimidated Lispector with "O Brasil para os brasileiros" and Lisbon *com programas de ódio e pureza*, Naples unsettled her with *os doentes*. Actively ministering to the injured Cobras Fumantes brought the vice consul's spouse face-to-face with the bodily price of war—the Brazilians suffered high casualties in the Monte Castello assaults, without receiving enough credit from the Allies (see McGann).

But in the same letter to Lúcio Cardoso, the immediate flesh-and-blood horror once more gives way to a meditation, now on pain enlarged and assuaged by the natural beauties surrounding Naples. Lispector paints a portrait of her visit to nearby Mt. Vesuvius, still smoking a year after its 1944 eruption, which piled devastation by lava on devastation by war, erasing whole villages as well as U.S. bomber aircraft. She then continues, moving from the visual to the emotional in what would become a characteristic writing tendency: "I've surely already told you about a place called Posillipo. It means 'respite from pain' in Greek. And pain is really suspended for a moment; the colors are so soft, so without savagery, the place is so beautiful, so beautiful, with the sea, the trees, and the mountain. I'm almost left with a bad impression: there are just too many pretty things, and it seems that I've neither the time nor the strength, the fact is that I'd be more at ease with just one." "E certamente já lhe falei em Posilipo, que é um lugar. Em greco quer dizer pausa da dor. A dor realmente fica um instante suspensa, tão doces são as cores, tão sem salvageria, tão belo é o lugar com mar, árvores, montanha. A minha impressão é quase ruim: há coisas bonitas em exceso, eu parece que não tenho tempo ou força, o fato é que ficaria mais calma com uma" (71).

An excess of nature's beauty amidst the ugliness: can even such loveliness be calming? And can human-made wonders, the Michelangelo, Botticelli, and Raphael masterpieces Lispector marveled at in Florence, the grand Middle Age and Renaissance palaces, be any more soothing, standing side by side with requisitioned hotel rooms and galleries still shut due to the fighting? How to take in and make sense of the conflicting vistas and emotions in a Europe still seething from fascist paroxysms?

The utter physical and moral exhaustion of the war comes through in Lispector's letter to her sisters on May 9, 1945, one day after VE Day marking the surrender of Germany. After some sisterly chitchat about hats and photos and wonderful carved wooden boxes (the boxes will play a novelistic role later), she says:

> Uma das coisas de que eu estou surpreendida e vocês certamente também é que no bilhete de hoje de manhã não falei no fim da guerra. Eu pensava que quando ela acabasse eu ficaria durante alguns dias zonza. O fato é que o ambiente influiu muito nisso. Aposto que no Brasil a alegria foi maior. Aqui não houve comemoraçoes senão feriado ontem; é que veio tão lentamente esse fim, o povo está tão cansado (sem falar que a Itália foi de algum modo vencida) que ninguém se emocionou demais. (73)
>
> ....
>
> One of the things that I'm surprised about and I'm sure you too is that in this morning's note I didn't mention the end of the war. I thought that when it ended I'd be giddy for a few days. The truth is that the environment has a lot to do with it. I bet that in Brazil the joy was much greater. Here there were no celebrations, just a public holiday yesterday; it's that the end came so slowly, people are so tired (without talking about the fact that Italy was in some sense defeated) that no one got overly emotional.

Berne: Instante Alpino, April 1946

April 1946: Clarice arrives in Switzerland by way of the great monuments of antiquity: in Egypt, she views the Sphinx and pyramids; in Greece, riding in an American jeep, she sees the Acropolis and Parthenon, on which the Nazi flag was raised a scant few years earlier, in 1941, only to be torn down by Greek patriots. After the loud and chaotic unruliness of Naples, the idyllic setting, penetrating silence, and methodical dignity—excessive dignity—of Berne strike her, she relates to Elisa in one of her first letters from the land of lakes unscathed by ruination (July 17, 1946, *Minhas queridas* 131–32). Yet the shadows of the just-ended hecatomb are not far away, particularly the stirrings of postwar thought, the endeavor to decipher how the road from Aristotle led to Auschwitz.

Once she was more settled in Berne (though hardly at home), Lispector's *crônicas* continued unabated, some now published in Brazilian newspapers. One is especially striking—the initial version of Lispector's much-reprinted chronicle "Berne," here headed "Instante Alpino" (An Alpine Moment) (1949). Against a clichéd sketch of pine trees and snowcapped mountains, the author perfectly strips away the apparent serenity with a penetrating moral assessment:

> The foreign visitor, confronted with such perfect beauty, may find it difficult to elucidate its mystery. The beauty of the Swiss landscape is all too evident. It's so crystalline, so orderly, in some ways so abstract that after an initial impression of accessibility, there comes a feeling of something impenetrable. At first, the guileless joy of a picture postcard; then little by little, the repose and symmetry begin to provoke unrest.
>
> The ancient and narrow city streets also betray a certain something not quite visible to the naked eye, an intimately austere way of life, a magical link with a past that barely reveals its History to the unknowing stranger. . . . In these fortified towns, with their towers, alleyways, arches and silence, the Devil has been expelled beyond the mountains. An uneasy peace has remained behind, the marks of a life molded by harshness . . . perfected in the Swiss obsession with cleanliness, with a desire to sacrifice the fatally impure and disordered human element to the pure abstraction of nature. Order is no longer a means, but almost an artistic necessity. Order is the only environment that the native of Switzerland can breathe.

As in Rio, Lisbon, and Naples, a sense of unrest, already intimated in her early letter to Elisa, seizes Lispector: too much cold(hearted) "order" at the expense of warm(hearted) "impurity"; frozen geography reinforcing fortified cities reinforcing fanatic cleanliness reinforcing frightening inhumanity. In "An Alpine Moment" Swiss "neutrality" borders literally and figuratively (and I think purposefully) on the Nazi mindset.[2]

Surrounded by this chilling natural, mental, and political topography, the copious chronicler will try to elaborate scenes of the late war into a novel. A novel that would be thought (always associated with Lispector), and be action (rarely associated with her). A novel that would attempt to understand through narrative why Socrates ended up in Buchenwald—the same questions vexing postwar philosophy—and also to stand firm before the menacing armies of purity and odium.

O FORASTEIRO, tendo diante dos olhos essa beleza perfeita, não saberá talvez elucidar o seu mistério. A cena suíça tem um excesso de evidência de beleza. E' uma paisagem límpida e sem confusões, em alguns pontos tão abstrata que, após a primeira sensação de facilidade, se seguirá a idéia do indevassável. De início a ingenuidade feliz de um cartão postal. Mas aos poucos a imobilidade e o equilíbrio começam a inquietar.

Também nas ruas antigas e tortuosas das cidades há alguma coisa que não se dá aos olhos, uma vida íntima e austera, continuação mágica do passado que cede ao estrangeiro incauto apenas a sua História. O que têm de tonto espaço as vistas das montanhas, têm de concentração as pequenas cidades altas, de casas e igrejas apertadas por muros que já tombaram. Nessas cidadelas de tôrres, becos, ogivas e silêncio, o Demônio terá fugido para as montanhas. Restou uma paz perturbadora, e marcas de uma vida que se formou com dureza, marcas da Reforma, sinais de conquista lenta, aperfeiçoamento obstinado e penoso. Obstinação que se trabalha mesmo nessa ânsia tão suíça de limpeza, quem sabe se vinda de um desejo de realizar em terra essa clareza do ar, essa lei de nitidez que a montanha dita. Asseio que é quase vontade de imolação das coisas humanas, fatalmente impuras e desordenadas, à límpida abstração dessa natureza. A ordem não é mais meio, é necessidade quase de arte. A ordem é sobretudo o único ambiente onde um homem suíço pode respirar.

Porque um tanto como essa natureza, são as criaturas dessa terra. Rostos ascéticos, economia de expressão, e, nas fisionomias pacíficas e às vêzes pesadas, uma fôrça silenciosa que lembra a do fanatismo. Disse alguém que o suíço não é soldado, é guerreiro. Poder-se-ia dizer que o homem suíço é um guerreiro porque a mulher suíça é mulher de guerreiro. E' um ser severo e duro, votado para algum sacrifício. E' de se vê-la nos concertos de igreja, o rosto sem pintura, impassível, banhando-se com um prazer sem manifestação nos sons antigos do órgão e nas vozes altas do côro, música purificada que responde à alegria austera dêsse povo. Ela não se encostará à cadeira, manter-se-á um pouco solene e indecifrável, sem o encanto da moleza, mas com alguma graça puritana que reponta não sei de onde, vencendo uma moda que tem pudor da vaidade.

Mas quando vem a primavera há uma pequena revolução sôbre os tetos medievais. O sol como é precioso depois de um longo inverno. Cada flor é um alívio. Blusas claras, pequenas golas brancas aparecem então nos vestidos escuros, tímido tributo à luz, delicada contribuição feminina à florescência da terra. As crianças pulam das casas e brotam nas ruas, os velhos se sentam sérios nos jardins — essa é a terra dos velhos respeitáveis. Dos bancos contemplam os lagos brilhantes, os Alpes nevados, e êsse ar de apressada alegria em cada ramo. Pois cada estação já é prenúncio perturbado de outra, e a natureza sensível é apenas mutação: a primavera é a espera do estio, quando tudo se perfuma com tepidez — as folhas se tornam mais ásperas e as flores, que a morte de outono já espreita, mais urgentes e violentas. O outono será o ocaso dêsse dia; águas, contornos de montanhas, superfícies, pequenas formas, tudo tomará, sob o vento mais frio e uma luz sem sol, uma intimidade de pensamento.

Por enquanto porém é de novo a primeira primavera e mal se tem tempo de manter-se nela um pouco mais — sob as pontes de Berna o rio frígido corre ligeiro. Homens e mulheres abrem as casas e recebem as primícias da claridade. Claridade, silêncio e mistério — eis o que se vê de uma janela suíça.

CLARICE LISPECTOR

Courtesy Archivo Clarice Lispector, Casa de Rui Barbosa, Rio de Janeiro.

The undertaking was a tall order, the little sister confided to her older sibling Tania:

> Estou trabalhando, mal ou bem; falta ainda o sentido do livro, uma razão mais forte para ele existir—aos poucos é que esta irá subindo à tona, á medida que eu for trabalhando. O que tem me perturbado intimamante é que as coisas do mundo chegaram para mim a um certo ponto en que eu tenho que saber como encará-las, quero dizer, a situcão de guerra, a situacão das pessoas, essas tragédias. Sempre encarei com revolta. Mas ao mesmo tempo que sinto necessidade de fazer alguma coisa, sinto que não tenho meios. Você diria que eu tenho, através do meu trabalho. Eu tenho pensado muito nisso e não vejo caminho, quer dizer, un camino verdadeiro. Talvez eu não esteja vendo o problema maduro, pode ser que a solucão venha daqui a anos, não sei. (Letter from Berne, May 8, 1946, *Minhas queridas*, 114)
>
> ....
>
> I'm working, for better or worse; the book is still missing a sense of direction, a stronger reason for it to exist—it will emerge little by little, as I keep working. What bothers me deep down is that the things of this world reached a certain point for me in which I need to know how to face them—the state of war, the situation people are in, those tragedies. I've always faced them with disgust. But at the same time that I feel the need to do something, I feel that I don't have the means. You'll say that I do have them, through my work. I've thought a lot about it and I don't see a way, a real way. Maybe I'm not seeing the whole problem, maybe the solution will come years from now, I don't know.

Tentative yet determined, Lispector divulges the impulse behind *A cidade sitiada* as coming from deep inside her, needing to find novelistic expression. What Borges termed the time of the wolf vexed her very being; she had *to do something*, even if incompletely. For a writer whose mode of speaking was susurration and stillness the statement couldn't be clearer; *The Besieged City* resounds with this loud whispering, this quiet assertion. I will "dare" to call *The Besieged City*, composed totally in Berne, Clarice's World War II novel, although it is set in São Geraldo, a fictional suburb in 1920s Brazil, although it centers on the protagonist Lucrécia Neves's womanly consciousness and successive love affairs, from a lieutenant, to a bourgeois whom she marries, to a doctor, none of which lasts, and so she runs away from the decaying town. This fraying summary scarcely conveys the semiotic power of the novel whose structure is allegorical, inviting a process of decipherment in order to find the "equivalencies" (Battella Gotlieb, 264).

Did no one notice that the suburb's iconic object, a cylindrical factory tower rising ominously above the houses, *a tôrre cilíndrica da usina,* elicits the remark: "If this were a world of heroes what a terrible face it would have" ("Fôsse éste um mundo de heróis que perfil assustador teria") (*cs*, 45)? Or that in the shadow of São Geraldo's "towers arched over the memory of wars and conquests," Napoleon and his troops behind him sit silently on their impatient horses, ready to attack: "Napoleão sôbre o cavalo de Naploeão . . . Atrás tôda a tropa em silêncio" (72)? This, along with references all through the book to the airplanes repeatedly flying over the city, the threatened food shortages, the digging of trenches for fortification, armored cars on every corner, victims described as sacrifices, the "reality" of wars and hospitals, trains that pose catastrophe. Throughout *A cidade sitiada*, technology menaces, the mercantile city ready to sacrifice everything for a much-vaunted "progress."

The allusions to Napoleon and to towers are less esoteric if we remember that throughout World War II, Napoleon was a not so veiled stand-in for Hitler. Thus, British historian Philip Guedalla in the *New York Times*, February 2, 1941, on the invasion of Russia: "If Napoleon Couldn't, Can Hitler?" Analogous comparisons appeared in other major newspapers and magazines. Threatening cylinders were similarly coded references to the war factories and crematoria—for instance, Borges's blood towers, *torres de sangre*, in his 1940 fantastic story "Tlön, Uqbar, Orbis Tertius," where the inhuman and totalitarian order of Tlön conquers the human disorder of our orb, third from the sun.

Looking elsewhere—and, to be fair, not possessing the documentation we now have—most exegetes neglected to read the signs and to discern that Lispector did not wait till the 1970s to insinuate "those tragedies" in Europe into her fiction. To my knowledge, Diane Marting is one of the few who briefly glimpsed between the lines in the introduction to her mammoth Lispector bio-bibliography: ". . . Clarice's nascent ability to translate grand political debates on moral issues into daily choices of her unpolitical protagonists can be seen in . . . [*A cidade sitiada*]. The frivolous and small-minded Lucrécia Neves, who is so chauvinistic about the suburb of São Geraldo, can be read as a coded, allegorical, and very understated replica in fiction of the hyperbolic Nazi madness of killing people for their ethnicity, sexuality, nationality, or political beliefs" (xxvii).

In the same bio-bibliography, however, the essay by Elizabeth Lowe on the novel itself says nothing along this vein, noting like most commentators that the book traces the metamorphosis of a small suburb into a modern Brazilian city: an external mutation through the mainly male forces of "progress," and an internal transformation through the female power of Lucrécia's mind, which metaphorically "besieges" and refashions São Geraldo in her own image (25).

Lucrécia, who in a sense *is* the suburb, stands against the external S. Geraldo but also becomes partially contaminated by its evils: intolerance, xenophobia, the cult of violence, denigration of personhood, and pursuit of industrial modernity at any price. But she has another side, a kind of internal foundational strength, a timeless power of rebirth linked to the ancient roots of Western civilization, Greece and everything that it represents. By means of this power, regeneration might be possible in the endless cycle of destruction and reconstruction of the city, the ordered polis continually threatened by the girded hosts of hell.

Read in conjunction with the *crônicas*, *A cidade sitiada* rings from its very title with Lispector's experience of the war, projected by a Latin American from a battered Europe on an imagined Brazilian geography. A twice-cited Berne-in-miniature found among Lucrécia's all-important bibelots, and obliquely observed (*um olhar de lado*, a view from the side), betokens the "real" site of writing: "a caixa de madeira com vista dos Alpes na tampa . . . a vista dos Alpes em extraordinária evidencia . . . A casa parecia ornamentada com os despojos de uma cidade maior" (*CS*, 51–52). "The wooden box with the view of the Alps on the cover . . . the view of the Alps in plain sight . . . the house seemed decorated with the spoils of a much larger city." The same mountains had elicited the frightful "Instante Alpino," the same move from viewing a landscape to moral, political, or emotional exegesis. We find the sideways Latin American perception here, the outsider/insider gaze that can make for fortunate results.

The creative eye, the perceiving or "spying" eye, as it is often called in the book, plays a major and dual role, on the one hand facing the Old Continent's tragedies, on the other seeking "respite from pain," *posillipo* in Greek, by conceiving a Brazilian space of possibility not entirely utopian, itself furnished with the detritus of the great Western capitals. Lispector does not sing the rose-colored wonders of Brazil à la her contemporary, the grateful Austrian-Jewish refugee from Hitler, Stefan Zweig, in his *Brazil: Land of the Future*, original title: *Brasilien: Ein Land der Zukunft*, 1941. Her vision is much more critical.[3]

São Geraldo I: Violence and Fascism

From its opening moment, the book thrusts us into a warlike zone; the first character we meet is *tenente* Felipe, Lucrécia's uniformed lieutenant boyfriend. A monstrous Walpurgis Night ensues—a nocturnal saint's day celebration lit by the explosion of (artificial) bombs and huge bonfires, horrible, ghostly, and reeking of disaster (8–10). There is nothing spiritual or calming about the religious commemoration, ringing as it does with hysterical bells, so the young woman flees despite the soldier's "protection," like an escapee from an auto-da-fé, to hide in the darkness behind the closed doors of her attic dwelling. *Lucrécia Neves escapara* (10). She had succeeded in escaping—for the time being. The suburb is what humanistic geographer Yi-Fu Tuan would name a topography of terror, the ghastly and murderous city also found in Borges's "El Aleph" or "Death and the Compass," Guimarães Rosa's "A Velha" or his "Páramo," all penned around the Hitler time, mirroring the dread, too. No space is safe, fleeing becomes the normal.

Poised between epochs, São Geraldo oscillates between old beliefs and modern technologies. Wild horses roaming its outskirts occasionally invade the not yet fully modern suburb, telluric animal forces ripe for harnessing or for unleashing destruction. In the breach between tradition and modernity, newfangled, fascist-like ideologies fill the void, spread by group indoctrination. Fascism seems the occult center of the narration, the never-pronounced word.

The same initial chapter gives us a sketch of such a group, the AJFSG, Associação de Juventude Feminina de S. Geraldo, S. Geraldo Young Women's Association. Lispector appears to be seriously spoofing on brainwashing organizations such as the Frauenschaft, the Nazi Women's League, the Jungmädel, the very young girls' section of the Hitler Youth, and the Bund Deutscher Mädel, the made-for-adolescents Union of German Young Women. Like these, the AJFSG is born (and dies) on the cusp of a new era full of threatening winds and frightening omens, quickly acquiring a hymn that thunders with barely concealed violence, vociferously sung at meetings full of agitation led by the fiery Cristina, a good orator and voice of a "progress" destined to consume its adherents. Cristina is *nossa vanguardista*, our guide to the future, the women smile.

Soon new principles and new *projetos de pureza* replace the innocently charitable good works previously undertaken by the AJFSG. All have to strive toward the Ideal that demands unthinking sacrifice, sacrifice of the flesh: *O ideal, o ideal! Mas que queriam elas dizer com o ideal!* The ideal! The ideal! But what did they mean by the ideal?

When Lucrécia, who joins the AJFSG in order to fit in, asks, what *is* the ideal, the confused young women stare at her angrily, and she is forced to resign, while Cristina, her body smelling of milk and sweat, gains strength, ever more happy, and more cruel. Cristina, the leader, represents the ideal of feminine beauty: short, a bit chubby, as befits a woman suited to life in the suburb in those heady days (14–16). Shades of the "new" woman?

I have paraphrased Lispector's description at length to illustrate just how she captures the spirit and, so sensitive to language, the shrill rhetoric of fascism.[4]

Again in the attic-refuge after her debacle, Lucrécia dementedly weaves her alternate reality, *writes* her alternate reality, just as her creator was doing, thinking, and scribbling self-referentially: "She stopped, holding the ostrich-feather pen in her hand, the half-written page on her desk. . . . Lucrécia Neves put the pen down on the desk, still submerged in thought. . . . She erased everything and started all over again" (70). Channeling the good/bad energy of the stallions, the colt-woman (who would be a recurring image in Lispector) fights for representation, attacking and retreating and again and again, finally, when words fail her, even resorting to nonverbal language, to gesturing and to minimalist signing with just one foot and one hand, so as to make thought break through, so as not to surrender: "And she would see things like a horse. Because . . . even at night the city was busy fortifying itself and by the morning new trenches would be in place. From her bed she at least tried to listen to the grassy hill where nameless horses were galloping in the shadows, returned to a state of hunt and war. . . ." "E veria as coisas como um cavalo. Porque . . . mesmo de noite a cidade trabalhava fortificando-se e de manhã novas trincheiras estariam de pé. De sua cama procurava ao menos escutar o morro de pasto onde nas trevas cavalos sem nome galopavam retornados ao estado de caça e guerra. . . ." (20). Lucrécia Neves declares war—war of the sexes, war on São Geraldo, war on exclusionist philosophies and limiting languages. The young woman, striking for *her* Ideal, becomes enmeshed, says Lispector before French poststructuralism, in the very logic she is striving to overthrow (59).

São Geraldo II: The Ruin(s) and Rebirth of Western Civilization

Lucrécia Neves belongs to the 1920s and 1940s, when the novel is set, to Napoleon's nineteenth century, with his mounted troop waiting, and hurling back in her dream through the tunnels of time to antiquity. In a visionary state she challenges space, thought, and language—and time, breaking down the chronotope of linearity and progress. At the novel's start she is said to possess an "archaic role that is reborn every time a town is founded, the story of her travails shaped the spirit of a city" (16). Her lover after the lieutenant is Perseu, named after the great Greek hero who slew the terrible filly of a mare, Medusa. The oracular voice of the city, the guardian of its memory, spirit, hardness, and pain also bears a Greek name, Efigênia, Iphigenia, in Hellenic lore "born to strength" but sacrificed by her father to appease the gods (21–22). Lucrécia herself is Efigênia redux, Medusa, and Centaur. Degraded and ironic versions, all retain the aura of a mythic time outside time, remembered and reenacted. Pindar, singer of the majestic odes to the Olympians, provides the novel's telling epigraph, "No céu, aprender é ver; na terra, é lembrar-se": In the heavens learning is seeing, on earth it is remembering.

These hints of a hoary temporality, long before the onset of modernity when things fall apart, come to full fruition in the same lengthy and meaning-laden visionary sequence in chapter 5, "No jardim" (In the garden), where everything is real but seen as through a mirror, where Napoleon and his troops wait to charge; the Corsican's impatient horses may be waiting for dawn, but Lucrécia is in no hurry, and she hallucinates on, until she discovers that she is a Greek maiden, draped in flowing skirts, her head encircled by a band (73). Armless Greek statues, torn from their place of origin, that Lucrécia distractedly glanced at in a magazine seem to have come alive with all their godly potency. "Appearance," the printed photographic image, morphs into "reality"—the "reality" of a vision.

But *phenomenon* and *noumenon*, surface flux and essential forms, names and things, constitute the heart of Greek philosophy, the foundational speculations of Western culture, and in the apparition Hellenic dress gives way to Hellenic thought, subversively done by a woman: she was, Lispector writes, "Greek in a still to be built city trying to name every single thing, so that through the centuries things would acquire the meaning of their names. Her life was built, along with other patient lives, of what later would be lost in the very form of things. She pointed with her finger, the faceless Greek woman. And her destiny as a Greek was as unconscious then as it was now in S. Geraldo. Would anything remain of what was so long ago? Insistence: she pointed." "Grega numa cidade ainda não erguida, procurando designar cada coisa para que através dos séculos elas tivessem o sentido de seus nomes. E sua vida erguia com outras vidas pacientes o que perderia mais tarde no própia forma das coisas. Apontava com o dedo, a grega sem rostro. E seu destino então era tão inconsciente quanto agora em S. Geraldo. O que retara de tão longe? A insistência: ela apontava" (73–74).

Lucrécia dreams the *ruin(s)* of Western civilization that Lispector has experienced throughout the Mediterranean: a broken statue, eyeless, lipless, hardened stone disarticulated in the shadows of a garden, ready to be carted away. As if tortured, she has been left to deteriorate head upside down, feet tied together, the capital column shattered, mosquitoes buzzing, rusty, empty cans tumbling in the mud, a buried bark's prow jutting pityingly out of the sand (74). The once-mighty Hellenic ships that carried Odysseus's and Achilles's progeny, sung to by Homer and Pindar, are reduced to archaeological trash. *O que retara de tão longe?* "Would anything remain of what was so long ago?"

Here lies the detritus of the glory that was Greece, a landscape of ruination, ravaged by the Nazis' proposed Thousand Year Reich, but waiting to reawaken at a rooster's crow, if only there were an insistence, a remembering, a pointing of the finger to a potential postcatastrophic day when names and things would no longer be split apart, and the polis would once again assume its rightful, civil heritage.

On that day of marvel, the vision goes on, the vessel's mast would burst forth from its misty grave, ready once more to set sail, a hued peacock would strut among the garbage, a new dawn would emerge. In the ever repeating cycle of destruction and reconstruction, wild horses would once more be tamed and tied to wagons, and men would innocently build cities made of "things," things that needed to be pointed to, and again called by their ancient names (74–75).

The sound of beating drums from the Boy Scouts' military march abruptly wakens Lucrécia from her reverie, pulling her back to the brutal "reality" from which her mind took flight, but centaurs still calmly float across the sky, and on one of S. Geraldo's streets three stone women, caryatids, hold up the portal of a modern building—the ancient order and promise never entirely shaken, if not fulfilled; at the book's end, Lucrécia flees S. Geraldo, her image, reproduced in a photograph, ever more distant from her "real" face—the gap ever wider between *phenomenon* and *noumenon*, existence and essence. (I can't help but think now of Walter Benjamin's "Art in the Age of Mechanical Reproduction.")

A Brazilian among the Ruins

Embattled in Berne, a woman and a Brazilian writing in Portuguese, on presumably domestic and amorous, not world-historical, matters, and hence neglected, through her ruination-filled book Lispector meditates on the "disaster of history that piles wreckage upon wreckage," as her frequently cited canonical contemporary Walter Benjamin, student of the ruin and the fragment, expressed it in German in 1940, on the cusp of annihilation (257). Hers too is a "debris text," wrestled with toil out of the rubble she had seen firsthand—the old remains of Greece and Classical civilization and the new fragments of the world war: the double destruction of the West. A conceptual rubble as well, an acknowledgment that "the cataclysmic events that have only recently transpired: the collapse of German power, the genocide of the Jews, the decimation of Europe, the atomic bomb" (which Clarice mentions to her sisters) were a "*caesura* in a philosophical as well as a political sense" (Rabinbach).

Lispector was entirely aware of the caesura. In her first note to Elisa from cool Helvetia, Clarice comments on a book she is reading about Jean-Paul Sartre's existential philosophy, attacked, she says, both in France and Switzerland but gaining many adherents—most of whom don't even really get what it's all about it—simply because "everyone is crazed to believe in something after this war, even if this belief is a disbelief." "Todo o mundo está doido para crer em alguma coisa depois dessa guerra, mesmo que essa crença sea uma descrença" (July 17, 1946, *Minhas queridas*, 131–32). Why the assaults on Sartre? Clarice explains: ". . . the story about this theory's having a German origin is stupid. Even if it did, it wasn't in a political sense" (131). Without going into depth, the author is referring to the 1945–1946 "Heidegger affair," the early controversy about Martin Heidegger's pro-Nazi past, and by extension about Sartre and his kinsmen within the orbit of French existentialism, who acknowledged their debt to the Freiburg sage; others, including Marxists like Henri Lefebvre, tarred Heidegger's devotees with accusations of fascism (Rabinbach).

Lispector touches on the heart of a debate that hasn't gone away to this day, whether the guru's nasty politics besmirched his philosophy. But since the novelist focuses on Sartre, she appears to follow the Frenchman's reasoning: Heidegger's membership in the Nazi Party didn't make his thought National Socialist (Sartre, "À propos de l'existentialisme," cited in Kleinberg 2005, 170). She herself wanted to read Sartre with a sense of hope, Clarice admits, perhaps expecting too much, not quite digesting Sartre, nor forming an opinion. Sartre, she summarizes for Elisa, believes that existence precedes essence, in the sense that existing precedes what we are; and we are what we ourselves choose to be (July 17, 1946, *Minhas queridas*, 132).

The rethinking of the Greek queries made urgent by the devastation, which philosophers such as Sartre, Karl Jaspers, Max Horkheimer, Theodor Adorno, Emmanuel Levinas, and Heidegger himself (in part trying to whitewash his Nazi past) struggled to elaborate, were the problems Lispector was vying to give a narrative expression, with tremendous difficulty (she rewrote the book some twenty times). Perhaps *The Besieged City*'s jagged and shadowy form, its agonizingly eked-out name-signifiers would somehow be commensurate with the catastrophe, somehow persist in motioning to things signified, like the battered yet potentially revived Greek statue of her protagonist's séance: *A insistência: ela apontava*. "Insistence: she pointed." Lispector didn't yet realize the originality of her forms in the struggle to represent the catastrophe.

It bears to recall Clarice's words to Tania: "What bothers me deep down is that the things of this world reached a certain point for me in which *I need to know how to face them—the state of war, the situation people are in, those tragedies*. I've always faced them with disgust. But at the same time that I feel the need to do something, *I feel that I don't have the means*. You'll say that I do have them, through my work. I've thought a lot about it and I don't see a way, a real way. Maybe I'm not seeing the whole problem, maybe the solution will come years from now, I don't know."

What were the means to "master" the trauma? How could philosophy and art both "tell" the collapse of the Road of Reason, and produce Adorno's much reformulated "poetry after Auschwitz," or Maurice Blanchot's later named "writing of the disaster"? Lispector's novel asks these same questions from the perspective of a Latin American with an eye seeing in multiple directions. And it asks them cognizant that answers may take years, the process requiring one to return to the beginning of Reason—the route of postwar philosophy—since "Greek poets and thinkers first produced the grammar of the West, [and] their view of Being—as essence and existence—prevailed" (Rabinbach 12).

The classical legacy was contested territory. Hitler also admired Hellenic autocratic principles and architecture, and Heidegger, for one, wanted to found a new age by revising the primordial achievement of the pre-Socratics, with Nazi Germany as the foundational nation and German as the new "Greek" tongue. But just as did Lispector, anti-Nazi postwar classicism wanted to go back to the Greek dawn in a quest for a move beyond barbarism, all the while recognizing that inscribing the Greeks held the seeds of barbarism, ready to sprout again, like Lispector's horses-on-the-brink.

São Geraldo III: Pale, Inside the Train Car

Back to the Greeks, but the ancient Hellenes didn't bodily suffer the Shoah. However grudgingly and slowly, philosophy and literature had to face the *specificity* of the Holocaust, seen as the ground zero of Western Reason.

Adorno in the late 1940s and Blanchot beginning in the 1940s and 50s were among the first, but the process was lengthy—Blanchot's *L'Ecriture du désastre* (*The Writing of the Disaster*) appeared in the 1980s—and many still refused to glance at, let alone express, the Other ethically (as Levinas did) in ways that conveyed the rupture and discomfort of traditional representation. How about Lispector? *A cidade sitiada*, arrhythmic, jerky, discontinuous, defying smooth representation, is filled with ominous insinuations and evocative icons: the cylindrical factory tower, mark of a terrible-faced "world of heroes"; the "purity projects" and authoritarian Ideal of the xenophobic, fascist-minded young women's association; the sacrificial victims (*vítimas eram hóstias*) flesh-and-blood hosts in the new universe on the brink of the abyss, in an intense imagistic phrase with all its echoes of the culminating ritual of Christianity (CS, 44).

During the crucial dream-chapter Lucrécia's spying eye switches from sign to sign with Lispector's signature fluidity, Napoleon's mounts streaming into the broken Greek woman-statue brought to semilife. But at the beginning of the nightmare another stark image murmurs volumes: Lucrécia entrapped in a catastrophic train: "O grito de uma locomotiva na estacão cortou o quarto em lamúria, sacudindo no sono todo o primero andar! Tocada! No meio da catástrofe, pálida dentro da carruagem, adormeceu mais" (The roar of a locomotive in the station cut through the room like a lamentation, shaking the entire first floor in the dream! The whistle! In the middle of the catastrophe, pale inside the coach, she fell into deeper sleep).

This mechanized time-space of physical calamity then jars into an irrational cipher, 5721387, useless for account keeping, etched on an inexplicable pebble that Lucrécia finds along the way, only to morph into a mad scene of labor on the stairs of the Library (with a capital letter), Lucrécia Neves moaning, scratching, scrubbing, rubbing, mopping, polishing, lathing, sculpting the stone steps, preparing her war materiel; Napoleon is set for battle, the Greeks to revive.

The thick juxtaposition of emblems, the dizzying layering of symbols, *emblemas e símbolos* (CS, 28), trigger an allegorical vertigo in the reader—it did in me: nothing declares the Shoah, yet everything seems to evoke it: the towers and trains, nullifying numbers, helpless hosts, even the stultifying stone scrubbing. Lucrécia, the demented master carpenter, *mestre carpinteiro demente* (71), masks and unmasks her creator, the anguished master writer scratching and sculpting the tough, perturbing, and tragic war materiel: "O que tem me perturbado intimamente . . . a situacão de guerra, a situacão das pessoas, essas tragédias."

The hard-as-stone materiel of the word as well: scratching out her own writing in the midst of the catastrophe, furiously taking on the great Library, and fitfully embracing an impossible certainty, but the "promising confusion of words" (134). Paper also cuts, "papel também corta," Lucrécia discerningly instructs Perseu (96).

Lispector's spark of a creation, her splintered, eked-out text, her *olhar de lado*, view from the side, full of temporal-spatial fissures; of realities split between consciousnesses, waking and sleeping, seeing and remembering; of differing languages, spoken, written, gesturing; of sentences begun and stopped and words hurled out or basted together; of breaches between *phenomenon* and *noumenon*; of images of authoritarianism, warfare, and mechanized suffering; and of inquisitions about the cost of Enlightenment and progress comes close to (and earlier than) Blanchot's *L'Ecriture du désastre*: his perception of writing as doubly disastrous, as negativity, violence, tear, fragment; and more specifically, as the process by which something called the disaster is written. That "something" is called the Holocaust, the "utter-burn" where all meaning "took fire" (47) (*sic dixit* Blanchot circa 1980).

I believe Lispector, tentative but discerning, knew exactly what she was saying in the 1940s: "Maybe I'm not seeing the whole problem, maybe the solution will come years from now, I don't know." In the 1940s she had some inkling, a murmur; then she internalized the disaster, never to forget till the end of her life in the 1970s.

Rio: Because the Germans Did What They Did, 1976

With Lispector's ambivalence and slipperiness, her open comments on her "Jewish condition" were few and in between. So it isn't surprising that what she said in a 1976 interview has been transformed into a locus classicus, always cited as proof of her identity as an oxymoron, barely affirmed, quickly repudiated: "Sou judia, você sabe. . . . Eu, enfim, sou brasileira, pronto e ponto." (I'm Jewish, you know. . . . In short, I'm Brazilian, and that's it, once and for all.) In Berta Waldman's poetically rendered opinion, for instance, the author alludes to her origin directly but then gives the sentence such a sharp turn that she ends up negating the initial affirmation; curiously, says Waldman, Lispector's texts bear the mark of this same operation, simultaneously affirming and denying the identity link (259).

I would like to regard the quote in its entirety from another perspective, the treatment of the Shoah. Here is the exchange between Edilberto Coutinho, the interviewer, and the author:

"Você certa vez escreveu, livrai-me do orgulho de ser judeu? Por quê?"

"Eu sou judia, você sabe. Mas não acredito nessa besteira de judeu ser o povo eleito de Deus. Não é coisa nenhuma. Os alemães é que devem ser, porque fizeram o que fizeram. Que grande eleiçao foi essa, para os judeus? Eu, enfim, sou brasileira, pronto e ponto."

....

Didn't you once write, free me from the pride of being Jewish? Why?

I'm Jewish, you know. But I don't believe in that foolishness about the Jews being God's chosen people. No way is that so. The Germans must be because of what they did. What kind of great election was that for the Jews? In short, I'm Brazilian, and that's it, once and for all" (Coutinho, 168).

It is interesting how the conversation has been truncated in the commentaries, the ellipses censoring the part about the Germans. Lispector gives the answer to a very specific query about the *pride* of being Jewish, the idea of Jewish superiority. To that, she responds, yes, I'm Jewish, but I don't believe in Jews as *Übermenschen*, if anything Jews suffered due to that tenet. If you want to espouse the doctrine of a chosen people, then take the Germans, who did what they did to the so-called nation of God precisely because they held that *they* were the master race. In short, let's not start the arrogance-of-identity thing again, who's Jewish, who's foreign, who's Brazilian, who's supreme.[5]

Three decades after the Shoah and *A cidade sitiada* Lispector lets on in her inimitable manner how much the catastrophe persisted in troubling her. Had the solution she was looking for in the 1940s come many years later? Her writing in the end became ever more fragment and absence, ever more meditation and void. Largely eluding decades of critical judgment, the germinating documents for this writing were her *crônicas* and her novelistic creations from the World War II and Holocaust era that ably chronicled the cataclysms, and engendered new literary modes. As with Borges, another so-called fantasist, the eyes of the exegetes were usually elsewhere and the Shoah particularly was out of sight. But each author, from slightly different vantage points, created astonishingly hybrid texts that enrich the corpus of Holocaust literature.

Works Cited and Consulted

Beccari, Vera D'Horta. *Lasar Segall e o modernismo paulista*. São Paulo: Editora Brasiliense, 1984.

Benjamin, Walter. "Art in the Age of Mechanical Reproduction." *Illuminations*. Translated by Harry Zohn, 1969. 217–51.

Blanchot, Maurice. *L'Ecriture du désastre*. Paris: Gallimard, 1980.

Braga, Rubem. *Crônicas da Guerra*. Rio de Janeiro: Editora do Autor, 1964.

Cixous, Hélène. *Reading with Clarice Lispector*. University of Minnesota Press, 1990.

Clarice Lispector: Cadernos de literatura brasileira. Vols. 17–18. São Paulo: Instituto Moreira Salas, 2004.

Coutinho, Edilberto. "Uma Mulher chamada Clarice Lispector." *Criaturas de papel*. Rio de Janeiro: Civilizaçao Brasileira/INL, 1980. 165–70.

Cytrynowicz, Roney. "Além do estado e da ideologia: Imigração judaica, Estado Novo, e Segunda Guerra Mundial." *Revista Brasileira de Historia* 22:44 (2002).

Dines, Alberto. E-mail to author. March 27, 2008.

Gotlieb, Nádia Battella. *Clarice: Uma vida que se cuenta*. Translated by Alvaro Abos. Buenos Aires: Adriana Hidalgo, 2007.

Guedalla, Philip. "If Napoleon Couldn't, Can Hitler?" *New York Times*, February 2, 1941. 3, 26.

Kleinberg, Ethan. *Generation Existential: Heidegger's Philosophy in France, 1927–1961*. Ithaca, NY: Cornell University Press, 2005.

Leonard, Miriam. "Creating a Dawn: Writing through Antiquity in the Works of Hélène Cixous." *Artheusa* 33:1 (2000): 121–48.

Lesser, Jeffrey. *Welcoming the Undesirables: Brazil and the Jewish Question*. Berkeley: University of California Press, 1995.

Lispector, Clarice. *A cidade sitiada*. Rio de Janeiro: A Noite, 1949.

———. *Correspondências*. Edited by Teresa Montero. Rio de Janeiro: Rocco, 2002.

———. *A hora da estrela*. Rio de Janeiro: Jose Olympio, 1977.

———. "Instante Alpino." Archivo Clarice Lispector. Fundaçao Casa de Rui Barbosa. Rio de Janeiro: N.p., 1949.

———. *Minhas queridas*. Rio de Janeiro: Rocco, 2007.

———. "Onde se ensinará a ser feliz." *Diario o Povo*, January 19, 1941.

Lispector, Elisa. *No Exilio*. Rio de Janeiro: Pongetti, 1948.

Marting, Diane, ed. *Clarice Lispector: A Bio-Bibliography*. Westport, CT: Greenwood, 1993.

McGann, Frank D. "Brazil and World War II: The Forgotten Ally; What Did You Do in the War, Zé Carioca?" *E.I.A.L.* 6:2 (1995). http://www.tau.ac.il/eial/VI_2/mccann.htm.

Moser, Benjamin. *Why This World*. Oxford: Oxford University Press, 2009.

Rabinbach, Anson. "Heidegger's *Letter on Humanism* as Text and Event," *New German Critique*, no. 62 (1994): 3–38.

Segall, Lazar. "Arte e política" (Art and Politics). *Revista Acadêmica*, no. 63 (May 1943).

Tucci Carneiro, Maria Luiza, and Celso Lafer. *Judeus e judaísmo na obra de Lasar Segall*. Granja Viana, Cotia, SP: Ateliê Editorial, 2004.

Varin, Claire. *Linguas de fogo*. Translated by Lucia Peixoto Cherem. São Paulo: Limiar, 2002.

Vieira, Nelson. *Jewish Voices in Brazilian Literature*. Gainesville: University of Florida Press, 1995.
Waldman, Berta. "Uma cadeira e duas maças: Presence judaica no texto clariciano." *Clarice Lispector*, 2004. 241–60.
Zweig, Stefan. *Brasilien: Ein Land der Zukunft*. Stockholm: Bermann-Fischer, 1941.

No tuve . . . la serenidad necesaria para trocar la pluma de combatiente por la pluma de hombre de letras . . .
I didn't have . . . the peace of mind to trade in my fighter's pen for the pen of a man of letters . . .
• • • Gerchunoff interview, 1947

3

Alberto Gerchunoff, Anti-Nazi

A Tale of Two Images

I am writing this chapter in the space between two images: one is a cartoon of a rotund, pudgy-faced Alberto Gerchunoff, outfitted as a Jewish gaucho, hacking at his typewriter; the other is a photo of a thin, hollow-eyed Gerchunoff, dressed in a dark suit, sitting under a Yiddish and Hebrew banner reading "Gedenk, Yizkor, 6,000,000," Remember the Six Million.

Both images date from the same decade, but the gap between them is yawning. The first was drawn by Clément Moreau, a renowned cartoonist and Don Alberto's colleague at the Buenos Aires newspaper *Argentina Libre,* where it appeared April 3, 1941. Moreau's sketch glows with warmth of feeling—a sheet of paper half-inserted into the typewriter reads, "Al gaucho Gerchunoff con muchas felicidades" (To the gaucho Gerchunoff with warm greetings); the jovial combination of the author pounding away decked out in his cowboy getup, with Stars of David on the gaucho belt and

¿QUIEN ES QUIEN?
Por Clement MOREAU
Alberto Gerchunoff

בוכענוואלד
דאכאו
די גאז-קאמערן
די קרעמאטאריעס
יזכור

the knife handle, leaves no doubt that Moreau is referencing Gerchunoff's best-known work, *Los gauchos judíos* (*The Jewish Gauchos*), the paean to Jewish settlement on Argentine soil first published in 1910 and reedited in 1936. Never mind that what Don Alberto was publishing in 1941 in *Argentina Libre* had little to do with gauchos, although a lot to do with Jews and Jewish stars.

The photo comes from 1947: just a scant six years later Gerchunoff still wears his signature round-rimmed black glasses, but everything else has changed: this is an ill Don Alberto, his hands crossed in front of him, listening to an orator. An inscription in Yiddish and Spanish on the back of the photograph, apparently in the author's own handwriting, explains the circumstances: "Oineg shabbes fin Tzentral-Farband fun Poilyshe Yidn in Argentine. Habla Rut Kliger, (enviada de Israel), 19/XII/1947, Buenos Aires" —Friday night Sabbath gathering of the Central Union of Polish Jews in Argentina, Speaker, Ruth Kliger (emissary from Israel), December 19, 1947, Buenos Aires. A prominent operative from the soon-to-be-born State of Israel, Ruth Kliger (also Klieger) was a member of the Jewish underground that tried to save European Jewry during the Second World War and a postwar fund-raiser to salvage the remnants of that Jewry in the ancestral homeland.

Wearing a pristine light dress embroidered with Israeli-Yemenite motifs typical of the period, Kliger is seen here addressing an organization devoted to rescuing not only its brethren's decimated bodies but also their souls. An example: in 1956 the Central Union published Elie Wiesel's first book, the Holocaust memoir in Yiddish *Un di Velt hot Geshivgn* (And the World Kept Silent) that later became the acclaimed *La Nuit* or *Night*, as volume 117 in its series about the destroyed communities of Europe.[1] Accordingly, the Yiddish banner behind Kliger, stark white letters inscribed on mourning black, says: "Majdenek, Auschwitz, Buchenwald, Dachau, the gas chambers, the crematoria." In every way, the photograph seethes with a historical and ideological context far removed from good old pampas days alluded to by Clément Moreau.

I found both the cartoon and the photo in the Gerchunoff Archive held at the Emilio Ravignani Institute of Argentine and American History at the University of Buenos Aires, and the distance traveled between the two struck me. Here, in 1941, is Gerchunoff wearing his "official" costume, arrayed as the "Jewish gaucho," the fantastically hybrid character he begot thirty years earlier in his inaugural writing, the complex story collection about the Baron de Hirsch Jewish agricultural colonies on the prairies, a collection inevitably understood as a rose-colored, utopian song of praise to Judeo-Argentine symbiosis. Jews would give up their ethnic markers, forget Yiddish and Yiddishkeit (Jewishness), Hebrew and the Holy Land, and morph into happy-clappy Spanish-speaking, lariat-swinging bronco

busters.

Tick, tick, tick, the fabulous creation emerging genie-like from Gerchunoff's typewriter was quickly folded in everyone's mind into Gerchunoff himself, so Moreau, looking for a pictorial shorthand, cast his friend and comrade in a familiar vein, perhaps also fueled by the 1936 reissuing of an emended version of *Los gauchos judíos*, the edition that became standard and largely buried the first.

And here, in 1947, is Gerchunoff seemingly so out of character, sitting under a flag brimming with Yiddish and Yiddishkeit: no more gauchos, no more gushing, just a somber realization that something had gone terribly wrong and, to the degree possible, had to be made right. This *other* Gerchunoff of the Second World War, and of the Shoah and its aftermath, has not received his due. Like Moreau, I myself (lovingly) began with the cartoon formula, even though I had picked at my own blind spots years ago beginning with the early essay "Alberto Gerchunoff, ¿gaucho judío o anti-gaucho europeizante?" (Alberto Gerchunoff: Jewish Gaucho or Europeanizing Anti-Gaucho?), and continuing in my book about Gerchunoff and his successors, *Books and Bombs in Buenos Aires*, and in my translation and study of the two versions of *Los gauchos judíos*, entitled *Parricide on the Pampa?*[2]

I would like to continue the task and correct the partial portrait of the author by looking at "Alberto Gerchunoff, anti-Nazi" and his writings, especially *La Estrella de David* (The Star of David), the never-published book that frames the end of his career just as *Los gauchos judíos* does the start. (He died in 1950.) This is a less familiar Gerchunoff, still partly hidden in the archives. If the task with Borges and Lispector was to challenge the fantasist-escapist label through the looking glass of the Shoah, the work to be done with Gerchunoff is to free him from his la-la gaucho local color suit. Unlike his two colleagues, who broke the generic molds of fiction under the pressure of war and genocide to create a new fictional discourse, the former farmer abandoned "belles lettres" in favor of journalism, as another way of representing Auschwitz, most especially in Argentine writing. But before I look at the "new" Gerchunoff, I'll take a backward/forward glance at the canonical *Los gauchos judíos*.

Hardly a Pure Aryan

When originally published in 1910, in honor of the centennial celebrations of Argentina's independence from Spain, *The Jewish Gauchos* contained twenty-four interrelated vignettes, opening with "Génesis" and closing with "El himno" (The Anthem). The trajectory was intentional—upward from the snowy village beginnings in Czarist Russian persecution to songs of liberation on the bountiful Argentine land. Gerchunoff's was a secular Haggadah, an updated Passover narration intended to celebrate, as Don Alberto voiced it with quasi-biblical locution, the "republic's . . . great feast, the paschal feast of liberation," more secularly and historically, the centennial of Argentine independence from Spain (Aizenberg 2000, 39).

The book fictionally mirrored Gerchunoff's own trajectory as a hounded Jew born under the czars in 1883; a young greenhorn brought to the Argentina settlements in 1889, and eventually making it in the big city Buenos Aires as a journalist and editor for the principal daily, *La Nación*. Enamored of his adopted Spanish language, Gerchunoff wrote incessantly—articles, essays, opinion pieces, and the book that contained the short stories about the troubles and triumphs of the newcomers as they learned the ways and idioms of their adopted land. No wonder the cartoonist Moreau sketched Gerchunoff as a writer- gaucho.

Although milk and honey do not constantly flow in the 1910 version of *Los gaucho judíos*—there is embittering violence and bad crops and antisemitism—the tone remains hopeful. The author wanted to believe, and the official discourse of centennial Argentina encouraged him to believe, that by the second centennial, or about the year 2010, the Jewish founders of the pampas towns would receive acclaim together with the Christian founders of the Argentine nation (Aizenberg 2000, 133). Much, much sooner than Gerchunoff or few others anticipated, the shadows glimpsed in 1910 spread like a deadly plague.

Just as the disconnect between the two archival portraits mirrors the changing and chilling winds, so does the divergence between the book's 1910 and 1936 editions. Aside from the numerous linguistic emendations, Don Alberto's most glaring revision is the inclusion of two new stories, "El médico milagroso" (The Miraculous Doctor) and "El candelabro de plata" (The Silver Candelabra), both placed right after "The Anthem." As a result of this tinkering, the internal cohesion of the book and its impact as a narrative of emancipation breaks down, no longer progressing from slavery to freedom. The first added tale relates the life of Dr. Nachum Yarcho, a beloved historical figure and one of the first physicians to serve the pampas settlements. More wonder worker than man of science, more dreamer of cities in the clouds than utilitarian builder—at least in Gerchunoff's relating—Yarcho's description contains a jarring touch: "He did of course wear glasses—he was a doctor after all—a pair of gold-rimmed spectacles that were always . . . perched warily on his thin, hooked nose. If I may be permitted an anachronism, I will confess that Dr. Yarcho was hardly what we would today call a pure Aryan. On the contrary" (174).

A strange interjection, rupturing the time frame—the narrator himself labels it "an anachronism"—and injecting into the fiction an ominously timely note, if satirically related: Yarcho looks stereotypically "too Jewish," not "pure Aryan," in the racialist parlance of Hitlerism. Gerchunoff is talking about the 1880s, in a book initially published in the early 1900s, from the perspective of the 1930s. Nazi "programs of purity and hatred," as his fellow Russo-Jewish immigrant author, the Brazilian Clarice Lispector, had called them, shade the story, demarking it from the earlier more buoyant vignettes.

"The Silver Candelabra," the other interpolated story that now closes *Los gauchos judíos*, heightens the negative effect. It tells of Jewish space and Jewish heritage raped, how an unknown stranger, sticking his hand through the open window, steals the beautifully precious and obviously iconic silver candelabra from Guedali, a pious Jewish settler, exactly while he is intoning the Friday night Sabbath prayers.

Anxious not to interrupt his devotions, the sad and emaciated Guedali barely mumbles a warning to the robber not to grasp the delicately worked seven-branched menorah, and profane the Sabbath, but to no avail. Without a glimmer of indignation, Guedali goes about the ceremonial of the Sabbath, swaying back and forth to the rhythm of the sacred verses, helpless to the thievery, concluding Gerchunoff's already then canonical book at the very moment when alien hands were reaching into Jewish homes, Jewish property was being summarily confiscated, and Jews, increasingly sad and emaciated, were largely unable to resist. These evil currents were swirling in Argentina as well, so Gerchunoff sends a fraught message, *rewriting* his centennial hymn a quarter of a century after the great feast of liberation.

On the one hand ever hopeful—some would say wishful thinking—he reiterates his faith in the good Argentina and the secure place of his coreligionists there. On the other, he tempers his Yarcho-like mirage of a bright and shining golden city on the horizon in the face of Benito Mussolini, Adolf Hitler, Francisco Franco, and José F. Uriburu, the right-wing general who in 1930 overthrew the elected government of Argentina, initiating the period of authoritarian, nationalistic, and later pro-Axis rule. I discussed some of its effects in the chapter on Borges.

Even the gaucho was by now "contaminated" by fascist-think, as shown

Illustration from the antisemitic *Clarinada*: a gaucho pointing to a cattle corral with the sign "Concentration Camp." The caption in rural-sounding slang reads: "What the f— did I put up this corral fer, if they've still got me keepin' it empty? By Yid Slayer." Courtesy of the Museo del Holocausto, Buenos Aires.

in the drawing from *Clarinada* (Clarion Call), the viciously antisemitic publication that blossomed in those years.

How the travails of the day were affecting literature makers comes home with a particular vengeance in the very year Gerchunoff republished *Los gauchos judíos*. In September 1936, the Fourteenth Congress of the International Pen Club met in Buenos Aires, with ninety representatives from thirty-nine countries, including such giants as Stefan Zweig, Jacques Maritain, Jean Giraudoux, and Emil Ludwig. The atmosphere was politically supercharged, to put it not so mildly, with delegates denouncing the presence of Filippo Tommaso Marinetti, official poet of Italian *fascismo*; adopting resolutions calling on world governments to safeguard peace in the wake of the Spanish Civil War and the imminent outbreak of World War II; disrupting the proceedings as the French and Italian delegations quarreled; and Stefan Zweig rising to denounce Nazi-fascist persecution of Jews, while Marinetti took on the defense of fascism. Victoria Ocampo's *Sur* reported abundantly on the goings-on—it had also helped sponsor Maritain's visit to the congress, which marked a parting of the waters as to what writers (nationalist, right wing) would no longer be published in the journal.

Among the authors at the conference was H. Leivick, the renowned playwright and critic, representing the Yiddish Pen Club, who defiantly opened his address in a language he knew none of the delegates understood, and spoke up for "minority" languages. Brazenly, Leivick attacked "literature for looking on while pogroms were visited on culture and people—and keeping still; for looking on while Hitlerism consigned its greatest works to the bonfire—and keeping still; literature," he cried, "masks its face behind words of falsehood; literature's conscience in these times is sick, on the verge of death" (125–26).

There was much talk at the meetings about the beauty of pure art, the beauty of pure poetry. Where, Leivick challenged the globe's master language-smiths, was the "mention of the beauty and holiness of human beings?" Wasn't human sorrow, the well-being of the "oppressed, helpless, devastated folk, whether Jew or Abyssinian," more important than beauty itself, "for they are testimony to the divine spark in human life"? "Bear that in mind, delegates to this congress," he ended, elevating ethics above art (126).

Did Gerchunoff hear Leivick's call to arms? He might well have, since he left descriptions of the meetings and discussions he attended. According to the artist Manuel Kantor, his son-in-law and literary executor, the Pen Club gathering was a culminating event in Don Alberto's life, and he became friendly with many of the participating writers; Kantor himself was a militant antifascist illustrator, and some of his cartoons appear in this book.[3]

But whether Gerchunoff heard Leivick's call or not, in the Yiddish the Argentine writer knew from childhood, his own response to the era of infamy was along the same lines, to push aside works of the imagination for works of combat (Kantor 13).

Ethics above Art

The premier of *Los gauchos judíos* led to a fruitful sixteen-year literary run —Gerchunoff published fifteen volumes of essays and fiction between 1910 and 1936; the reedited story collection gave rise to exactly the opposite. With the exception of *La clínica del Doctor Mefistófoles* (Dr. Mephistopheles' Medical Office), a timely fantasy cum philosophical dialogue based on the Faust legend, and published a year after the second edition of *The Jewish Gauchos*, twelve protracted and arduous years passed with only one book, along with several posthumous editions.

Did Don Alberto suffer from writer's block? Quite the contrary. But new times demanded new writing. Or to cast it in more lit-crit terms, the crisis of belles lettres denounced by Leivick troubled Gerchunoff, as it did Borges, Lispector, and Guimarães Rosa. How could one be faithful to the hellish history, could one ethically document catastrophe and battle evil, yet "do" fiction or poetry? This remains the dilemma haunting the Holocaust and the arts.

Every one of the intellectuals in this book made statements to that effect, Borges when he said in 1945 that since 1939 he has tried not to pen a single word that would permit a condoning of Nazism; Guimarães Rosa in the 1940s when he called Hitlerism's anti-Jewish decrees infamous while he and his wife helped Jews escape from Nazi Germany; Mistral when she wrote at the end of the 1930s that Latin America was consciously and unconsciously falling into fascism, and everything good that freedom lovers had fought for was on the border of the abyss; and Lispector in 1946 when she noted that the war's suffering and tragedies had hit her hard, necessitating an as yet unformed mode of expression (*Borges en "Sur,"* 302; Guimarães Rosa, *Diario da guerra*; Mistral, 233).

Capturing the war through narrative was problematic, Lispector had acknowledged. What, then, was the intellectual to do? Gerchunoff's reaction to the fighting and the Shoah, and to the problem of its representation, has never been looked at in depth, even though (celebratory tone notwithstanding) Manuel Kantor's assessment rings true: "En el idioma castellano apenas existe ejemplo de un escritor que, con esa altura, desarrollara una labor diaria tan constante y sin desfallecimientos y que dejara un testimonio de esa época infame y gloriosa a través de medio millar de sus escritos" (There is scarcely another example of a Spanish-language writer who engaged in such untiring daily work, with such distinction, and who left testimony of that infamous and glorious era through some five hundred of his writings) (Kantor 37).

As an antifascist activist, and head of the Anti-Nazi Press Aid Committee (Ayuda Periodística Antinazi), Gerchunoff did not stop authoring, but his *immediate* response to that *época infame y gloriosa* was to abandon "disinterested or pleasurable speculation," *la especulación desinteresada y placentera*, as Kantor fittingly says (37). More directly, he gave up fiction, or to hear his own words from an interview in 1947:

> Soy, antes que nada, un escritor, tengo escritos ensayos, novelas, diálogos filosóficos, cuentos. Tengo *saudade* de mi literatura. Y, entretanto, estoy condenado, como todos los escritores, a luchar contra problemas que nada tienen que ver con la literatura. ¡Mas el monstruo fascista no murió aún y no llegó el tiempo del descanso! Es el problema de todo escritor, particularmente del escritor sudamericano. . . . Desde que comenzó la guerra me transformé en un soldado de la libertad, combatí en los diarios, con conferencias, las ideas tenebrosas que amenazaban dominar el mundo. No tuve más tiempo de pensar como escritor de imaginación, ni la serenidad necesaria para trocar la pluma de combatiente por la pluma de hombre de letras. . . . Tengo fe en el futuro, pienso que en breve podremos dejar la lucha para volver a nuestras ocupaciones individuales. Entonces

seguiré nuevamente mi aspiración de producir obra de imaginación. Sin libertad verdadera, sin libertad para todos, no hay vida, no hay orden, no hay humanidad, no hay nada. . . . (Jaroslavsky de Lowy, 26).

....

I am, before anything else, a writer; I've written essays, novels, philosophical dialogues, stories. I miss my literature very much. In the meanwhile, I'm condemned, just like all writers are, to fight against problems that have nothing to do with literature. But the fascist monster still hasn't died, and the time for rest still hasn't come! It's the problem of every writer, particularly the South American writer. . . . Since the beginning of the war I've become a soldier of liberty, I fought against the sinister ideas that threatened to transform the world, in newspapers, through lectures. I no longer had the time to think like a writer of the imagination, nor the peace of mind to trade in my fighter's pen for the pen of a man of letters. . . . I have faith in the future, I believe that in a short time we'll be able to end the struggle and go back to our own professions. Then I'll follow my aspiration: to produce works of the imagination. Without true freedom, freedom for all, there is no life, no order, and no humanity, there is nothing . . .

On the ever-shifting continuum between journalism and belles lettres, the imperative of combating or imagining, witnessing (*dejar un testimonio*) or inventing, Gerchunoff tended to the first options, reflecting what Sidra DeKoven Ezrahi terms "regard for the primacy of the *report* that was exemplified during the war years by Thomas Mann and other writers who served as broadcasters or journalists devoted to publicizing the little-known facts of the atrocities" (24; emphasis added). Such reportage, argues Ezrahi, paved the way for documentary *fiction* of the Shoah, which slides a step further along the continuum toward "artistic reconstruction of the actual" (48).

Alas, Gerchunoff did not put down his journalistic fighter's pen as quickly as he had hoped, battling after the war for the establishment of the State of Israel. I'd like to surmise that the ongoing endeavor, and his premature death in 1950, prevented him from novelizing "the sinister ideas" in the way he had subjects as varied as Jewish gauchos, Don Quixote's quixotic belief in the right (*La jofaina maravillosa* and *Retorno a Don Quijote*), corrupt and ignorant South American politicians and authoritarian generals (*El hombre importante*), pompous Argentine intellectuals (*El hombre que habló en la Sorbona*), and the hardships of making a living on the streets of Buenos Aires ("El día de las grandes ganancias").

When Don Alberto says that he is above all an author, not a journalist, he echoes an old debate about the relation between the two, primarily the allegedly noxious effects of newspaper reporting on the literary calling. Borges, for one, claimed that the idiom of reportage was ephemeral, aiming to tell the evanescent facts without concern for the lasting weight and timbre of the verbal violin; and Lispector, who started out as a journalist and made a living through newspapers and magazines her entire life, including pseudonymous advice columns on beauty and femininity, fretted that that transparent and "easy" language of the press would debase her intricate, agonizingly wrung-out, philosophical-fictional word craft.

Yet Don Alberto was as much a journalist, a brilliant conversationalist, and a lecturer as a fiction maker, long affiliated with *La Nación*; a pressman who founded a newspaper, *El mundo*, and who published in periodicals known and unknown, of all shades and stripes; his books were often collections of articles or stories first placed in the media. José Luis Lanuza, a colleague on *El mundo*, recalled how Don Alberto was criticized for wanting to run a paper with writers and not reporters, because the two were considered incompatible. But Gerchunoff, a man of strong convictions, was adamant, he had "faith in the efficacy of the word" (*tenía fe en la eficacia de la palabra*) and "polished his editorials as if they were works of art" (Jaroslavsky de Lowy 19–20).

So despite his comments, the dichotomy soldier of liberty/writer of the imagination is not sharp and immovable (it rarely is), and Gerchunoff's literature of combat rings with the powers of fictional recourse, just as his fiction does with the strength of denunciation and political thought. The Shoah pushed him to the creation of a scorching combat prose that dropped fiction in the service of fact; yet this *escritura de combate* was unafraid to take hold of fiction's resources if they buttressed his fighter's pen.

Argentina Libre and Argentine Antifascism

Don Alberto's main platform was the antifascist weekly *Argentina Libre*. Starting on March 7, 1940, the weekly was published every Thursday till 1949, under the more outspoken name *Antinazi* from 1945 to 1946. Its main editor was Luis Koiffman, who had ties to the Socialist Party, but the paper was open to all opponents of fascism, whatever their affiliation. By the time its offices were raided and shuttered by the Perón government, *Argentina Libre* had printed 297 consecutive issues, extinguishing an "editorial experience of vital importance," in historian Jorge Nállim's accurate appreciation (103). Andrés Bisso, another major scholar of the period, concurs, calling *Argentina Libre* and *Antinazi* "indispensable sources for the detailed study of Argentine antifascism" (10).

Nállim, like Bisso, is part of a recent scholarly upswing in the study of Argentine *anti*fascism, as opposed to the earlier emphasis on fascism, and he has examined the publication in detail, primarily within the context of his country's turn to the right after General Uriburu's 1930 coup, with the attendant rise of the army and a militant Catholic Church, along with conservative, antidemocratic elements. These kept Argentina from embracing the Spanish Republican and Allied causes; Argentina reluctantly declared war on the Axis powers on March 27, 1945, under intense U.S. pressure, when the war was mostly over. *Argentina Libre* was born out of the need to defend civil liberties and to openly push Argentina to the Allied cause. Argentina's mainline press, newspapers like *La Prensa* or *La Nación* (where Gerchunoff continued to write), initially kept a more restrained attitude, and took a firmer stance only as the war progressed (Efron and Brenman, 221–27). There were other antifascist magazines and newspapers—*Acción Argentina, Orientación, Por la Francia Libre* among them—but *Argentina Libre* was a major one.

Argentine radicals, socialists, and democratic progressives, expectedly more split than united, coincided in their defense of antifascism, and linked the domestic front with the international scene: Uriburu and his successors, among them Perón, were viewed as imposing their homegrown fascism on the liberal, open Argentine tradition to which Gerchunoff had sung at the century's start, and which he, like Borges, continued affirming. After the Peronist triumph of 1945, *Argentina Libre* turned its ire on the new leader and Evita, the "Saint of the Poor," labeling the couple's flamboyant rule "a simian imitation of Nazism," a posture that Nállim and other Argentine historians consider simplistic in its misunderstanding of Peronism's embrace of a changing, laboring Argentina through its social welfare policies (February 22 1945, 3, 100).

Many intellectuals participated heatedly in the antifascist/anti-Peronist camp, and the activity wasn't without a price. Continually harassed, some of its contributors exiled and jailed by the military governments, *Argentina Libre* served as one antidote to a host of antisemitic, Axis-supporting broadsheets, such as *Clarinada* and the equally infamous *Crisol*, which had as early as 1933 accused Borges of "maliciously hiding" his Jewish ancestry, prompting his deliciously satiric response, "Yo, judío" (I, a Jew). No less acute was Gerchunoff's vehement penning, since he was at one with *Argentina Libre*'s stand from his opening salvo, the editorial "La posición ante la guerra" (Position on the War), published in the inaugural issue. From that moment on, Don Alberto was a constant presence, often on the front page, to the tune of some three hundred articles.

He was joined by the finest voices in the Argentine opposition—historians Emilio Ravignani and José Luis Romero, writers Luis Emilio Soto, Roberto Giusti, Guillermo de Torre, Samuel Eichelbaum (a well-known Judeo-Argentine dramatist), as well as prominent South American, U.S., and European antifascists from Gabriela Mistral, recipient of the 1945 Nobel Prize in Literature, to Max Lerner, Emil Ludwig, Stefan Zweig, and Jacques Maritain.

Gerchunoff and the Graphic War

Writing was not *Argentina Libre*'s only weapon—that is why Moreau's cartoon of Gerchunoff serves as one of my guiding images. More modern than some of Argentina's traditional, somewhat staid newspapers, *Argentina Libre* used abundant picture warfare—telling photographs and sardonic political cartoons. Huge photo collages dominated its front page at significant junctures in the conflict: LAS DEMOCRACIAS EN OFENSIVA (The Democracies on the Offensive), the gigantic banner head shouted out jubilantly when the Allies landed in Vichy-held North Africa, atop a picture montage of the Operation Torch invasion, with Franklin D. Roosevelt at the center (November 19, 1942). Frequent photographs from England showed the grit of the British under Hitler's Blitz.

Local events likewise provided photo opportunities, such as the massive memorial meeting for Stefan Zweig, whose suicide in Brazil especially riled the antifascist Latin American intelligentsia, since he was one of their own, on their continent (see chapter 5, on Gabriela Mistral, Zweig's neighbor and friend in Petrópolis, Brazil). Hollywood too furnished grist for the pro-Allied snapshot mill; one example was the full-page montage on German-Jewish director Ernst Lubitsch's political satire *To Be or Not to Be*, starring Carole Lombard and Jack Benny, about a troupe of actors in Nazi-occupied Poland who use their wits and skill to fool the Germans (November 12, 1942).

Cartoon art played an even greater role, deserving a yet to be written study that takes its title from *Argentina Libre*'s front-page headline: "Como reaccionaban los artistas contra la opresión" (How Artists Reacted to Oppression). The feature was accompanied by drawings by the nineteenth-century French master of the political cartoon Honoré Daumier and, closer to home, by one of the newspaper's duo of resident cartoonists, Toño Salazar; the other was Carl Meffert aka Clément Moreau. Salazar, a Salvadoran

caricaturist living in Paris who escaped to Buenos Aires after Hitlerism occupied France, only to be unceremoniously deported to Uruguay in 1945, and Moreau, a German Expressionist anti-Nazi exiled to Argentina in 1935, were the vanguard of Argentine cartoon warfare.[4]

Just like Don Alberto's fiery columns, Salazar and Moreau's acerbic caricatures jumped out of issue after issue, black-on-white sketches forming a persuasive antifascist shuttle space. Moreau's work in particular was often placed near Gerchunoff's, whether as intentional collaborations or by editorial decision. Moreau's cartoon "Fin de año" (New Year's Eve) is printed near Gerchunoff's December 24, 1944, article, "Matanza científica de judíos" (Scientific Slaughter of Jews), registering a sleeping Hitler blanketed in a blood-oozing copy of *Mein Kampf*, blissfully unaware of midnight bewitching hour for the noose around his neck to tighten as payment for his crimes.

By late 1944, Hitler was wasted on the Russian front; the Red Army had reached the eastern concentration camps, allowed the press to enter Majdanek, near Lublin, and the world saw the first atrocity photos, uncovering how, Gerchunoff darkly writes, Jews were "scientifically" eliminated. He bases his report on the largest display of these pictures, which appeared in the *Illustrated London News* on October 14, 1944, and he provides for his Spanish-language audience part of the accompanying apology: "It is not the custom of the *Illustrated London News* to publish photos of atrocities, but in view of the fact that the enormity of the crimes perpetrated by the Germans is so wicked . . . we consider it necessary to present them" (original quoted in Zelizer, 57).

Don Alberto then pauses on the photos exhibiting the accoutrements of atrocity, on the captions and livid commentary, often in a verbatim translation: the annihilation camp buildings, the ropes used to hang prisoners, cylinders containing asphyxiating Zyklon B gas, crematoria ovens, and ashes shipped to Germany as garden fertilizer. And he quotes: "Este campamento . . . será 'un recuerdo horrible de ese pedazo de inhumanidad que descubrimos en cada alemán'" (This camp . . . is a grim reminder of that streak of utter inhumanity which is found in every German) (Zelizer 59). Extending the charge to Christendom as a whole, the man who once passionately palavered pro Judeo-Christian symbiosis makes this "grim reminder" the heart of his essay.

Remarkably from a twenty-first-century perspective, the paper placed the simulacrum of Hitler, not one of the horror transparencies, near Don Alberto's article, indicating perhaps snags with reproduction rights (although, as I have noted, war photos from Allied sources appeared in *Argentina Libre* all the time) but, more to the point, the difficulty of imaging the Shoah right from the start, and the tug not only between word and image but between types of images, drawing versus snapshot. Talking about the British and American press, Barbie Zelizer in her authoritative and relentless book, *Remembering to Forget: Holocaust Memory through the Camera's Eye*, observes that the Majdanek shots were published "unevenly and infrequently," and not all major newspapers even included them (56). *Argentina Libre* was not different.

More chilling than the sleeping Hitler was Moreau's design near Don Alberto's cri de coeur "El crematorio nazi en los cines de Buenos Aires," a gut-wrenching reaction to the newsreels of the Nazi gas chambers screened "in the comfort" of the Argentine capital's movie houses, as Gerchunoff barbs with characteristic irony (May 24, 1945). This article, too, deals with

EL SALDO DEL "NUEVO ORDEN"

EL CREMATORIO NAZI EN LOS CINES DE BUENOS AIRES

Por Alberto Gerchunoff

DESDE hace algunos días se exhiben en las salas cinematográficas de Buenos Aires, cintas informativas sobre los campos de concentración. El público bonaerense dispone ahora de comodidad para observar los procedimientos que aplicaban los alemanes en los lugares de exterminio. Los visitaron los fotógrafos militares y periodísticos, las comisiones parlamentarias de Londres, y cronistas como Paul Ghali, corresponsal del "Chicago Daily News", instruyeron con datos precisos respecto al número, la nacionalidad y la definición étnica de las víctimas. En Auschwitz, en Tremblinka, en Dachau, en Ohdruff, en Buschendal, en Nordhausen, perecieron muchos alemanes antinazis, extranjeros insumisos, políticos disconformes con el hitlerismo; sumarán varias decenas de millares. Pero, en esos laboratorios refinados de matanza murieron seis millones doscientos mil judíos, sobre un total de osho millones que habitaban los distintos países de Europa. Esta cifra, aceptada por los gobiernos aliados, nos demuestra que los campos de concentración habían sido organizados principalmente para exterminar la población israelita y de un modo secundario a los no judíos que por cualquier razón merecieran la hostilidad nazi. Lo que se puede apreciar en las películas que muestran actual-

images as the indisputable evidence of Hitler's handiwork—the atrocity pictures were quickly turned into film and shown to "mesmerized" audiences "on both continents" (Zelizer 148).

To go together with Don Alberto's (once again) caustic condemnation of Christendom for seeding the ground for genocide, we see Moreau's rendering of a kind of atrocity shot eventually transformed into an icon fraught with the symbolic weight of the Shoah—jumbled piles of corpses, foregrounded and spilling out of the picture. Moreau's caption reads, "El saldo del 'nuevo orden'" (The Tally of the New Order), referring to Hitler's Thousand Year Reich. Moreau's portrayal and Gerchunoff's article had a double life: they were reproduced in a special pamphlet issued by the Delegación de Asociaciones Israelitas Argentinas, or DAIA, the Argentine-Jewish community's umbrella organization, to highlight the hell uncovered through the documentaries.

In her book Zelizer spells out the sources of such drawings on pages labeled "not for the squeamish" (I still have a hard time seeing and thinking about these semblances); she explains how "turning out roll after roll of black-and-white film, photographers depicted the worst of Nazism in stark, naturalistic representations of horror," first and foremost "bodies turned at odd angles to each other" (89). The exact place and time of the snapshots (what *Konzentrationslager*, or KZ, on what day) seemed less important than what the image told, above all the mounds of dead repeated to numbness.

Most of these photographs—the one I show comes from Buchenwald, and as U.S. government property is in the public domain—were shot immediately after Allies reached the concentration camps of the western front. They surfaced in the British and U.S. press in April and May of 1945, along with the newsreels; the release in Argentina was contemporaneous with these dates, as was Gerchunoff's angry account.

The "tally of the new order" was not Moreau's only illustration to appear near the erstwhile "Jewish gaucho" in portraying the *lagers*. Don Alberto's article "Los culpables del gran crimen" (Those Guilty of the Great Crime), about an Allied declaration (finally) condemning the Nazi extermination campaign, came out in *Argentina Libre* on Christmas Eve, December 24, 1942. Just a week earlier, on December 17, British foreign secretary Anthony Eden had introduced the declaration in the House of Commons, and its members rose for two minutes of silence: those responsible for the coldblooded war against the Jews would be punished, Eden assured.

Right below Gerchunoff's derisive retort to this preholiday gesture of "Christian charity" toward the massacred and stateless Jews, the stateless

German cartoonist sent his own "Christmas card": a tableau of hollow-eyed men, women, and children behind barbed wire, some gazing straight at the viewer, with the greeting "Navidad en Europa" (Christmas in Europe) (p. 4). The stark chiaroscuro closely resembled another early photographic image of the Shoah turned icon: up-close views of barbed wire fences separating blank-eyed survivors from the outside world, such as one from Auschwitz.

Moreau's cut, with the sad imprisoned mother nursing her (dead?) baby in the foreground as a kind of counter–Madonna and Child, had lasting power: three years later, in 1945, it was printed on the front cover of the DAIA flyer; like the photos of the piled corpses that modeled Moreau's other drawing, used inside the flyer, the exact place and time of the image seemed less important than what it told.

In this case the snapshot-sketch dialogue had a twist. While the piled bodies sketch *followed* the snapshots, the barbed wire drawing from 1942 *preceded* them, as if the artist were eerily prescient. Artists often are, but Moreau had been hunted by the Gestapo before he fled Germany, and he produced harsh cartoons about the Nazis' methods from the 1930s; he likely drew on those experiences to give visual substance to the macabre knowledge "revealed" by Anthony Eden.

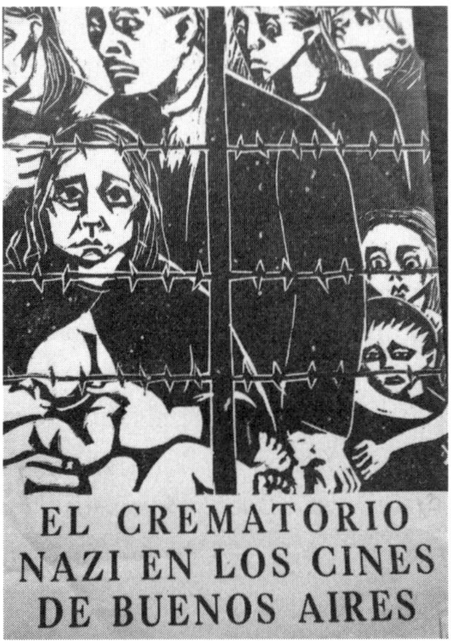

The vagaries of Moreau's work accentuate the knotty relation between Holocaust drawing and photography. Images soon superseded words as more effective carriers of the genocide story—witness Gerchunoff on Majdanek and on the newsreels—but ambivalence about the role of photography in witnessing atrocity, and the harshness of the pictorial record, sometimes led to the use of drawings, considered more bearable—exactly what happened in the DAIA brochure. Photographic documentation of atrocity was hard to come by before the war's end, so drawing did its part, initially anticipating, ultimately depending on photography, with transparencies "turning up as reality markers in other modes of Holocaust representation" and artists using photos as "visual cues" (Zelizer, 144, 147).

In the reflection *On Photography*, Susan Sontag ponders the relation between painting and photography and the potency of her first encounter with the photo images of Bergen-Belsen and Dachau in 1945, as an adolescent in California: "Something broke . . . some limit had been reached, something went; something is still crying." Her life was divided into a before and after

(19–20). In Argentina something also broke in Alberto Gerchunoff. The displaced cartoonist and the immigrant in the round-rimmed black glasses afford a powerful example from the South of the interplay of word, drawing, and photography in the early search to represent the unimaginable.

The Star of David

Don Alberto wrote about every aspect of the conflagration in this pugnacious multimedia environment. For five arduous war years his hammering articles delved into the Third Reich, its military advances and (ecstatically) its defeats, alliances, bombings, conquering, speechifying, distortions, leaders (later war criminals), and surrender (in the piece "Rendición de Alemania," May 3, 1945). France, torn between the true France, "la verdadera Francia," beacon of liberty, and the false France of Vichy often vexed Gerchunoff's pen (see "La verdadera Francia," June 19, 1941).

So did the threat to Latin America: German incursions into South American waters; pan-Americanism as an anti-Nazi force; and the infiltration of Nazism and Franco's Spanish Falangism into Argentina and other countries (e.g., "Nazis en Bolivia," July 24, 1941, and "Neofalangismo argentino," March 1, 1945). He commented on Italian fascism and Mussolini, on the Red Army, and constantly on Churchill and Roosevelt's conduct of the war and British resistance to Nazism (as in "La roca británica," August 29, 1940).

When the hostilities ended, he didn't stop and encyclopedically dissected the postwar panorama, the price of victory, the founding of the United Nations, women's reaction to the conflict, the Nuremberg Trials, the atom bomb, and over and over the lingering legacy of Nazism in Europe and his own nation (see "Sir Oswald Mosley y el nazismo," December 6, 1945, or "Nazismo posnazi," November 15, 1945). He wrote and wrote till the newspaper was shut down, and then wrote elsewhere.

Where did the war on the Jews and its aftermath fit into this overflowing production? At the archive in the Institute for Argentine History I came across an unpublished manuscript with a cover page in Don Alberto's own hand, entitled "*La Estrella de David* por Alberto Gerchunoff 1938–1946." Right below the title he had a crossed-out parenthetical subheading: "(Temas Judíos II Tomo)," or Jewish Topics II Volume [*sic*]. The next two pages show the presumed table of contents: a first section, "La Estrella de David," with twenty-four articles, all but two originally published in *Argentina Libre* and *Antinazi*; and a second, "Israel," mostly the reports Gerchunoff sent to Jadla, the Spanish-language press service of the Jewish Agency for Palestine, which after the war spearheaded the campaign for the establishment of

Israel. (In this period "Palestine" referred to British Mandatory Palestine, and the Jews of the area were "Palestinians.")

The volume that never saw the light of publication does not incorporate the author's every Jewish-themed or Holocaust-related article. Before *Argentina Libre* started appearing, and even while he contributed there, Gerchunoff wrote in venues such as *Repertorio Americano, Judaica, La Nación, La Semana de Buenos Aires*. On the bottom of the first contents page he scribbled and erased a reminder to himself to "look for" essays in *La Semana de Buenos Aires* from 1938, "Hombres y judíos" (Men and Jews) and "Antisemitismo activo" (Active Antisemitism). Another jotting just says, "El destino de Israel y el imperio británico" (Israel's Destiny and the British Empire) — Nov. 1941."

So we don't have a full record, but a representative one, self-fashioned by the author to show what was important to him. The two parts of *La Estrella de David* together shape an emotional, intellectual, and ideological trajectory, Gerchunoff's anthology of his journalistic struggle to absorb and pillory the burgeoning Holocaust, and to militate after the catastrophe for a state that would give Jews refuge and, as significantly, juridical and collective political personhood. What nation among the nations will demand justice for the murdered Jews, he repeatedly asks.

Since Gerchunoff did not collect his other press work on the Second World War, *La Estrella de David* presumably reveals what mattered most to the old "Jewish gaucho" at this agonizing juncture in his career, when the personal and the political meshed more than ever. If *Los gauchos judíos* gives us the young rosy-eyed Alberto eager to be one with the pampas, even as he already recognizes that prejudice hasn't all disappeared in the South American "Zion," *La Estrella de David* shows a wizened, battle-scarred warrior whom the Nazi genocide turned totally toward the homeland in Zion he thought Jews no longer needed in his rural-romanticizing days. "Zion is where peace and happiness reign. We'll all go to Argentina," he had believingly sung in *Los gauchos judíos* (Aizenberg 2000, 43). Don Alberto had moved away from this extreme position before Hitler, but now he was of a mind with those who drew a straight line (with eyes open about the political and military tussles with the British and the Arabs) from the Nazi yellow star to Israel's Star of David; the book's title comes from an article he published when the Nazis decreed the sign of infamy, and the article ended with his vision of the resurgent Jewish star defeating fascist ignominy ("La Estrella de David," *Argentina Libre*, September 11, 1941).

Just as Gerchunoff's thinking on Zion evolved, so did his coverage of the

Shoah. When he turned journalism into his antifascist fighting machine, he did not drop the signature style—linguistic richness, historical erudition, poetic diction, irony. But congruent with the burgeoning tempo of the genocide, he became more direct ("the bare facts"), fuller of a sense of purpose, moral indignation, and condemnatory tone: a prose of urgency becomes prominent. Some examples: the opening article, "Genios en emigración" (Emigrating Geniuses), about Sigmund Freud and Stefan Zweig's expulsion from Vienna, converting them into men without a country, "*Heimatlos*, in today's sad parlance," typifies the early pieces (*La Semana de Buenos Aires*, June 10, 1938).

Brief, sardonic, it skewers the Nazi persecutor baroquely with its own racist mumbo jumbo based on alleged head measurements of "Nordic" and "inferior" peoples: "dolicocéfalo esencialmente rubio, con entronque en los compañeros de Atila" (a basically blond dolicocephalus [long-head], cognate with Attila's comrades). Still, Gerchunoff's positive thinking continues to blossom: the transfer of genius from intellectually dead Vienna to London and other civilized locales will allow for culture's survival, and redemption of the now beastly homeland through the ministry of the word.

The springy tone remains in Gerchunoff's next selection, the first from *Argentina Libre*, a much longer article of September 19, 1940, entitled "La colina de la espiga madura" (The Hill of Ripe Wheat), his reaction to the aerial bombing on September 9 of Jewish Palestine's chief city, Tel Aviv—the spring hill of his title—as part of the Italian campaign against Mediterranean "strategic targets." (What was strategic about Tel Aviv wasn't quite clear; the oil refineries in the port of Haifa were also bombed by Il Duce.)

Don Alberto the reporter starts with the inverted pyramid of modern journalism—straightforward recitation of the major data, spiraling down through the article to elaboration: "Tel Aviv conoció en estos días la lluvia de fuego" (In recent days Tel Aviv suffered an attack by air). But this initial statement of facts swerves sharply in the next sentence: "No pudieron suponer los habitantes de esta recientísima y blanca ciudad que Jehová, cuyos servidores son, en el sentido histórico y poético, aunque no en el aspecto áridamente ortodoxo, volvía a castigarles por algún pecado o alguna abominación" (The inhabitants of this brand-new white city couldn't imagine that Jehovah, whose servants they are in a historical and poetic sense, if not in the strictly orthodox one, was once more punishing them for some sin or abomination).

After starting in the present Don Alberto the author makes an anachronistic-literary turn, waxing biblical just as he had in *Los gauchos judíos*, where the early twentieth-century Jews were hocus-pocused into scriptural maidens and patriarchs. The residents of what he himself says is a modern, secular "white" metropolis (called so because of its many Bauhaus-style buildings designed by refugees from Germany) are similarly Harry Pottered, while he shuttles between a copious account of the material and cultural achievements of the contemporary denizens, and the tug of the types he had invented in *The Jewish Gauchos*, dreamy, venerable Jews, not unrelated to Jesus, with majestic brows and gleaming pupils. The miraculous spiritual power of these idealists will ultimately overcome the "seeders of death, the spreaders of sparks"—nary a word about the Jewish fighters in the British armies or the local Jewish defense organizations whose resistance helped the Allies and fledgling State of Israel.

These sorts of historically drenched, metaphorically rendered meditations, generally soft on Christianity, abound on the early pages of *The Star of David*. Gerchunoff seems anxious to teach his mainly Catholic readership, win their sympathy, and reiterate the cultural-moral legacy of Judaism and its relevance to its sister religion. "La noche de Pascua" (The Eve of Passover; *Argentina Libre*, April 10, 1941) begins with a reflection on how the surviving ghettoized Jews of Poland might commemorate the solemn holiday beginning just two days later. Gerchunoff the informant takes care to explain that the first night of Passover will coincide with Holy Saturday, part of Easter (also named Pascua in Spanish), and he then launches into an account of Passover as a time of persecution throughout history, again invoking the miserable ghetto Isaacs of the Middle Ages, Inquisition eras, and Czarist days. Why are we continually oppressed, the Jews ask, with the specter of a crucified Christ hovering nearby? Now that all of the European nations are suffering too, they will understand their own Savior and the Jews better and will join with them in "patient resistance" to overcome the contemporary Pharaoh.

Succeeding articles, "La Estrella de David" (as noted, on September 11, 1941), "El decálogo nazi" (The Nazi Ten Commandments; November 20, 1941), and "Los nuevos ghettos" (The New Ghettos; April 9, 1942), likewise proceed from news—the imposition of the yellow star, Nazi propaganda chief Joseph Goebbels's authoring of an Antisemitic Decalogue, the establishment of sealed ghettos—to historical narrative and poetic flights: Hitler's Germany is the Anti-Bible, the Anti-Gospel, the Anti-Decalogue.

But as Hitler implements the Final Solution, Don Alberto does not sustain the same level of historical-poetic flights. In 1942 he writes five articles on the Shoah, as well as the text of a public poster illustrated by Manuel

Kantor, "Al pueblo argentino" (To the Argentine People), issued by DAIA on Christmas Eve, informing viewers of the extermination and of the Allies' declaration and asking for solidarity.

In the most denunciating of his articles, "Exterminio de judíos" (Extermination of Jews; December 3, 1942), "Matanza científica de judíos" (Scientific Slaughter of Jews; December 10, 1942), "Más de 1,000,000 de judíos muertos" (More than a Million Jews Dead; July 2, 1942), passion more than ever trumps any purported impartiality—the dam between telling and opining—a supposed pillar of journalistic practice (Stephens 220).

Nevertheless, reporter that he is, Gerchunoff anchors his comments in the best available information, noting the travails of news gathering in conditions of Nazi censorship, occupation, and war, and the purposeful mendacity and obfuscation of Hitler's death projects, especially the Final Solution. The article "Más de 1,000,000 de judíos muertos," for instance, opens with irony shading reportage:

> El comité británico del Congreso Judío Mundial ha publicado el resumen de sus informaciones sobre la situación de las comunidades israelitas en los países ocupados por los alemanes. Es difícil investigar en los lugares dominados por los nazis lo que éstos hacen con los grupos de población a los cuales distinguen con la preferencia de su hostilidad. Sin embargo, se acaba por conocer sus métodos . . .
>
> . . . .
>
> The British Committee of the World Jewish Congress has published the summary of its information about the situation of the Jewish communities in German-occupied countries. In areas dominated by the Nazis it is difficult to investigate what they do to population groups singled out for their preferential hostility. Nevertheless, their methods have just been made known . . .

The news of the press conference held in London on June 29, 1942, at which Sidney S. Silverman, a member of Parliament, and Ignacy Schwarzbart, of the Polish National Council, spoke of murders and gassings of Jews in Poland and gave the death toll as close to a million was disseminated and reprinted internationally, but with varied emphasis. The British press generally headlined the item in boldface on its main news pages of June 30, as in the *Daily Telegraph*: "More than 1,000,000 Jews Killed in Europe." In the United States the story was usually downgraded to the lower part of inner pages under much more qualified titles; the *New York Times* buried the item on the lower half of page 7 on the same day (Leff, 139–40; Lipstadt, 164). In Buenos Aires *La Nación* published the same information on

July 8, under the misleadingly vague headline "Declaración judía" (Jewish Declaration). This placement reflected the general posture of the popular daily—providing coverage of the horrors, but not overly generously given their magnitude (Efron and Brenman, 227). In *Argentina Libre* on July 2, the news was put on the front page, at the Thursday weekly's first opportunity.

The hard-hitting tenor of "Más de 1,000,000 de judíos muertos" and similar articles not only gives the facts but also asks the difficult, still-resonating questions: Why didn't the Allied governments protest the mass massacre of Jews earlier? Why did the Allies wait till they themselves documented the death of millions and the proposed obliteration of millions more? Would Hitler have carried out his plan of extermination had Great Britain or the United States threatened to bomb German cities for each step in its implementation? Why didn't Pope Pius XII speak up more forcefully about Nazi atrocities?

Why did the proposal to constitute an international tribunal to judge the guilty immediately meet with the "they were only following orders" defense—expressed in an anonymous letter to Gerchunoff for allegedly having "the gall" to apply the *lex talionis*, an eye for an eye, to the "poor" German soldiers ("Los anti-hombres," or The Anti-Men, March 11, 1943)? Once the Nazis were defeated and their criminal heresiarchs imprisoned or escaped, would the German collectivity wash its hands of its direct or indirect complicity in the anti-Jewish enterprise, adducing that it was the "other" Germany that carried it out? Would the terribly specific Jewish suffering be subsumed under the general rubric of war suffering? And most important, as far as Gerchunoff is concerned, who would speak for the Jews, who have no national or judicial entity? How would they pursue their claim for tangible and moral compensation without "personalidad nacional," a legally constituted and internationally recognized national entity, like Holland or Czechoslovakia, Romania or Hungary? ("La postguerra y los judíos," or The Postwar and the Jews, April 15, 1943).

In the postwar why did Great Britain through its foreign minister, Ernest Bevin, renege on its own legally recognized commitments to support a Jewish homeland in Palestine alongside Arab populations? Why did it only lukewarmly pursue the Grand Mufti of Jerusalem, a Hitler supporter wanted as a war criminal? Why were there internment camps for displaced Jews in British-controlled Cyprus? Why was Britain free to apply to Jews the immoral practices identified with the Nazis? ("Tierra Santa," or The Holy Land, October 10, 1946)

Good-bye Jewish Gaucho

In 1940 Leonides de Vedia, the chief editor of *La Nación*, made Gerchunoff an offer most writers wouldn't refuse: Vedia would organize a special homage to mark the thirtieth anniversary of the first publication of *Los gauchos judíos*. To the editor's probable surprise, especially since the second edition had come out just four years earlier, Gerchunoff turned down the honor. He explained his motives in a letter. How could he complacently worry about his ego when the world was burning? How could he agree to the tribute of his democratic friends when every ounce of energy was needed to fight the Nazis conquering Europe? (Letter to Vedia, June 26 1940; cited in Senkman, 148)

The question goes to the heart of Gerchunoff's passage from "Jewish gaucho" to anti-Nazi and to the rejection of belles-lettres for armored prose. His brothers and sisters were going up in smoke; fiction seemed a luxury, personal honor a smug satisfaction.

A transformed Don Alberto emerged in the process, shaking up the firm believer in Judeo-(Christian) Argentine coexistence, and in Argentina the Promised Land. He became the resolute if haggard man under the banner "Gedenk, Yizkor, 6,000,000," Remember the Six Million, sharing a spotlight and a stance with an Israeli emissary.

He no longer had the time to think like a writer of the imagination, nor the peace of mind to trade in his fighter's pen for the pen of a man of letters. But the old did not completely stop nurturing the new. To mark the creation of the State of Israel, open-eyed political realities found expression in misty-eyed ancient verses:

"Sing a new song to the Lord for He has done wonders" (Psalms 96:1).

Works Cited and Consulted

Aizenberg, Edna. "Alberto Gerchunoff, ¿gaucho judío o antigaucho europeizante?" *Anuario de letras* 15 (1977): 197–215.

———. *Books and Bombs in Buenos Aires: Borges, Gerchunoff, and Argentine-Jewish Writing*. Hanover, NH: Brandies University Press published by University Press of New England, 2002.

———. "Gerchunoff y la representación gráfica de la Shoá." *Hispamérica* 38:114 (2009): 75–84.

———. *Parricide on the Pampa? A New Study and Translation of Alberto Gerchunoff's "Los gauchos judíos."* Madrid and Frankfurt am Main: Iberoamericana/Vervuert, 2000.

Bisso, Andrés. *El antifascismo argentino*. Buenos Aires: CeDinCi, 2007.

Borges en "Sur," 1931–1980. Buenos Aires: Emecé, 1999.

Chinski, Milena. "Ilustrar la memoria: Las imágenes de tapa de la colección Dos poylishe yidentum (El judaísmo polaco) Buenos Aires, 1946–1966." Paper delivered at the XV International Research Conference, Latin American Jewish Studies Association, Arizona State University, Tempe, Ariz., June 12–14, 2011.

Efron, Gustavo, and Dario Brenman. "La prensa gráfica argentina ante el nazismo y la Shoá." *Indice* 37:25 (2007): 201–35.

Englebert, Beate, Luca Englebert, and Ulrich Merkel. *Clément Moreau: con el lápiz contra el fascismo*. Buenos Aires: Instituto Goethe, 1994.

Ezrahi, Sidra DeKoven. *By Words Alone: The Holocaust in Literature*. Chicago: University of Chicago Press, 1980.

Gerchunoff, Alberto. *La clínica del Doctor Mefistófeles*. Santiago: Ercilla, 1937.

———. *La Estrella de David*. 1938–1946. Unpublished manuscript.

———. *Los gauchos judíos*. La Plata: Joaquín Sesé, 1910; Rev. ed. Buenos Aires: Gleizer, 1936.

Guimarães Rosa, João. *Diario da guerra*. Unpublished manuscript.

Jaroslavsky de Lowy, Sara. *Alberto Gerchunoff: vida y obra, bibliografía, antología*. New York: Hispanic Institute in the United States, 1957.

Kantor, Manuel. *Alberto Gerchunoff*. Buenos Aires: Congreso Judío Mundial/ Biblioteca Popular Judía, 1969.

———. *De Munich a Nuremberg*. Buenos Aires: Standard Publishing, 1946.

Leff, Laurel. *Buried by the Times: The Holocaust and America's Most Important Newspaper*. Cambridge: Cambridge University Press, 2005.

Leivick, H. *Di heiligkeit fun mentschlechn lebn* (The Sanctity of Human Life). In *Eseyen un redes*, edited by Y. Zilberberg. New York, 1963. 124–26.

Levinas, Emmanuel. *Difficult Freedom: Essays on Judaism*. Translated by Seán Hand. Baltimore: Johns Hopkins University Press, 1990.

Lipstadt, Deborah E. *Beyond Belief: The American Press and the Coming of the Holocaust, 1933–1945*. New York: Free Press / London: Collier Macmillan, 1986.

Mistral, Gabriela. *Castilla, tajeada de sed como mi lengua: Gabriel Mistral ante España y España ante Gabriela Mistral, 1933 a 1935*. Edited by Luis Vargas Saavedra. Santiago: Universitaria, 2002.

Mixco, Miguel Huezo, "Toño Salazar expedicionario del siglo XX." *Letras Libres*, February 2005. http://wwww.letraslibres.com/index.php?art=10266.

Nállim, Jorge. "Del antifascismo al antiperonismo: *Argentina Libre, . . . Antinazi* y el surgimiento del antiperonismo político e intelectual." In *Fascismo y antifascismo: Peronismo y antiperonismo; Conflictos políticos e ideológicos en la Argentina, 1930–1955*. Edited by Marcela García Sebastiani. Madrid and Frankfurt am Main: Iberoamericana/Vervuert, 2006. 77–105.

Senkman, Leonardo. "Los gauchos judíos: una lectura desde Israel." *EIAL* 10:1 (1999): 141–52.

Sontag, Susan, *On Photography*. New York: Farrar, Straus and Giroux, 1977.

Stephens, Mitchell. *A History of News*. 3rd ed. New York: Oxford University Press, 2007.

Szurmuk, Mónica. "Home on the Pampas: Alberto Gerchunoff's Jewish Gauchos." In *Jews at Home: The Domestication of Identity*, edited by Simon J. Bonner. Vol. 2, *Jewish Cultural Studies*. Oxford: Littman Library of Jewish Civilization, 2010. 241–56.

Wiesel, Elie. *Un di Velt hot Geshvign*. Buenos Aires: Unión Central Israelita Polaca, 1956.

Zelizer, Barbie. *Remembering to Forget: Holocaust Memory through the Camera's Eye*. Chicago: University of Chicago Press, 1998.

O diabo na rua no meio do redemoinho
The devil in the street, in the middle of the whirlwind
... Guimarães Rosa subtitle

4

João Guimarães Rosa, Consul in Hamburg

Against the Stereotypes

Borges weaver of fantasy, Lispector author of intimacy, Gerchunoff purveyor of gaucho sagacity: in the previous chapters I questioned each of these stereotypes, and through the lens of the Shoah I found human beings for whom turning away from horror was a tempting option not always chosen.

Borges and Gerchunoff, however different in personal background and artistic response, shared the challenge of the Shoah at a remove. Well informed, both reacted vehemently—but they were safe. Despite Nazi propaganda, hatemongering, and spy missions, Hitler did not establish a Fourth Reich in Patagonia, as Borges and many others had plausibly feared (as the illustration with the alligator shows). Gerchunoff, needless to say, was particularly fortunate as a Jew spared from destruction by virtue of earlier immigration. Even so, identification with his hunted breth-

A menacing Nazi crocodile poised to swallow up (unsuspecting?) Latin America, represented by a pre-Columbian-like Native American figure. Illustration by Mexican painter Chávez Morado, from *El libro negro del terror nazi* (The Black Book of Nazi Terror), Mexico, 1943. The picture accompanied an essay by Vicente Lombardo Toledano outlining Nazis' plans for dominating the "inferior races" of Latin America.

ren undercut his sense of relief. He couldn't watch the first newsreels of the concentration camps. Too close for comfort, he said, his nerves couldn't take it.

Lispector's situation was even more tangled. At the war's start she lived far from the fighting in a "tropical paradise," aware of what was going on but more concerned with the immediate—gaining Brazilian citizenship, marrying a Brazilian, and disengaging from the "foreign" (Jewish, Yiddish, Russian). Then, almost suddenly, she was thrust into the battle, into the Italian zone of killing and rationing, protected by her consul husband's diplomatic immunity, with her origin largely masked, yet behind the camouflage chilled by German propaganda, projects of hatred and purity, and the icy xenophobia and surgical orderliness of postwar Switzerland. She still was not totally immersed in the day-to-day challenges of diplomacy around the war and the war itself.

On the other hand, João Guimarães Rosa and Gabriela Mistral faced the brunt of the Nazi machine head-on in their consular assignments in Germany, Portugal, Spain, and France, as the Old Continent was self-destructing. Seen through the Shoah, conventional wisdom about their diplomatic and literary work, as with Borges, Lispector, and Gerchunoff, begs further nuance, complicating the image of Rosa, the playfully experimental wordsmith and practitioner of Brazilian regionalism, and Mistral, the "poetess" and prototype of tender maternity.

In large measure due to the war and the Shoah, Guimarães Rosa, to whom I now turn, innovated in fictions that go beyond reality to propose another reality and another language antithetical to Nazism and its propaganda. This counterlanguage helped produce his long-unknown and still unpublished "War Diary," his *éstorias* (his name for his special kind of stories), and his linguistically and anecdotally ingenious novel *Grande Sertão: Veredas* (1956; translated into English as *Devil to Pay in the Backlands*).

Hamburg: Two Years of War and Hell, 1938

May 1938: five years after Hitler's takeover and one before the war, João Guimarães Rosa, like Maury Gurgel Valente a recently minted young Brazilian consul, is dispatched by the authoritarian Vargas regime to his first assignment, Hamburg, Germany. He writes sometime after, diplomatically measuring his words as he would learn to do more and more: ". . . seguiu para Hamburgo, 1o posto, lá teve ano e pouco de paz e dois anos e tanto de guerra, bombardeios aéreos, o diabo; veio, na troca dos diplomatos" (. . . I left for Hamburg, my first post, there I had a little more than a year of peace and two or so of war, aerial bombardments, the devil; I came back in the exchange of diplomats) (Kutzenberger, 27). (The historian Haim Avni has written about the importance of what the Germans termed *Austausch*, exchange, as Nazi leverage for repatriating diplomats and Reich supporters subject to arrest in Latin America; see Avni, 30–31.)

Guimarães Rosa's words might be curt and deliberate, but they insinuate a complex geographic, linguistic, professional, and political landscape that took Brazil's greatest twentieth-century novelist (Lispector is the other stellar name), born in 1908 in the provincial city of Cordisburgo, Minas Gerais, from the steppe-like Brazilian uplands, or *sertãos*, to the great port of Hamburg; and from the perks of a polyglot diplomat fluent in German and loving of German culture to the privations of his consulate's destruction and house arrest by the Gestapo in January 1942, after Brazil, the only South American country to fight with the Allies, broke relations with the Axis.

A landscape that also took Guimarães Rosa from a first-rate education by German friars, the practice of medicine, and an unhappy marriage that produced two daughters to overseas diplomacy, a beloved soul mate—his second wife, Aracy Moebius Carvalho, a consular attaché whom he met in Hamburg—and to sharp opposition to Nazism, especially Nazi antisemitism. Among the horrors shortly after his arrival was Kristallnacht (Night of Broken Glass), the pogrom of November 9–10, 1938, when on a single night Nazis murdered 91 Jews and deported 25,000–30,000 to concentration camps, demolished more than 200 synagogues, and ransacked thousands of Jewish enterprises and homes.

We have a meticulously researched study on how these atrocities played out specifically in Hamburg, where Jews were an integral part of commercial life. German scholar Frank Bajohr's detailed and chilling book *"Aryanisation" in Hamburg* spells out the ever-growing exclusion, confiscation, humiliation, and pauperization to which the Hanseatic metropolis's shrinking community of 16,000 Jews was subject, with 1938 as the watershed annus horribilis that literally smashed any lingering thoughts of economic survival in Hitler's Reich.[1]

Far from being incidental to his future life and literature, these devilish years in Germany left a traumatic mark on the novice consul, who after surviving the bombings, the pounding of Hitler's propaganda, the indignities visited on the Jews who crowded the consulate begging for visas, and, finally, the house arrest in Baden-Baden, was summarily sent to high-altitude Bogotá, Colombia, as second secretary of the legation (1942–1944). His story "Páramo" (Barren Plateau), set in this inhospitable terrain, captures a consul-protagonist's state of life-in-death and his identification with cadaverous humans and refugee Jewish exiles.

Immediately after the war, in 1946, Guimarães Rosa served as secretary to the Brazilian delegation to the Paris Peace Conference, and he visited devastated postwar Germany, including Berlin, Munich, and Nuremberg, where the Nuremberg Trials were being held (November 20, 1945, to October 1, 1946). He wrote to his daughters, "Vimos muita miseria e ruinas em quantidade. . . . Em Nuremberg, estive na sala do julgamento dos criminosos de guerra nazistas" (We saw a lot of misery and a tremendous amount of ruins. . . . In Nuremberg, I was in the courtroom of the Nazi war criminals) (AMBL, Doc. O.8462, Paris, September 3, 1946).

In her thoughtful essay on Guimarães Rosa's German years and their Holocaust connections, Florinda Goldberg rightly asks: Was Guimarães Rosa's quick removal from Hamburg to Bogotá with barely a month's stopover in Rio de Janeiro a slap on the hand for defying his generally anti-Jewish superiors by facilitating visas together with his future wife, exactly when Itamaraty, the Brazilian Foreign Office, limited such permits? Maybe it was, illustrating the contradictions both in Brazil's policies and in Guimarães Rosa's attitudes (admiring and working for the authoritarian Vargas but not at one with all his directives) (see Goldberg; see also chapter 2, on Lispector). Another story, "A Velha" (The Old Lady), portrays the frustration of a sympathetic Brazilian consul stationed in Hamburg at his inability, after realizing the murderous implications of the Night of Broken Glass, to grant a lifesaving visa to the daughter of an aged matriarch: *Eu, o homem do sertão, não posso presenciar injustiças* (I, a man of the *sertão*, can't witness injustice).

Guimarães Rosa was a master of verbal hide-and-seek, akin to his countrywoman Lispector, whose reluctant answer to an interviewer has become the locus classicus on her Jewishness, German Holocaust culpability, and chosenness. Guimarães Rosa too divulged the little he cared to about his role in rescuing Jews only with prodding, in an interview conducted many years later. Ambiguity and indirection were the two great contemporaries' stock-in-trade, probably a consequence of diplomatic training, a need to censor information and shield identities, and, from a rhetorical-ideological perspective, a distrust of declarative, self-assured language—for instance German under the Nazis—purporting to be the idiom of the "Chosen" trumpeting the "Truth."

What Guimarães Rosa wrote to his much-admired uncle Vicente from Hamburg in June 1939 is quite different from what he told his interviewer, Günter Lorenz, in January 1965. On the former occasion, he wrote:

> Você me pede que lhe fale da minha situação como Cônsul. Mas a materia referente ao assunto é, nas coisas interessantes, eminentemente reservada, secreta mesmo, de tal maneira que não me arriscaria a dizer a minima palavra a respeito numa carta. . . . É um trabalho intenso e cheio de responsabilidades, mas subterrâneo e de penumbra. Também, não se esqueça que eu sou clouro na carreira, pelo menos na práctica no estrangeiro. (Guimarães 2006, 157)
>
> ....
>
> You ask me to tell you about my situation as Consul. But anything interesting related to that subject is extremely sensitive, even secret, so I wouldn't risk saying even a single word about it in a letter. . . . It's intense work, full of responsibility but covert and shadowy. Don't forget too that I'm new to the career, at least when it comes to assignments abroad.

After his tight lips on the diplomatic front—what covert work is he doing?—the nephew launches into a lengthy itinerary of his tourism all over Germany, with the emotional highlights his visits to the well-preserved houses of Schiller and Goethe in Weimar "fazendo-me enorme bem" (doing me a lot of good) (Guimarães 2006, 159). This represents the Germany Guimarães Rosa looks up to, not the Germany of Hitler's raspy, rabid voice, with the Nazi eagle and swastika fluttering on every street corner (see "A Velha").

A quarter of a century after, here is the interview with Günter Lorenz:

JGR: . . . A política é desumana porque dá ao homem o mesmo valor que uma vírgula em uma conta. Eu não sou um homem político, justamente porque amo o homem. Deveríamos abolir a política.

GL: Foi isto que em Hamburgo levou você a se arriscar perigosamente, arrebatando judeus das mãos da Gestapo?

JGR: Foi alguma coisa assim, mas havia também algo diferente: um diplomata é um sonhador e por isso pude exercer bem essa profissão. O diplomata acredita que pode remediar o que os politicos arruinaram. E também por isso mesmo gusto muito de ser diplomata. E agora o que houve em Hamburgo é preciso acrescentar mais uma coisa. Eu, o homem do sertão, não posso presenciar injustiças. No sertão, num caso desses imediatamente a gente saca o revólver, a lá isso não era possivel. Precisamente por isso idealizei um estratagema diplomático, e não foi assim tão perigoso. E agora me ocupo de problemas de límites de fronteiras e por isso vivo muito mais limitado. (41–42)

. . . .

JGR: . . . Politics is inhuman because it gives man the same value as a decimal point on a bill. I'm not a politician precisely because I value man. We should abolish politics.

GL: Was that what led you to put yourself dangerously at risk in Hamburg, snatching Jews from the hands of the Gestapo?

JGR: It was something like that, but there was also a different reason: a diplomat is a dreamer, and that's why I was good at my profession. The diplomat believes that he can set right what the politicians ruin. That's also why I like being a diplomat a great deal. Now about what I faced in Hamburg, there's one more thing to add. I, as a man of the *sertão*, can't be witness to injustice. On the *sertão* in such a case, people reach for their guns right away, and over there that was impossible. That's why I came up with a diplomatic maneuver, and it wasn't all that dangerous. But now I deal with border demarcation issues, so I'm much more bordered in.

João Guimarães Rosa, who by this time held full ambassadorial rank, knew full well that his stratagems in Hamburg were supremely political; but even in parsing between the dreaming diplomat and the poisonous politician, the justice-seeking backland man and the inhumane practitioner of Realpolitik, he reveals almost nothing about what he actually did, talking in sound bites and ending with a verbal legerdemain: "I now deal with border [*limites*] . . . issues . . . I'm much more bordered in [*limitado*]."

Enough suggestive information does seep through. Guimarães Rosa's statement that politicians reduce human beings into decimal points elicits the question about the Hamburg Jews and the Gestapo from Lorenz, one of Guimarães Rosa's main German commentators. Are there shades of Hitler's Final Solution here, the ciphering of the suffering? Then, diplomats can remedy what politicians ruin: as in Itamaraty's secret antisemitic instructions, circumvented by consular manipulations?

And further: on the *sertão*, the battle between what was seen as good and evil was ferociously fought between bands of *jagunços*, gunmen loyal to a chief or rancher, and the raging background to Guimarães Rosa's great postwar novel, *Grande Sertão: Veredas* (1956). On the streets of Hamburg the same conflict, in Rosa's view, was transposed into diplomatic ruses, pullulating in the novel's subtitle, *O diabo na rua, no meio do redemoinho* (The devil in the street, in the middle of the whirlwind). Could the semi-said be intimating how subterranean activism and shadowy storytelling went hand in hand?

Righteous among the Nations

At Yad Vashem, the austere Holocaust Martyrs' and Heroes' Remembrance Authority in the Jerusalem hills, I walked from the state-of-the-art exhibitions in the showcase museum to a modest side building, where I followed nondescript corridors to the Department of Righteous among the Nations, devoted to honoring non-Jews who took risks to save Jews during the Shoah. Now numbering some twenty thousand from more than forty countries, the list contains two rescuers from Brazil, Luis Martins de Souza Dantes, Brazil's ambassador in German-occupied France, and Aracy de Carvalho de Guimarães Rosa.[2]

The woman in charge of the department led me to a small reading room lined with shelf after shelf of yellow manila dossiers. In these unassuming surroundings, seated at a simple metal table, I was transported back, low-tech style, to the eeriness of Nazi-era Hamburg, sifting through correspondence, press clippings, testimonies, and photographs. The oldest item was a typed letter dated December 27, 1941, with the letterhead Reichsvereinigung der Juden in Deutschland abt. Wanderung (Hilfsverein), or Reich Congregation of Jews in Germany, Emigration Dept. (Aid Society). It read in part:

> Sehr geeherte Frau Carvalho:
> Bei Gelegenheit der Einstallung unserer Tätigkeit möchten wir es nicht versäumen, Ihnen herzlichen Dank auszusprechen . . .
>
> . . . .
>
> Dear Mrs. Carvalho:
> On the occasion of the cessation of our activities, we cannot neglect to express our deep gratitude to you. . . . Advising and helping us with your vast experience as a highly qualified consular official, you did not hesitate to put yourself at risk for anyone who came to solicit your help; many applicants succeeded in emigrating thanks to your support. . . .

The letter's polite language simmers with the desperate juncture: late 1941, when the Nazis forbade Jewish emigration and those who hadn't escaped were trapped. More audaciously under the circumstances, the text hints at Aracy de Carvalho's stratagems to save lives.

What exactly had she done? Affidavits from refugees whom Dona Aracy had helped, newspaper articles about her actions, and correspondence between Israeli consular officials in Brazil and Yad Vashem soliciting evidence all flesh out the details, as part of the careful search for information always conducted by Yad Vashem. The search culminated in 1983 when Guimarães Rosa's wife was named a Righteous among the Nations; in 1985, Dona Aracy traveled to Jerusalem to receive the Certificate of Honor in a ceremony held at Yad Vashem. She came alone—João Guimarães Rosa, her great accomplice, had died prematurely in 1967.

A second letter—more a declaration—dated April 28, 1985, and handwritten by Dona Aracy on the stationery of the Jerusalem Ramada Renaissance Hotel, tells the story from her perspective, possibly explaining her husband's "something like that" of the Lorenz interview. We can't discount the vagaries of time, memory, personal views, and narrative-shaping in considering the affidavit-like account, the answer to a set of questions posed by Yad Vashem. My research in the file, together with information I gleaned from additional interviews and articles, shows that Mônica Raisa Schpun, who has studied Dona Aracy's endeavors meticulously, is on target when she says there are many "lacunae" in relation to Dona Aracy and Guimarães Rosa's work, due to the discretion of the operation and the fragmentary records as a result of the war. But this very vagueness, claims Schpun, gives a sense of the fraught climate of the time, increasing the "density" of the historical events (see Schpun and Carvalho). Dona Aracy's Yad Vashem letter has to be read with this lack of sharpness and thick effect in mind.

She begins by introducing herself as the widow of the writer and diplomat João Guimarães Rosa, ex-Brazilian consul in Hamburg, where she worked in the passport and visa department as a diplomatic assistant (*auxiliar diplomática*). My husband, Dona Aracy writes, always signed the documents that I prepared, no questions asked — an indispensable requirement. (Guimarães Rosa and Carvalho were formally married only after the war.)

Around 1938, when German Jews started to come to the consulate daily begging for visas to Brazil because they were being persecuted — many of their fellow Jews had even disappeared — Dona Aracy, at great personal danger despite her diplomatic immunity, obtained or facilitated visas (the exact number is one of the lacunae), overcoming the hurdles of President Vargas's secret anti-Jewish circulars as well as the antipathy of fellow consular officials who were Nazi sympathizers.

At the other end of the spectrum, Guimarães Rosa, who already had the reputation for issuing "more than his share of immigrant visas," according to historian Jeffrey Lesser, requested that he receive a special quota of a thousand visas related to a Vatican plan to aid converted Jews. Hamburg was suggested as the place to effect the rescue operation in some measure because of Guimarães Rosa's sympathies, which were apparently known to the Nazis (see Lesser's discussion, 149–50, 157–58).

In the rest of her testimony, Dona Aracy fleshes out remaining aspects of the operation: her need to accompany refugees to the departing ships; her hiding the persecuted in her apartment; her bringing food to Jewish families who weren't allowed to receive rationed items; and her safekeeping precious belongings for emigrants, returning them when she met them again in Brazil. According to Schpun's investigations, some immigrants gave Dona Aracy valuable gifts in gratitude for her assistance, but she never asked for payment for her services, they reported. (Stories, some true, were common at the time about extortion by diplomats and immigration authorities.)

After ending with the episode of the internment in Baden-Baden and the exchange for German diplomats at the Spain-Portugal border, Dona Aracy adds an afterthought, as if summing up the whole underlying motivation for the Guimarães Rosa couple's behavior: "Asisti muitas cenas deprimentes como vea judeus professoães universitários varrendo ruas, com a Estrela de David nas suas roupas" (I witnessed many depressing scenes, such as seeing Jewish professionals with university degrees sweeping streets, with the Star of David on their clothing). Her words recall her husband's: "I, as a man of the *sertão*, can't witness injustice. . . . That's why I came up with a diplomatic maneuver, and it wasn't all that dangerous." She reported in another interview that Guimarães Rosa would always say, if he didn't give them the visas, those people will end up dead, and "I'll have that weighing on my conscience" (*vou ter um peso na minha consciencia*).

Guimarães Rosa, holding consular status and doing less of the "dirty work," was more protected than his partner, but even allowing for wifely hero-making, he may have well underplayed his own exposure in a regime that knew he was not friendly to its cause. This was his position throughout, even when he received an award from the German ambassador to Brazil decades after the occurrences (see Goldberg 2007).

Doing and Discourse: The "War Diary"

At the same time that he was performing his overt and covert professional duties, the consul thrown into the maelstrom was also writing. Cloak-and-dagger-like, portions of that private notebook from 1939, 1941, and 1942 were preserved in a photocopy and only made widely known in 2003, after six decades of repose in the Acervo de Escritores Mineiros, an archive. Professors Eneida Maria de Souza, Georg Otte, and Reinaldo Marques have edited what they have named the "Diario de Guerra" (War Diary), but to date the fragments remain unpublished; Professor Otte was kind enough to give me a copy.[3]

A treasure trove for Guimarães Rosa scholars, and an eyewitness testimony for students of early stages of the Shoah in Germany from the perspective of a "neutral" consul-writer, the "War Diary" constitutes a sort of "missing link" between João Guimarães Rosa, the diplomat, polyglot, and word meister, and Joãozinho, the sensitive and antiracist "Johnny" known to family, friends, colleagues, and Doña Aracy (Ara, to him).[4]

The destructive immediacy of the war hangs heavily over the log, whose major topic, if you will, is the nonstop hammering of Hamburg by the British Royal Air Force (RAF)—the sirens, antiaerial flak cannons, searchlights, air raid shelters, blackouts, ruins, victims, and bombs falling near Guimarães Rosa's home, breaking windows and destroying part of the embassy building. "A coisa está brutal" (It's brutal), he writes darkly on July 4, 1940. And with greater foreboding on October 10: "Será que començou o fim do mundo?" (Is this the beginning of the end of the world?)

In the face of a possible apocalypse, Guimarães Rosa tries to maintain a semblance of normality whenever possible, working, dining, and going to the opera, spending time with friends and strolling with Ara, enjoying nature, a particular refuge from the disorder and an element that would appear frequently in his fiction. In a respite from the sirens, he makes a record of (part of?) his varied library, noting titles, authors, and shelving locations (June 12, 1940). Many German volumes sit alongside French, Spanish, English, and some Portuguese ones, with writers of multiple nationalities and religions, from the Austrian-Jewish Stefan Zweig and Franz Werfel to the Spanish Federico García Lorca and the British Rudyard Kipling. Guimarães Rosa spoke and knew dozens of languages.

Some of the volumes are unsettling. The German Nazi ideologue Alfred Rosenberg's infamous *Der Mythus des XX Jarhunderts* (The Myth of the Twentieth Century) also sits on the bookcases, as does a section of then regnant German ethnographic, archaeological, folklore, and myth studies —Albert Richter and Guido Görres on the Niebelunglen, for example— including the likes of Professors H. F. K. Günther, Carl Schuchhardt, and Gustav Schwantes, all connected to the Nazi mania with Volkskunde and "racial prehistory." Günther was the chief "racial theorist" of the Reich, defaming Jews and extolling the Nordic "race." As the RAF explosives detonated, Guimarães Rosa the anti-Nazi read those he agreed with and those he decried, quite obviously fascinated and affected by Germanic myths, legends, and sagas but evidently taking his own tack on ethnicity, regionalism, language, purity, fact, and fiction. To the contemporary reader, his diary notations, and his reading, move jarringly from one sphere to the other, bookish and banal, mundane and terrifying.

But it isn't only the reporting of the bombing by air that makes the diary noteworthy, with Guimarães Rosa, despite the suffering, cheering on the RAF "boys," or "brave fellows," as he calls them in English. It is more the intertwining of verbal experimentation—word juggling, poem fragments, term lists in Portuguese and German, neologisms, translations of phrases and sentences—with sarcastic commentary on the failings and falsehoods of Nazi Germany, highlighting its vicious antisemitism.

The autobiographical mode amalgamates with testimony, the culture shock literature of the traveler-observer with the resultant need to think through new forms of enunciation antithetical to Nazi discourse. Guimarães Rosa develops this amalgamation in *Grande Sertão: Veredas* and his *estórias*, the first of which he was rewriting during his Hamburg consular stay and Baden-Baden confinement, at times overlapping the sounds in the tales—the braying of a burro—with the sounds of war: "Mugiram as sirenes. Alarme!" (The sirens brayed. Alarm!) (Otte 2003, 290; "Diario de Guerra," May 30, 1940). (He published the *estórias* right after the war in 1946, under the title *Sagarana*, "saga-like," one of his invented words, overlapping the Germanic "saga" with "rana," meaning "similar" in Tupi, a Brazilian indigenous language.)

Historically shattering, the German period shaped the *éstoria*, a form meant to break down History with a capital H: "a *éstoria*, em rigor, deve ser contra a História," as the author explained, more like an anecdote with an unexpected ending, like a phosphorescent match, lit and blown out, but in that flash opening a path of poetry, transcendence, and analysis (cited in Fantini, 221).

A telling diary entry from March 25, 1940, exemplifies the combinatory of language, critique of Nazism, day-to-day living, and solace in the natural order. Guimarães Rosa notes: "Almocei em casa do cônsul Geral. . . . Às 7 horas, na Staatliches Schauspielhaus fui ver O FAUST. . . . Um acontecimento! Maravilha! . . . Heil Goethe! . . . O dia foi bonito. E, ao sairmos do teatro, fazia luar" (I had lunch at the General Consul's house. . . . At seven o'clock I went to see *Faust* at the State Theater. Quite an occasion! Marvelous! Heil Goethe! . . . It was a nice day. And when we came out of the theater the moon was shining.)

As he recounts the day's activities, "normalcy" in a time of gross terror, Guimarães Rosa's compact and caustic take on the Nazis' ubiquitous salute deflates the unsavory *political* verbiage, retooling the phrase to express his admiration for the lasting *cultural* achievement of Goethe and his *Faust*. But the entry isn't politically innocent, since the Faustian theme of the struggle for people's souls, between saint and devil, continually vexes Guimarães Rosa in the notebook; it would become the central dilemma of *Grande Sertão: Veredas*, again suggesting the strong connection between Hitler's Germany and the brutality-filled "Brazilianist" novel.

Lingua Tertii Imperii

I'd like to pause further on two aspects of Guimarães Rosa's diary: his emphasis on what Victor Klemperer named the Lingua Tertii Imperii (LTI), the language of the Third Reich; and directly connected to the Nazi-speak, the persecution of the Jews. The vice-consul filled his log with articles cut and pasted from the German-language newspapers of the day, often as exemplars of Hitler's manipulation of facts through words. Georg Otte, who translated these articles into Portuguese, writes himself a perceptive memo in a footnote: "To look into further—the strong presence of war rhetoric in an apparently informational text: The link between Nazism and propaganda and its relation to fictions that go beyond reality." Put another way, the fact-fiction link as construed by Nazism infuriated yet intrigued Rosa, whose writings sought precisely to explore the murky fact-fiction in-between, but in a way that questioned deceit.

Borges, another explorer of that twilight zone through a creative narrative style, the *ficción*, had similar discomfort about Nazi "unreality": "El nazismo adolece de irrealidad, como los infiernos de Erígena. Es inhabitable: los hombres sólo pueden morir por él, mentir por él, matar y ensangrentar por él" (Nazism suffers from unreality, like Erigena's hell. It is uninhabitable: men can only die for it, lie for it, kill and maim for it) ("Anotación al 23 de agosto de 1944," OC, 728). Could "unreality," both Borges and Guimarães Rosa ask, be used differently, by means of linguistic multiplicity and polyvalent sense, not bloodying foreclosure of sense?

Many of the articles pasted into Guimarães Rosa's diary deal with the aerial bombing, and they open with the salute that signals entry into the "unreality" of the LTI, staged by the master of the Big Lie, Joseph Goebbels: "The Hamburg Ministry of Propaganda announces." The diplomat skilled in diplomatic lingo was keeping a record of the official version of events perfectly concordant with Klemperer's descriptions of the "fairy-tale quality" of Goebbels's production (Klemperer, 202).

The communiqués emphasize veracity in a set pattern. The RAF raids injure and kill, and inevitably miss their targets thanks to the marvelous flak antiaerial defenses, hitting civilian buildings. The Führer, in contrast, has forbidden destruction of the enemy's nonmilitary interests. One lengthy pasted item reads in part, "This crime also cannot be justified in the eyes of the English people when it finds out the truth. Suffice it to say that Mr. Churchill should anxiously wait for the day of reckoning both with us and with his own people, when together with his war strategy against Greater Germany that he hates, his huge, never-before-seen edifice of lies will crumble. As we have already said: the future will bring the truth" ("Major Aerial Attack on Hamburg," or "Ataque aéreo extenso a Hamburgo," November 16, 1940).[5] What makes this dispatch especially heinous is that it appeared right after the English city of Coventry was wiped out by Luftwaffe bombers on November 14, 1940, one of the watershed blitz raids of the world war, in which civilians were indiscriminately slaughtered and the cathedral was reduced to ashes.

What did Guimarães Rosa have to say about the RAF bombardments? "Estou escutando a mensagem de Churchill . . . radiografada, aos franceses. E escuto o roncar dos aviões dos Tommies. Duas mensagens. Viva!" (I'm listening to Churchill's message . . . radio-telegraphed to the French. And I can hear the noise of the Tommies' [British soldiers'] airplanes. Two messages. Hooray!) (October 21, 1940). Or: "Ontem, foi assinado pelo Presidente Roosevelt o *lend-and-lease bill*! Tiroteo da *Flak* ligeira . . . Será que vai começar a tremenda ofensiva aérea, tão anunciada? . . . Nestas últimas semanas, parece que os ingleses supercoventrizaram Wilhelmshaven; dizem que 'a cidade não existe mais' . . ." (Yesterday, President Roosevelt signed the Lend-Lease Bill! [The program supplied vast amounts of war material to the Allies.] Minor shooting from the flak . . . Could the heavy air offensive that's been announced so many times actually be starting? It seems that in the last few weeks the English supercoventrized Wilhelmshaven; they say that "the city no longer exists" . . . (March 2, 1941).

In both excerpts, the future novelist offers alternate versions. "Supercoventrizaram" is his invented sendup of an LTI building block, the verb "Coventrieren," coined by Goebbels after the devastation of Coventry to describe a city's total annihilation by air. One-upping the LTI's benumbing abuse of the superlative—a trait that Klemperer emphasizes—Guimarães Rosa talks about the "*super*coventrizing" of *German* cities; he uses *coventryzada* again when Kiel is exploded by the *boys* later in the year (April 10, 1941).

"What remains?" Klemperer asks in a moving short chapter devoted mainly to the verb *coventrieren*, peeling back just as Guimarães Rosa did the reality of "coventryizing." Hiding from his tormentors, the Jewish professor surveys the rubble of German cities, the gutted rooms, everything reduced to dust, and the birth of a new painting and literature of ruins unlike the sweet melancholic ruination writing of the eighteenth century: "And, when the bitterness at this sight evokes the word 'coventrieren' a desolate train of thought is summoned up. It is called crime and punishment" (Klemperer 119).

Two decades after, Guimarães Rosa still echoes the desolate train of thought, of language buried under ash heaps, leading philosophers led astray: "O idioma é a única porta para o infinito, mas infelizmente está oculto sob montanhas de cinzas. Daí resulta que tenha de limpá-lo, e como é expressão da vida. . . . Soa a Heidegger, não? Ele construiu toda uma filosofia muito estranha, baseado em sua sensibilidade para com a língua, mas teria feito melhor contentando-se com a língua." (Language is the only gateway to the infinite, but unfortunately it is hidden under mountains of ashes. It sounds like Heidegger, right? He developed a very strange philosophy based on his sensitivity to language, but he would have done better by just sticking to language) (Lorenz, 47).

Antisemitism and the Language of the Third Reich

Nazi criminality in word and works combines with special vehemence in Guimarães Rosa's condemnation of the antisemitic crescendo: "Os judeus não têm dereito de comer todas as coisas que ainda estão ao alcance dos estômagos arianos" (Jews don't have the right to eat all the things that are still available to Aryan stomachs), he opens acidly on March 29, 1940, going on to detail the red J stamped on the ration cards, and the restrictions on food, clothing, shoes, radios, shopping, yet observing at the end that food often materializes when the poor persecuted shell out extra cash.

If the frightful paragraph reduces to absurdity the LTI's über-term, "Aryan," reportage shading into storytelling, almost a proto-*estória*, this reduction is much more striking in Guimarães Rosa's perturbing jotting just a few months later:

> 13.VII. 1940—Passei hoje, com Ara, à tarde. Fomos pela beira do Alster.
> Num recanto da margem, perto da Lombardsbrücke, para o lado de cá (da minha casa), vi uma praiazinha para crianças. Pequenina enseada, protegida, de um lado, por um pernambuco de pedra, ganho pelas ondas do lado, que vão e vêm por entre as pedras, convertendo-o em cachoeira. Marrecos flutuam, dando o peito redondo ao ímpeto em miniatura das ondas, ou mergulhando as cabeças. A 2 metros da terra, uma tela, firme em estacas. Os garotos podem nadar alí dentro. Há um quadrado, espécie de vasto caixão de areia, para os garotos brincarem. Perto, os salguieros-chorões. Ondazinhas vêm lamber a praia de brinquedo. E . . . mas . . . para estragar toda a mansa poesia do lugar: arvoraram, num poste, uma tabloletazinha amarela: "Lugar de brinquedo para crianças arianas" . . .

....

> July 13, 1940—I went for a walk, with Ara, this afternoon. We went to the bank of the Alster.
> In a recess at the water's edge, close to the Lombard Bridge, on this side (toward my house), I saw a little beach for children. A small inlet, protected on one side by a stone outcropping, bathed by the waves on the side that flow back and forth between the stones, turning into a waterfall. Ducks float, puffing out their chests to the slow rhythm of the water, or diving in with their heads. About two meters from land, a cloth, stretched out on poles. The kids can swim inside of it. There's a square, a kind of large sandbox, where the kids can play. Close by, weeping willows. Little

waves lick the toy beach. And . . . alas . . . to spoil the gentle poetry of the place: they put up, on a post, a small yellow sign: "Playground for Aryan children" . . .

Now *Aryan* isn't so much reduced to absurdity but exposed as a linguistic and human poison that besmirches even a space of innocence, where we expect the joy of childhood to defer the suffering of adulthood. The yellow sign (the color of infamy, of the despicable star) fissures the poetry of a carefully manicured *locus amoenus*, the paradisiacal place of safety and comfort, with its trees, water, and naives at play.

The authorial eye structures the scene in a way later familiar to Guimarães Rosa's readers: the uncanny laden with human guilt and pain interrupting the apparent calm of nature, leading to a meditation on right and wrong and the possible structuring of other realities, or unrealities. We see this characteristic most famously in his emblematic *estória* "A Terceira Margem do Rio" (The Third Bank of the River), where on the shores of another, unnamed river the bizarre that wasn't supposed to happen does, in a drama of sin, remorse, and penitence again centering on children. A Noah-like father drifts his life away in a canoe, while his son struggles with the burden, why was he doing it? What was he atoning for? Why couldn't the son take over the load? "To look into further: The link between Nazism and propaganda and its relation to fictions that go beyond reality."

Infamante! Horrivel! Mentira!

The three words in my subhead define particularly forceful diary entries on the subject of antisemitism:

1. * 26.IX. 1941 (Sexta-feria)—Passei de automóvil com Ara. Passamos na Grindelberg. A venda dos judeos. Até crianças de 4 anos, ou menos, com o distintivo amarelo. Infamante!
   E o povo do partido, vendendo *Abzeichen*: hoje é a *swastika* a través os tempos.
2. * 20.X. 1941—Judias chorando no Consulado, por terem recebido a ordem de evacuaçao de Hamburgo, para o dia 24. Horrível.
3. * 13.III. 1941—Mentira! O que houve foi o leilão.

. . . .

September 26, 1941: (Friday) I went for a car ride with Ara. We drove through Grindelberg [Grindel quarter was the heavily Jewish area of Hamburg]. Jewish emporia. Even four-year-olds, or younger, wearing the yellow patch. Despicable!

And the party people, selling *Abzeichen* [badges]: today it's the swastika through the ages.

October 20, 1941: Jewish women crying in the consulate after receiving the order to evacuate Hamburg by the 24th. Horrible!

March 13, 1941: It's a lie! It was an auction.

Infamante! Guimarães Rosa chronicles the growing victimization, bringing to mind his widow Aracy's testimony for Yad Vashem — the painful confinement to so-called Jewish houses mainly in the Grindel quarter and the imposition of the "Judenstern." He contrasts the yellow star, again using sarcasm, with the true badge of infamy. The discriminatory mark particularly vexed him throughout the diary. He pastes in the text of the obligating decrees, makes a sketch of the star, and comments on the first one he saw, in another uncanny mininarration where youthful innocence and disability suffer semiotic vileness: a sweet little boy in knickers, marked with the patch, was helping a blind man, who had a special blind-emblem on his arm, to cross (September 20, 1941). Tuned in to the ironic absurdity, Guimarães Rosa pays as close attention to the semiotics of badges, a visual aspect of the LTI manifesting the Nazi obsession with symbols, as he does to their written and oral language.

Horrivel! In October 1941, the junior consul evidences the first transport that euphemistically "evacuated" the harried Hamburg Jews to the Lodz ghetto, a way station to extermination; the single word pits Nazi versions to his own, and such scenes remained etched in his memory, to be reworked in the story "A Velha."

Mentira! The third entry repudiates lies about the pillaging of Jewish property in possibly his most succinct answer to the cut-and-pasted antisemitism: his rejection of an article claiming that the Jewish goods "generously" brought to Hamburg from all over Germany for safekeeping in so-called giant "Jew boxes" until they could be forwarded to their emigrating owners were destroyed by none other than the Jewish-directed British air attacks. ("The Boomerang Hit the Jews," or "O bumerangue acertou os judeos," the headline trumpets.) Guimarães Rosa handwrites the article's date, March 13, 1941, along with his short retort: *Mentira! O que houve foi o leilão.* (It's a lie! There was an auction.)

German historian Götz Aly's book *Hitler's Beneficiaries: Plunder, Racial War, and the Nazi Welfare State* confirms Guimarães Rosa's testimonies: "The contents of many of the containers that had been stored in Hamburg in the spring of 1941 were auctioned off, with the lion's share being bought by the Social Services Administration. The goods were then distributed to various warehouses throughout the city as a 'handy reserve in case of catastrophe.' . . ."

Hamburg, which because of its size and proximity to Britain was hit especially often and hard by RAF raids, represents a case in itself. In February 1941 at the behest of the local gauleiter (Nazi district leader), the Gestapo confiscated three to four thousand lifts in Hamburg's duty-free port and ordered the contents immediately sold off by a Hamburg auction house (125, 127–30).

O diabo na rua no meio do redemoinho

Similarly to Georg Otte, editor of Guimarães Rosa's diary, critic Marli Fantini sees the writer's years in Germany as essential to the development of his expansive narrative perspective. She reiterates that the neophyte diplomat's immersion in war logic, his living as a foreigner through the dislocations of the Second World War, along with his need to survive imprisonment allowed him to operate with a "vetor fronteiriço" (frontier vector), favoring fluid identities, immigration and otherness, territorial permeability, and socio-cultural-linguistic plasticity (106; see also 82–83). In short—everything that Hitlerism and the LTI did not.

Seen through the kaleidoscope that the war log anticipated, the distance appears to shrink between Hitler and Hermógenes, evil incarnate in *Grande Sertão: Veredas*, although we obviously can't reduce any facet of such a multistranded six-hundred-page fictional tour de force to one historical or literary source. Goethe's *Faust* also lurks in the background (see Kutzenberger).

Riobaldo, the novel's protagonist, tells the story of his *jagunço* band's warfare against the cruel Hermógenes's henchmen in a hybrid Portuguese language that refuses to be neutral, almost a grammar of its own. The work, it has been often said, is untranslatable, or at least poses impossible challenges to those who have dared to take it on, since it brims with neologisms, archaisms, popular, regional, and scholarly expressions, and foreign loan words. Nilce Sant'Anna Martins has edited a large lexicon of Guimãraes Rosa's language, with hundreds of words that aren't in standard dictionaries. Nothing "pure" or one-voiced about Guimãraes Rosa's prose, as the diary already shows.

And the *sertão* where the novel occurs is itself an imprecise, fantasy-ridden locale, hence the *veredas*—the byways, the lateral (in Lispector's view), the "third margin" of the river (*Rio-baldo*), where the uncanny laden with human pain interrupts the apparent calm of nature, as it did on the Alster River, leading to a meditation on right and wrong and the possible structuring of other realities, or unrealities. Sexuality also ceases to be "straight" as Riobaldo feels a homoerotic attraction to his fellow *jagunço* Diadorim, and he finds out only at the end when Diadorim dies vanquishing Hermógenes that s/he is a woman.

Time, too, flows back and forth: even though the book supposedly talks about early twentieth-century Brazil, it is a maze of remembrance and action, with the violent local backlands filtered through the lens of a broader globe where only a few years before its writing millions died in a world war and a Holocaust.

Recalling his Hamburg days, Rosa told a colleague, "Você não sabe mas o fascismo é o Demo. Porque eu sei, eu estive lá e eu sei que é o Demo. Eu tive que lidiar com alemães para proteger refugiados judeos." (You don't know it but fascism is the devil. I do know, I was there and I know that it's the devil. I had to fight with Germans to protect Jewish refugees.) Recalling his battles, Riobaldo says:

> O Hermógenes—demônio. Sim sô isto. Era êle mismo. . . . Repenso . . . soante que mesmo vi e assaz me contaram; e outros—as ruindades de regra que executavam . . . baleando, esfaqueando, estirpando, furtando os olhos, cortando linguas e orhelas, não economizando as crianças pequenas, atirando na inocência do gado, queimando pessoas ainda meio vivas, na beira de estrago de sangues. . . . (*GSV*, ed. 4a, 40)
>
> ....
>
> Hermógenes—devil. Yes, that was it. He was the devil himself. . . . I think back . . . what I saw for myself and what I heard; and other things—the atrocities which they committed as a matter of course . . . : shooting, stabbing, gutting, putting out eyes, cutting off tongues and ears, not even sparing little children, firing on the innocent cattle, burning persons still half alive in a welter of blood. Did not such things come from hell? Of course. . . .

Riobaldo's ruminations on Satan form a large part of the narrative, and they address a Guimarães Rosa–like stand-in who listens yet never speaks, hinting at the androgynous author, two sides of the same creature—hinterland man and urban sophisticate. Riobaldo palavers and philosophizes. Why is there evil, why suffering? Is there a God? Does the devil exist? What are his many names? Did he, Riobaldo, also pact with him? Don't all religions merit the same respect? Aren't foreigners with their broken Portuguese that Guimarães Rosa reproduces, Middle Easterners and (pointedly) Germans, okay people, if they live and let live?

Guimarães Rosa's *sertão* isn't the homogeneous *sertão* of a sloganeering xenophobe of the "Brazil for Brazilians" ilk, or of a *Heimatschriftsteller*, a German regionalist writer praising Fatherland and Folk and singing paeans to an idealized peasant life, a type of generally back-looking author much favored by the Nazis who took the blood and soil, *Blut und Boden*, ethos to its extremes. Guimarães Rosa, intentionally using the German term, rejects the label for himself and his book in his interview with Günter Lorenz, showing his repulsion at its implications: ". . . não gostaria que na Alemanha me considerassem um *Heimatschrifsteller*. Seria horrível . . ." (31). Guimarães Rosa works regionalism from another perspective, just as Lispector fiddles with regionalism in her own way, ostensibly also setting *The Besieged City* in early twentieth-century Brazil but likewise shifting times, interiorizing observations, breaking apart language, tackling postwar philosophical questions, and building in Nazi hideousness.

Estoria and Shoah

I'd like to circle back to "La Velha" and "Páramo," the two *estórias* most directly tied to Guimarães Rosa's shell-shock exposure to the Shoah. They are part of a group of fictions that crack regionalism further apart, narrating the war's traumas in the interstices of reality and unreality. They have cross-woven settings and linguistic thickness in a Portuguese peppered with German and other languages: sometimes occurring primarily in Nazi Germany, with touches of Brazil, as in "O mau humor de Wotan" (Wotan's Bad Mood, published in 1948; Wotan, or Odin, was the war god of Germanic myth), "A senhora dos segredos" (The Lady Who Had Secrets, in 1952), and "La Velha" (1961); sometimes in the gaps between the European war theater and the *sertão*, "Dois soldadinhos mineiros" (Two Soldiers from Minas [Gerais], 1957); or in the estranging Latin American exile of those who survived damaged, "O cavalo que bebia cerveja" (The Horse Who Drank Beer, in 1962), and "Páramo (1969)." When the stories appeared isn't necessarily when they were written, since a number were published only after Guimarães Rosa's death in 1967.

Brazilian critic Jaime Guinzburg discerningly places these *estórias* at what he calls "a hybrid juncture, hard to classify, at which biography intersects with fiction, and history with literature. We could say that we find a testimonial tone in these stories" ("um ponto híbrido, difícil de submeter a classificações, em que a biografia se cruzaria com a ficção, e a história com a literatura. Poderíamos considerar que nesses contos encontramos um *teor testemunhal*"). As testimony, says Guinzburg, they approach the category of "Holocaust literature" (Guinzburg, "Guimarães Rosa e o terror total").

Hitlerocidades: La Velha

The Brazilian consulate in the great Hanseatic city (Hamburg) receives a vague call one morning: something about a sick old lady, Frau Wetterhuse, who would like the (unidentified) consul to come to her house on the matter of a will.

> O recado se perdia, obrigacão abstrata, no tumulto diário de casos, o Consulado invadindo-se de judeus, sob mó de angústias, famintos de partir, sofridos imenso, em desengano, público pranto e longo estremecer, quase cada rosto prometendo-se a coativa esperança final do suicídio. Vê-los, vinha à mente a voz de Hitler ao rádio—rouco, raivoso. Contra êsses, desde novembro, se implacara mais desbordada e atroz a perseguição, dosada brutal. Viesse a guerra, a primeira ordem seria matá-los? (*Ave, palabra*, 108).
>
> ....
>
> The message, an abstract demand, was lost in the daily whirlwind of cases, the consulate overrun by Jews, full of anguish, anxious to leave, etched with suffering, disillusioned, weeping openly, convulsed, nearly every face marked with the forced promise of suicide, the final hope. Seeing them conjured up Hitler's voice on the radio: raspy, raging. Since November, an ever more implacable and atrocious persecution had been unleashed against them, a brutal assault. If war broke out, would the first order be to kill them?

"Since November . . .": A reference to Kristallnacht, when desperate Jews started coming to the legation in search of visas. And grafting biography onto fiction, Guimarães Rosa evidences Hitler's omnipresent howl, blasted everywhere through the fairly newfangled instrument of the radio, the LTI made sound and fury. From the *éstoria*'s opening he immerses us in the *heimlich* melded with the *unheimlich* (a vague call, an abstract demand, an anonymous diplomat), confronting History with *petite histoire*—the anecdote with an unexpected ending, serving as a path of poetry, transcendence, and analysis.

I'd like to enter the story where the proto-*estórias* of the "War Diary" flower into full-fledged fiction, through the Hitler shriek that haunted Guimarães Rosa just as it terrified Victor Klemperer, who returned to it obsessively. On first hearing the Führer Klemperer notes: "Hitler always spoke, or rather screamed, convulsively. . . . Composure and musicality

were never to be heard in his voice . . ." (49). And on Hitler on the radio: "an excessively agitated, hectoring, often rasping voice" (35). How, asks the language professor, could such a voice with its crude sentences and bombastic rhetoric have won over the masses?

Guimarães Rosa doesn't directly ask the question, but he structures the *éstoria* as a clash of voices, loud and low, hunter and hunted, male and female, German and Portuguese, even a hint of Hebrew. A third voice narrates omnisciently but barely speaks—the consul, who after a second, insistent call, goes to see Frau Wetterhuse and learns that her problem isn't a will but a half-Jewish daughter who must be saved from the annihilation actualized by the hectoring scream. Perpetrator, victim, and bystander play a role, to use Raul Hilberg's important if sometimes contested terminology, in an *éstoria* that refuses to serve as a lie (*mentira!*) or a fiction of salvation.

While the consul traverses wintry Hamburg with its streets and neighborhoods—Glockengiesserwall, Lombard Bridge, Haversterhude—spacetime contorts and the cityscape turns into a nocturnal Nazi Nifelheim, the mythic Germanic realm of ice and death:

> Sumia-se no dia noturno a bela, grande cidade hanseática. . . . Dava-se, que nem caudas de cobras, delgados glaciais chicotes—nevando, fortes flocos—o vento mordaz. . . . Saindo para o Glockengiesserwall . . . Via-se, a cada canto, o emblema: pousada num círculo, onde cabia oblíqua, a swástika, a águia de abertas asas. A fora, as sombras dos troncos de árvores, na neve, e as curvas dos corvos, o corvo da desdita. Dizia-se que . . . morriam muitos pássaros. O coraçao daquela natureza era manso, era mau? Sentia-se um, ao meio de tal ponte, à face do caos e espírito de catástrofe, em tempo tão ingeneroso, ante o critério último—o pecado de nascer—na tese anaximândrica. Todos pertencíamos, assim mesmo, à vida.
>
> A casa era no Harversterhude, umbrosa . . .
>
> ....
>
> The beautiful and grand Hanseatic city vanished in the night-like day. . . . Sharper than snakes, thin, frigid whips of wind—huge flakes of snow were falling—cut the air. . . . Going toward Glockengiesserwall . . . On every street corner you could see the emblem: perched inside a circle filled with the crooked swastika, the eagle with open wings. Outside, the shadows of the tree trunks in the snow, and the curves of the crows: the crow of ill fortune. People said . . . many birds would die. Was the heart of this nature benign or evil? One felt face-to-face with chaos in the middle of that bridge, and a sense of

looming catastrophe, the harsh weather, confronting the ultimate — the sin of being born — in Anaximander's teachings. And yet, we all belonged to life.

The house was in Harverterhude, shaded . . .

The Führer's screech, a bird of prey gripping the vicious swastika rune, the crow of evil fortune, and the silenced, dying birds — a synecdoche for savage Nazis and savaged Jews. As in the diary, symbol, sound, and scenery evoke the bridge between life and death, the Shoah, and the very act of being in an Anaximandrian cosmos of ultimate erasure. And yet, optimism tries to reign.

Not for long: the old lady's house reeks of the Brothers Grimm — an abandoned garden, drafty, seemingly subterranean rooms, antique chandeliers dripping with candles, worn furniture, and worn old women, Frau Wetterhuse, her daughter, Angélika, and three relatives. There is an eerie throwback feeling of lurking hobgoblins and evil spirits ("duendes e lémures"). These turn out to be Hitler's very real, of the moment poltergeists when Dame Verónika begins to speak in fluent, if archaic, Portuguese, with an asthmatic, determined voice, drawing the consul into the whirlwind through his own language and history: she and her late husband, who was Jewish, lived in Petrópolis, the imperial city of Brazilian royalty, respected by the good emperor (Dom Pedro II, ruled from 1841 to 1889), a renowned Hebraist, "Êle estudava o hebraico . . . ," she remembers.

But back to the present: in her frigid homeland the Hebraic is in peril: "prison camps, hitlerocities, murderous methods, fanatic hatred, tortured Jews" ("campos-de-prisão, as hitlerocidades, as trágicas técnicas, o ódio abismático, os judeus trateados"). Guimarães Rosa supercoventrizes the LTI with a portmanteau exclusive to this story, "Hitler" + "atrocities." Then, directly to the point, the problem at hand was "mixture" in Nazi vocabulary, a result of the 1935 Nuremberg Laws, which parsed the "gospel" of "racial cleanliness." The daughter was a "Teutonic-Hebrew, a *mischling*, 'a first-degree mixed race,' according to the hideous code" ("teuto hebréia, uma mischling, 'mestiça do primero grau,' segundo o código hediondo"). She was in grave danger; the mother had to do something (*Ave, palabra*, 110).

Guimarães Rosa may have defamiliarized (or entirely made up) Frau Wetterhuse, her house, and her doomed daughter, but he fine-tunes the details of the "blood purity" edicts, saturated as he was in the *mischling* versus the hitlerocities he recorded so precisely; in comparison Borges didn't have this acute directness, for all his penetration of Nazism. You had to be there to feel it.

And yet, the old lady's voice comes up again, there is an out, a long-buried secret heartrendingly dredged up that can save her child at the cost of staining herself, tearing up the family for the little time she has left to live—Angélika is really the love child of an affair between Frau Verónika and a Brazilian aristocrat, a family friend, she doesn't have the "birth stain," she's Brazilian. Can't the consul, representative of a strong, noble country, save her?

"No, in fact. No. I had to shake my head" ("Não, em fato. Não. Tive de sacudir a cabeça"). While the Führer screams and Frau Wetterhuse beseeches, the diplomat shakes his head, emitting the requisite bureaucratese: Angélika isn't even Brazilian, there's no documentation, just a romance lost in time, is it real, invented, so long ago, who would believe it? Gathering her remaining strength one last time, sobbing, the voice cries out: "He was your countryman, a nobleman, the love of my life!"

There's no response: "Levantei-me; eu nem era um cooperador passivo do destino. . . . Alí borbulhavam pensamentos. Desfalecidos espíritos. Só silêncio . . . Todos nós jazíamos de pé, em volta dela. A longa mulher. O sistema do mundo. A velha vida" (I stood up; I wasn't even destiny's passive collaborator. . . . Thoughts were bubbling up there. Dejected spirits. Only silence . . . We all stood around her. The long-lived woman. The way of the world. The old life) (110).

From scream to silence, fiction uncovers facts, and facts ensnare—even those who don't fancy themselves "passive" collaborators are willy-nilly part of the "system." These may be large statements, but they comport with Lawrence Langer's argument in his hammering study *Admitting the Holocaust*. A literary "tradition of avoidance," a language warmly snuggled up in its "discourse of consolation," simply won't do for an event for which there is none, when normal notions of time, space, and humanness fragmented (Langer, 5). We can only enter the realm of the Shoah through a "discourse of ruin," says Langer, echoing Klemperer's "What remains?" Death defeated us on such a massive scale that redemptive words—"prevailing," "liberation," even "survivor" and "martyr"—ring hollow, without logic or meaning (Langer, 6–7).

Strikingly, Guimarães Rosa offers up no redemptive rhetoric: "Dejected spirits. Only silence." Since Nazi doom left the individual no simple way of surviving with dignity, the price was often the disruption of family integrity (Langer, 164). In "A velha," the mother cannot rescue her offspring even after debasing everything she holds dear, even after revealing she had lived a lie. Vice-consul João Guimarães Rosa and *auxiliar diplomática* Aracy de Carvalho might have been feted for the lives they snatched from the crematoria, but it is *estória* maker Guimarães Rosa who tells the truth—they couldn't save most of the *judias chorando no Consulado,* "Jewish women crying at the consulate." *Horrivel! Infamante! Mentira! Hiterocidades. Desfalecidos espiritos. Só silencio.* These are the debris words that "admit" the Shoah. Beyond testimony, the story's unvarnished insightfulness brings it close to the category of "Holocaust literature."

The Corpse-Man: Páramo

> O homem com a semelhança de cadáver / Homem com o aspecto de cadáver / Homem com o ar de cadáver / Homem com fluidos de cadáver / Homem com a presença de cadáver / Homem frio como um cadáver / Homem com alguma coisa de cadáver / Homem com o todo de cadáver / Homem que é um cadáver / Homem com o frio de cadáver.
>
> ....
>
> The man who resembles a corpse / man who looks like a corpse / man with the air of a corpse / man with the fluids of a corpse / man with the appearance of a corpse / man as cold as a corpse / man with something of a corpse / man with everything of a corpse / man who is a corpse / man with the cold of a corpse.

Like a ritornello, these linguistic variations on a corpse-man reverberate throughout "Páramo," set, uniquely for Guimarães Rosa, on the high Andean plateau. But it isn't all a departure: we again find a nameless protagonist diplomat-narrator; again, a frantic grapple to stave off death; and again, a hostile twilight zone of world and word. Except here the diplomat himself morphs into a victim, chased, menaced, spooked, embraced by a corpse-man, repelled by the apparition and yet aware that he is one of his own kind, "é da minha raça," he's of my race, the human race. Even more, he is his funereal and inseparable brother, "meu lúgubre e inseparável irmão"—in short, a doppelganger (183, 189).

Through the kinship of our humanness, Guimarães Rosa draws us into the *éstoria*, not letting us off the hook. "Sei, irmãos." "Irmãos, acreditem-me" (I know, brothers. Believe me, brothers), he urges, while he introduces us to a dying amid living and living amid dying. For some, the perilous emptying-filling-emptying gyre never ceases; for others like the narrator, a temporary limit experience triggers the crisis, be it loss, dislocation, or condemnation. The trial should lead to a resolution. But does it? Here is the tale:

> Aconteceu que um homem, ainda moço, ao cabo de uma viagem a êle imposta, vai em muitos anos, se viu chegado ao degrêdo em cidade estrangeira. Era uma cidade velha, colonial . . . numa altiplanície na cordilheira . . . uma das capitais mais elevadas do mundo . . . Lá, no hostil espaço, o ar era extenuado e raro. . . . Tôda uma pátina sombria . . . com cheiro de sarcófago . . .
>
> Não sou daqui, meu nome não é o meu, não tenho um amor, não tenho casa. Tenho um corpo? (178–79)
>
> ....
>
> Once, many years ago, a young man found himself banished to a foreign city, after a forced journey. It was an old colonial city set on a plateau in the cordillera . . . one of the world's highest capitals . . . The air was thin in that inhospitable setting, barely there. . . . Everything was enveloped by a somber patina . . . reeking of coffins . . .
>
> I'm not from here, my name isn't my own, I don't have a love, I don't have a home. Do I have a body?

All special, temporal, and linguistic markers of solidity and personhood tumble in this place of exile (*degrêdo*)—home, love, name, one's very body literally vanishing into thin air. The narrative voice veers from the initial third person with the aura of folktale to first person testimony, and later from the deathly present to various deathly pasts. Descriptions of the torturous plane ride through six countries to get to this forbidding posting, and of a night spent drinking with an alcohol-guzzling colleague on the last layover, mix with the portrait of the customs agent who shades into the guardian of the netherworld's dead souls clearinghouse, and with the ominous warnings that the narrator is trapped *en la cárcel de los Andes*, the prison of the Andes, as the living-dead of the story call it in the frequently interpolated Spanish. Although the diplomat understands and speaks the language, and we might expect a kinship with Portuguese, Spanish largely serves to underline linguistic displacement.

Just then the *homem com a semelhança de cadaver* first appears, too close for comfort. "Êsse, por certo eu estava obrigado a defrontar, por mal de pecados meus antigos, a tanto o destino inflexível me obrigava" (And I had no choice but to confront him, because of my old sins, an ironclad destiny was forcing me to do it) (181). What sins? Why a cadaver-figure to conjure them up over and over?

Cold, short of breath, burdened by guilt, hallucinating, feeling in the grip of death, an attack of *soroche*—altitude sickness—triggers much more than ordinary malaise, but a crisis of being, and an obsessively repeated identification with the corpse-man. Couldn't Guimarães Rosa be narrating the symptoms of trauma—belated distress, death imprint, shattering of the "I," estrangement, arousal, and persistent reexperiencing—a concept now inevitably wedded to the Shoah, with its mountains of cadavers and cadaverous survivors?

A voluminous literature exists on the connection, its benefits and drawbacks, applications and misapplications, and on its signs in all manner of representation—from survivor testimony to national memory, from visual art to literary texts. Often the term post-traumatic stress disorder (PTSD) appears instead—with all the necessary caveats about levels of trauma, low and high responsibility, structural and historical—employed as a framework for understanding the psychic wounding brought about by intense physical and emotional shock (see Förster and Beck).

Poised between biography and fiction, the *estória* irradiates the weight of Guimarães Rosa's hard years under Hitler—the desperation at the consulate, unspeakable persecutions, hush-hush operations, screaming radio; the bombs that cracked windows in Guimarães Rosa's own house and hit the consulate; the hunger-ridden house arrest and immediate posting to Bogotá without Aracy, with the war still raging and his health undermined by *soroche*.

The eyewitnessing of Germany's postwar's ruination, in his words, *como se la gente tivesse baixado ao inferno em escafandros de amianto* (as if people had descended to hell in asbestos diving suits), and the being-there in the Nuremberg courtroom, could only have reinforced the hard legacy: "Perdí o contrôle emocional. Eu sou pessimista agora" (I lost emotional control. I'm very pessimistic now), he drearily wrote to a colleague after his visit (Letter to Antonio Azevedo da Silveira 1946).

Post-traumatic stress affected wartime populations in varying intensities. Alice Förster and Brigit Beck's nuanced study focuses on the exposure of the World War II home front in Germany, mentioning Kristallnacht, the deportation of neighbors, and the constant cruelties. Carefully understanding that these were not concentration camp inmates, and not falling into a "we were more traumatized than you" quagmire, the authors ask what proportion of the civil population felt that they had failed to prevent a killing, and thus experienced a trauma high in responsibility. The bombing of German cities, and the attendant blackouts, burnings, and death, was especially shattering to the psyche (23, 28). Guimarães Rosa had said it while it was happening in all its ferocity: "A coisa está brutal" (It's brutal.) "Será que começou o fim do mundo?" (Is this the beginning of the end of the world?)

Still, can we establish a clearer link between war and Shoah trauma and "Páramo"? I believe that we can. The motif of doubling provides an entry point, first, through the corpse-doppelganger, with the associations that inevitably come to me: Elie Wiesel's closing words in *Night*: "From the depths of the mirror, a corpse gazed back at me. The look in his eyes, as they stared into mine, has never left me"; or Primo Levi's description of the "mummy men," the "living dead" of the *lager* called Muselmänner: ". . . if I could enclose all the evil of our time in one image, I would choose this image . . .: an emaciated man, with head drooped and shoulders curved, on which there is no trace of thought" (1979, 96);[6] or even Giorgio Agamben's meditations on the Muselmänner and the third-realm "limbo between life and death" (48). I am in no way implying an equivalency between Guimarães Rosa and Wiesel or Levi, who went through the hellfire of the camps, but it's impossible to escape the reverberation of trauma on the home front.

A second kindred spirit inserts the baggage of Shoah trauma explicitly into the tale. He is summoned by the maid at the point the narrator lies almost lifeless after his first shock-meeting with the cadaver-man:

> Chamou o médico, um doutor que ela dizia ser o melhor—clandestino e estrangeiro. Moço ainda, e triste, êle carregava longos sofrimentos. Era um médico judeu, muito louro, tivera de deixar sua terra, tinha mulher e filhos pequenos, mal viviam, quase na infima miséria.—"Aqui, pelo menos, a gente come, a gente espera . . . Não é como nos Llanos . . ." Nos primeiros tempos, fôra tentar a vida num lugarejo perdido nas tórridas planuras, em penível desconfôrto, quase que só de mandioca e bananas se alimentavam. Lâ, choravam. Longe, em sua patria, era a guerra. Homens louros como êle, se destruíam, de grande, frio modo, se matavam. Ali, nos Llanos, indios de escuros olhos olhavam-no, tão longamente, tão afundamente, tão misteriosamente—era como se o próprio sofrimento pu-

desse olhar-nos. Ao sair, apretamo-nos as mãos. Era uma maneira viril e digna de chorarmos, um e outro ("Páramo," *Estas estórias*, 182).

....

She called the doctor, a physician who she said was the best—a clandestine foreigner. He was young and sad, weighed down by long suffering. He was a Jewish doctor, very blond, he was forced to flee his country, he had a wife and little children, they all lived badly, in almost total poverty. "Here, at least people eat, people hope . . . It's not like on the plains . . . " At first, he had gone to live in a godforsaken backwater on the burning plains, in disheartening penury, eating almost nothing but manioc and bananas. There, they cried. Far away, war was raging in his homeland. Blond men like him were destroying each other, killing each other violently, coldbloodedly. On the plains dark-eyed Indians stared at us, so insistently, so piercingly, so mysteriously—it was as if suffering itself were looking at us. When he left, we shook hands. It was a manly and dignified way of crying for one another.

If *o homem cadaver* most embodies (and disembodies) trauma's death mark, the mirror-image European-Jewish physician underlines trauma's role in estrangement from others. The cadaver man, in Robert Jay Lifton's telling, fits "the radical intrusion of an image feeling of death or an end to life. That intrusion may be sudden, as in war experience . . . or it may take shape more gradually over time. Of great importance is the unacceptability of death contained in the image—of prematurity, grotesqueness, and absurdity . . ." (169). The refugee physician, on the other hand, suggests a fictive elaboration of Guimarães Rosa the young diplomat-doctor's own foreignness, covertness, and engulfment in the German-Jewish tragedy, exacerbated by suffering in the Andean landscape.

A handshake and a "macho" shedding of tears seal the identification, as does the carefully constructed language: the diplomat is "ainda moço," the doctor "moço ainda," the diplomat "ao degrêdo em cidade estrangeira," the doctor "clandestino e estrangeiro." Edna Tarabori Calobrezi's pointillist study on death and otherness in "Páramo" mentions the physician as the only character with whom the protagonist can identify but doesn't pick up on either his Jewishness or his "refugeeness." To explain the association, she recalls that Guimarães Rosa was a medical doctor, was posted to Colombia, and suffered from *soroche*, but she quickly pulls away from any purported "taint" of "biografismo," when in fact life and letters intertwine, slipping and sliding into each other, making impossible any "pure" mimetic or nonmimetic logic (139).

Leo Spitzer's memoir, *Hotel Bolivia: The Culture of Memory in a Refuge from Nazism*, itself an "impure" amalgam of life and letters, poignantly recollects just how common the trauma of "refugeeness" was in the Andes during the 1930s and 40s, as Jews from Germany and Austria grabbed any visa they could: "For incoming refugees, the rugged, severe physical terrain was also their first impediment to adjustment. When they arrived . . . anywhere in the Andean highlands, most of them came down with altitude sickness—*soroche*—and suffered shortness of breath, sleeplessness and aches in the head and body. . . . But aside from the adjustment difficulties and medical dangers, it was the immense *foreignness* of the environment that compounded their feelings of alienation—the refugees' sense of being distinct 'outsiders,' truly strangers in a strange land" (1999, 87; emphasis in the original).

Metaphorically and psychologically, the diplomat-protagonist resembles a "Jew," mirror-imaged by the corpse-man, mirror-imaged by the Jewish escapee, against the background of an infernal European war dripping with killing, and a hellish Andean milieu filled with atrocity and malice; in one particularly tormenting scene, a woman is mutilated, starved, and shut in behind a wall still semialive, until her liberators find the remains of what was once a human being, a pile of worms and excrement (*Estas estórias*, 187).

At the *estória*'s closing, the protagonist-diplomat succeeds in "coming back" with the help of a mysterious book of poetry, the Book, "o Livro," as he calls it. Can language rename the world, as Guimarães Rosa repeatedly tried to do in his literature, standing against the Language of the Third Reich, digging language out from under the piles of ashes, saving language while saving lives? "Não se trata de vitória plena," Tarabori Calobrezi says, "it isn't a total victory" (198). As in "A Velha," Guimarães Rosa doesn't offer redemptive rhetoric, he testimonies, renames, resists, but ends with the words:

> Eu voltaba, para tudo.
> A cidade hostil, em sua pauta glacial.
> O mundo.
> Voltaba, para o que nem sabia se era a vida ou se era a morte.
> Ao sofrimento, sempre.
> Até ao momento derradeiro, que não além dêle,
> quem sabe?
> . . . .

I came back, to everything.
The hostile city with its glacial aura.
The world.
I came back to life or to death, I didn't know which.
To suffering, always.
Until the final moment, maybe even beyond it,
who knows?

Gabriela Mistral, about whom I'll write next, would have understood Guimarães Rosa perfectly.

Works Cited and Consulted

Agamben, Giorgio. *Remnants of Auschwitz: The Witness and the Archive*. New York: Zone Books, 1999.

Aly, Götz. *Hitler's Beneficiaries: Plunder, Racial War, and the Nazi Welfare State*. New York: Metropolitan Books, 2007.

Avni, Haim, "La guerra y las posibilidades de rescate." In *Entre la aceptación y el rechazo: América Latina y los refugiados judíos de nazismo*, edited by Avraham Milgram. Jerusalem: Yad Vashem, 2003. 13–36.

AMBL Doc. O 8462. Paris, September 3, 1946.

Bajohr, Frank. *"Aryanisation" in Hamburg*. Translated by George Wilkes. New York: Berghahn, 2002.

Borges, Jorge Luis. *Obras Completas*. Buenos Aires: Emecé, 1976.

Carvalho, Aracy de Guimarães Rosa. Yad Vashem file.

Fantini, Marli. *Guimarães Rosa: Fronteiras, Margens, Passagens*. São Paulo: Senac-Ateliê, 2004.

Förster, Alice, and Brigit Beck, "Post-Traumatic Stress Disorder and World War II: Can a Psychiatric Concept Help Us Understand Postwar Society?" In *Life after Death*, edited by Richard Bessel and Dirk Schumann. Cambridge: Cambridge University Press, 2003. 23, 28.

Goldberg, Florinda. "La palabra que (no) salva: João Guimarães Rosa y el holocausto." *Noah-Noaj*, nos. 16–17, edited by Berta Waldman and Moacir Amâncio (São Paulo: Editorial Humanitas, 2007): 109–19.

Guimarães, Vicente. *Joãozinto: A infância de João Guimarães Rosa*. São Paulo: Editora Original, 2006.

Guimarães Rosa, João. *Ave, palavra*. Rio de Janeiro: José Olympio, 1970.

———. *Cadernos de Literatura Brasileira*. Vols. 20–21. São Paulo: Instituto Moreira Salas, 2006.

———. *The Devil to Pay in the Backlands*. Translated by James L. Taylor and Harriet de Onís. New York: Knopf, 1963.

———. "Diário de Guerra." Edited by Eneida Maria de Souza, Georg Otte, and Reinaldo Marques. Unpublished manuscript.

———. *Estas estórias*. Rio de Janeiro: José Olympio, 1969.

———. *Grande Sertão: Veredas*. 4th ed. Rio de Janeiro: José Olympio, 1965.

———. Letter to Antonio Azevedo da Silveira. September 23, 1946.

———. *Sagarana*. São Paulo: Nova Fronteira, 2001.

———. *The Third Bank of the River, and Other Stories*. Translated by Barbara Shelby. New York: Knopf, 1968.

Guinzburg, Jaime. "Guimarães Rosa e o terror total." http://www.brasa.org/Documents/BRASA_ix/Jaime-Ginzburg.pdf.

Hirsch, Marianne, and Irene Kacandes, eds. *Teaching the Representation of the Holocaust*. New York: Modern Language Association of America, 2004.

Klemperer, Victor. *The Language of the Third Reich*. Translated by Martin Brady. London: Continuum, 2008.

Kutzenberger, Stefan. *Europa in "Grande Sertão: Veredas" / "Grande Sertão: Veredas" in Europa*. Amsterdam: Rodopoi, 2005.

LaCapra, Dominick. *History and Memory after Auschwitz*. Ithaca: Cornell University Press, 1998.

———. *Writing History, Writing Trauma*. Baltimore: Johns Hopkins University Press, 2001.

Lang, Berel. *Primo Levi: The Matter of Life*. New Haven: Yale University Press, 2013.

Lesser, Jeffrey. *Welcoming the Undesirables: Brazil and the Jewish Question*, Berkeley: University of California Press, 1995.

Levi, Primo. *"If This Is a Man" and "The Truce."* Translated by Stuart Woolf. Introduction by Paul Bailey. Afterword by the author. London: Penguin, 1979; 2005.

———. *Opera*. Vol. I. Turin: Einaudi, 1987.

Lifton, Robert Jay. *The Broken Connection*. Arlington, VA: American Psychiatric Publishing, 1996.

Lorenz, Günter. "Diálogo com Guimarães Rosa." *Ficçao completa*. Vol. I. Rio de Janeiro: Aguilar, 1994. 27–61.

Martins, Nilce Sant'Anna. *O Léxico de Guimarães Rosa*. São Paulo: EDUSP, 2001.

Otte, Georg. "O 'Diario Alemão' de João Guimarães Rosa." *Veredas de Rosa*. Vol. II. Belo Horizonte: PUC Minas, 2003.

Patterson, David. *The Shriek of Silence: A Phenomenology of the Holocaust Novel*. Lexington: University Press of Kentucky, 1992.

Schpun, Mônica Raisa. *Justa: Aracy de Carvalho e o resgate de judeus*. Rio de Janeiro: Civilizacão Brasileira, 2011.

Spitzer, Leo. *Hotel Bolivia: The Culture of Memory in a Refuge from Nazism*. New York: Hill & Wang, 1999.

Tarabori Calobrezi, Edna. *Morte e alteridade em "Estas Estórias."* São Paulo: EDUSP, 2001.

Veredas de Rosa. Vol. II. Belo Horizonte: PUC Minas, 2003.

Los que hemos sobrevivido en las afueras del holocausto, hemos estado muriendo día a día . . .
Those of us who have survived on the edge of the holocaust have been dying day by day . . .
• • • Letter to Pedro Zuloaga y Sanz, January 1947

5 Not Just Children's Poetry

Gabriela Mistral, Consul in Nice

A Slight Dissonance

The picture seems innocent enough. A group of well-attired men and women sit in an audience, heads turned toward a speaker. Their clothing is 1930s, the men in suits and ties, the women in dresses and hats, proper ladies and gentlemen looking clean-pressed, impeccable.

But there is a dissonance: an empty chair in the first row, and right next to it, all the way in the corner, a woman who doesn't appear to belong. She isn't wearing a hat, and her short hair is slicked back like a man's. Enveloped in some sort of loose-fitting, indiscriminate frock, she holds papers in her lap instead of gloves and a dainty purse. And yet she is about to be the center of attention, introduced to the crowd as Gabriela Mistral, "distinguished poetess and current diplomatic representative of Chile in Portugal," *la eximia poetisa y representante diplomática de Chile en Portugal.*

We know this from the article accompanying the photo: Gabriela Mistral is about to give an illustrated lecture about

"Chile's Human Geography" (*Geografía humana de Chile*) and to read from her unpublished poetry before a select public—Latin American diplomats, academics, press representatives. The description goes on: "Nada más decidor para un alemán sobre la geografía humana de Chile que la trayectoria ascendente que la carrera y la popularidad bien merecida . . . de Gabriela Mistral. Coordina con nosotros el orgullo que siente por su raza y que justifica con su propio valer" (For a German nothing speaks more eloquently about Chile's human geography than Gabriela Mistral's own successful career and well-earned fame. . . . We share the sense of pride that she feels in her race and that she more than justifies through her own worth) (Galleguillos 1937, 21).

The dissonance in the photo has taken an ominous turn: a German, pride of race? We are in Hamburg in March 1937 at the port city's Latin American Institute, Instituto Ibero-Americano, presided over by the illustrious Argentine-German Hispanist Prof. Dr. Rudolf Grossmann, and we are looking at the March issue of the *Revista Alemana* (German Review). Its

cover illustration shows one of Columbus's cross-adorned caravels sailing from Europe toward America, overlapping with the swastika-decorated zeppelin *Hindenburg* flying right behind it: Paul von Hindenburg was the president who gave way to Hitler, and the rigid airship named after him regularly flew the transatlantic route before it blew up suspiciously in New Jersey in May 1937. What Spain did in 1492—coveting new worlds—Germany was doing some five hundred years later.

We get more information from the journal's masthead. *Revista Alemana* is published by the Ibero-Amerika Verlag, or Press, located on Börse Street, third floor, Hamburg, under the general direction of Dr. G. Kurt Johanssen. We aren't told that Johanssen acts as a chief Nazi propagandist, cited in the hearings of a congressional special committee on un-American Nazi activities as maintaining offices at precisely the same address, nor about his vicious antisemitism even before Hitler's rise and his premier role in shutting Jews out of Hamburg's business community through the ruthless "Aryanization" of their properties (see Bajohr 33–34; and chapter 4, on Guimarães Rosa).

What we do find in the same issue is an interview entitled "Conversando con Gabriela Mistral en Hamburgo" (A Conversation with Gabriela Mistral in Hamburg), conducted by the Institute's secretary-general and a fellow Chilean, Antenor Rojo Galleguillos, and placed right under a paean to the National Socialist "reforms" to the German school system with a photo of uniformed Hitler Youth members "playing happily" (Galleguillos 1937, 17). "In the National Socialist schools of the future," the text says in Spanish, "the teacher will also have to possess the Führer's outstanding mental capacity." Rojo Galleguillos wrote his dissertation at the University of Hamburg on "foreign influences" and "current issues" in the Chilean school system, and published it under the college's auspices in 1941.[1]

His interview proceeds poetically enough, detailing Mistral's multifarious biography and sweet verse, repeatedly using the tags "superior spirit" and "love of race" and speaking of a "fanatical," "sacred" love for "primitive roots," particularly for the indigenous peoples of the Americas. The interview then meanders to current events, such as the recent death of Mistral's friend, the great Spanish writer and philosopher Miguel de Unamuno, broken by the spectacle of his "country in flames." "What will become of Spain?" Mistral asks over and over, alluding to the Spanish Civil War. (No mention of Hitler's support of Franco's Nationalists and Unamuno's demise while under house arrest by the Franco forces.) The conversation finally turns to Germany, and Gabriela is quoted as confessing to Antenor:

> Es curioso . . . que no haya descubierto antes a Alemania. Me siento aquí tan segura y cuando yo digo segura es mucho decir. . . . Me agradaría volver en el verano a Alemania para conocerla mejor. Me llevo ahora sólo la impresión de un film. Lo que he visto de Alemania como país me parece muy hermoso y en otros aspectos sólo conozco algunas preciosas leyendas germanas, que he puesto en un poema. De las personas me llevo el recuerdo de su exquisita gentileza. Ya que hablo de Alemania debo confesar que a medida que he ido conociendo la cultura sajona la avalúo mucho más. Observo que a nosotros nos falta mucho de su benéfica influencia. De la cultura latina la que más conocemos es la francesa e ignoramos otra que también es muy valiosa, la italiana (21).
>
> . . . .
>
> It's strange . . . that I hadn't discovered Germany before. I feel so secure here, and when I say secure, that's saying a lot. . . . I'd like to come back to Germany in the summer to get to know it better. For now I'm only taking away the impression of a movie. What I've seen of Germany as a country seems very beautiful and as for other aspects I'm only familiar with some wonderful German

legends that I've used in a poem. My impression of the people is that they're extremely polite. And since I'm talking about Germany I must confess that as I've gotten to know Saxon culture better I appreciate it much more. I think that we're lacking its positive influence. As for Latin cultures, we're most familiar with the French and not with the other important one, the Italian.

An Expert at Ambiguity

If *Revista Alemana* manipulatively omits certain facts, Gabriela Mistral knowingly leaves out others. As the regime's propaganda tool for Latin America, the journal obviously keeps quiet about the situation of the Jews and other persecuted groups, and about its publisher's noxious work; Mistral, in turn, says nothing about the German government and its policies that she abhorred, and she takes cover in her feigned ignorance of the Teutonic homeland and heritage. She mouths generalities about the loveliness of the landscape, the courteousness of the Germans, and the appreciation of Saxon culture. She also doesn't mention that she had already visited Germany in 1931 or that she is reporting back to her government about what she is "taking away." To put it bluntly, she says something by saying nothing—just *la impresión de un film*, presumably superficial images sliding by, moving snapshots that linger only a second and leave little trace.

But superficiality may not be the case if we know that Mistral believed mightily in the power of the image, especially film, early on recognizing its impact on the processing of information, in a way that was "more rapid, more vertical" ("más rápida, más vertical"). Disserting on movies in the essay "Imagen y palabra en la educación" (Image and Word in Education), she writes, "I've always considered the Image to be a kind of super-word that leaves no room for error and persuades much more than just the written or spoken word" ("Desde siempre consideré la Imagen como una especie de superpalabra, que evita todo error y que convence mucho más que la mera palabra escrita o hablada") (204). So the phrase "impression of a film" doesn't have to mean frivolity, but a perception that (censored) words may not be able to relay.

Mistral's expertise in managing the subtleties of the image was solidified by her credentials: a poet and a diplomat, and before that an educator, each requiring careful crafting of utterances. We saw similar dexterity in Guimarães Rosa and in Lispector, where the stifling of communication shaped their speech and writing. Mistral understands what she can express and what she can't, even as she rails continually against the thought police she bumped up against in and out of the diplomatic legations. She writes in a letter to her friend Victoria Ocampo in the same year as her German visit: "no tengo boca libre, mano de escribir libre" (I can't open my mouth, I can't write what I want) (*Esta América nuestra*, 59). And to her consular supervisor in Santiago while she was consul in Portugal: "Artículos para mis diarios no puedo escribirlos sino sobre asuntos que sean de otro planeta, que no toquen el medio" (I can't write articles for my newspapers except on topics from another planet that don't touch on what's going on) (See Horan 2009). During the time Mistral was consul in Lisbon, Portugal was ruled by the pro-fascist dictator Antonio de Salazar; *consulesa* Gurgel Valente / Clarice Lispector had also complained in a private letter about the "purity projects" of the proper ladies and gentlemen she met in Salazar's Portugal.

But if Mistral, fluent in consul-speak and hampered by speech control, couldn't *always* open her mouth, she defied Big Brother whenever she could through her activism, poetry, and, often most forcefully, her prose. A sharp-eyed, sharp-tongued observer and narrative stylist, her articles, essays, messages, lectures, diplomatic correspondence, and private letters fill many more pages than the verse that earned her the 1945 Nobel Prize for Literature, the first for a Latin American. That prose is receiving more of its due now as a broader portrait of the writer emerges. In the prose, Mistral minces no words, or in the more pungent Spanish saying, *no tiene pelos en la lengua*, has no hair on her tongue. When she had the opportunity to write about her 1937 visit to Germany in a confidential letter that reached Chile's president, there was no pretty talk, but "a hairless" comment about the "two liberal-devouring" Chilean pro-fascists she met while visiting Chile's Berlin embassy, and had to listen too "ashamed to be a Chilean" ("con vergüenza de chilena") (Letter to Carlos Errázuriz, July 13, 1939). It is important to remember that Chile had a homegrown fascist movement, Partido Nacista (Nacista Party), that in 1938 attempted an unsuccessful coup against the government.

Lucila Godoy / Gabriela Mistral

Mistral's lessons in the subtleties of the image began early in life. Born Lucila Godoy Alcayaga in 1889, surrounded by the green village splendor of Chile's Elqui Valley, she was raised in near poverty in an all-female household after her father abandoned the family when she was three. Despite these inauspicious beginnings, the rural orphan progressed from uncredentialed classroom aide to teacher to school principal in various parts of Chile, including Punta Arenas in Patagonia, then to educational system reformer in postrevolutionary Mexico. She also leaped from Lucila Godoy, a provincial poet publishing in local newspapers, to "Gabriela Mistral," winner of the first prize in the Juegos Florales, a prestigious national literary contest, for her *Sonetos de la muerte* (Death Sonnets; 1914). The nom de plume she chose, various versions have it, evoked the poets Gabriele D'Annunzio and Frédéric Mistral, along with the Archangel Gabriel, and the Mistral wind of Provence — all high-reaching cognomens for orphan-of-father with little formal education and no status.

Still, Lucila Godoy didn't disappear as Gabriela Mistral gained fame. Together, they spent their life wandering, first from north to south throughout Chile as Lucila/Gabriela moved from school to school; then to cities and pueblos in Mexico; and, from the 1920s on, back and forth to Europe and the Americas, a constant whirl until 1957 when they/she died in Roslyn Harbor, New York. Lucila/Gabriela never returned to Chile, except for occasional visits.

Officially the perpetual motion was a result of Mistral's — or perhaps Lucila's — career. After her time in Mexico she became secretary of the League of Nations Committee on Intellectual Cooperation, a forerunner of UNESCO headquartered in Geneva, and held a high-level post in the affiliated International Educational Cinematographic Institute, based in Rome. (Recall her remarks on film and the image.) In 1932 she entered Chile's diplomatic service, and was named consul in Naples. Benito Mussolini's government promptly rejected her credentials, since Italy didn't accept women as diplomats. After this initial debacle she moved from consular post to post, among them Madrid (1933), Lisbon (1935), Nice (1939), Niterói and Petrópolis, Brazil (1940), Los Angeles (1945), Veracruz, Mexico (1948), Naples (1950), and New York (1953), where she represented Chile at the UN. The diplomatic uprooting was punctuated by nonstop lecture tours and visiting professorships, as the onetime schoolmarm boarded ships and airplanes, shifted in and out of hotel rooms and apartments, switched from Spanish to Italian to Portuguese to English, and carried on a global correspondence. In consular documents and official letters she was "Lucila Godoy, Consul de Chile"; in other personal and public writings, "Gabriela Mistral."

The rootless existence wasn't only a product of a diplomatic job, however. If we examine the photograph from Hamburg again, we see that Mistral didn't look conventional, didn't dress conventionally, and she didn't lead a conventional life. Antenor Galleguillos Rojo may have gushed about Mistral as a supreme exemplar of "Chile's human geography," sharing a common "pride of race," but she hardly fit the exaggerated "Kinder, Kirche, und Kuche" ideal of the Third Reich, nor for that matter the traditional Hispanic veneration for matrimony and biological motherhood that became codified in state programs in early twentieth-century Latin America (Fiol-Matta, 79–83). She had deep, lifelong concern for children and their education and welfare but never married, didn't dress in a "feminine" fashion, had women secretary-companions, and a son, Juan Manuel Godoy, or Yin-Yin, supposedly the illegitimate son of a half-brother born to her father after he walked out on Lucila's mother.

These were touchy issues in Mistral's lifetime, and the touchiness has waned but hasn't completely gone away (see Fiol-Matta and Agosin). The subtleties of the image could hardly have been lost on a talent who removed herself from Chile, lived as she wished despite its difficulties, and built government and male-supported careers as both Lucila Godoy and Gabriela Mistral, all the while exalting motherhood and the schoolteacher as caring nurturers, especially in the children's poetry and the rounds and lullabies for which she grew famous. Each of her main poetry collections, *Desolación* (1922), *Ternura* (1924), *Tala* (1938), *Lagar I* (1954), and the posthumously published *Poema de Chile* (1967) and *Lagar II* (1989), contains touching verse for or about children. Poems such as "Piececitos" (Little Feet) and "La maestra rural" (The Rural Teacher) are among her most cited lyrics. She was acclaimed as the "School Teacher of America" and "Saint Gabriela."

So Lucila Godoy / Gabriela Mistral spoke "Mother Tongue" as fluently as she did consul-speak. Constrained by both lingos, she pushed against their boundaries and used them as tools to express her views. She wasn't just a writer of saccharine children's poetry but a highly sophisticated political writer whose complex merits (and demerits) are being recognized after decades of hagiographic pruning. The totalitarian terrorism of the mid-twentieth century, and the Holocaust, brought her strong position-taking to the fore and changed her lyric. But the relation between her activism and writing in the specific context of the Shoah hasn't been explored meaningfully as a way of understanding the "complex" Mistral. I would like to do just that by layering Mistral's varied life and letters around three key texts, the poem "Al pueblo hebreo" (To the Hebrew People), the essay "Recado sobre los judíos" (Message on the Jews), and, returning to verse, the "Poema de los hebreos" (Poem of the Hebrews).

"Al pueblo hebreo": A Holocaust Poem?

On March 25, 1946, Walter Grohmann, director of *La hora alemana*, a German-language hour transmitted in Chile's port city of Valparaíso, wrote a letter to Gabriela Mistral. He had been featuring both Spanish and German readings of some of her poems from *Desolación* for some time, but would she now give him permission to translate more poems into German and to publish them? He explained why:

El ánimo de efectuar este trabajo serio y difícil me lo dio la firme convicción de que sus poesías, traducidas en mi idioma podrían ayudar a franquear el abismo que el sistema nacista ha abierto brusca y brutalmente entre el pueblo alemán y los demás pueblos del mundo. Pero le ruego creerme que no pienso conducir a mis compatriotas sobre este puente en un mundo soñado de arte donde pueden dedicarse a la veneración de la belleza olvidando fácilmente así el conocimiento de la propia culpa. . . .

Ud. entendera que tal concepto espiritual de nuestra responsabilidad me obliga a traducir un poema como "Al pueblo hebreo," un poema que, ideal en el sentido poético y conmovedor en el sentido humano, mantiene despierto el recuerdo del asesinato en masa de nuestros hermanos israelitas. Esta matanza no debiera desaparecer ni un instante de la memoria de nosotros los alemanes cristianos, pues pertenece a lo más indigno y abominable que jamás cerebros humanos proyectaran y manos humanas realizaran. . . .

Sus poesías podrían ayudar a efectuar la obra de esclarecimiento y—en toda la desolación—de consolación que hoy día necesitamos tanto nosotros los hombres y aparentemente no menos nosotros los alemanes. . . .

The incentive to undertake this serious and difficult work came from my strong conviction that if translated into my language, your poems could help bridge the chasm that the Nazi system has so brusquely and brutally opened between the German people and the rest of the world. Rest assured that I have no intention of using this bridge to lead my fellow countrymen into an artistic dreamworld where they can devote themselves to the worship of beauty, and so, easily forget the need to acknowledge their own guilt. . . .

You'll surely understand that this . . . view of our responsibility mandates me to translate a poem like "To the Hebrew People," a poem that—ideal in its poetic conception and moving in its human sensibility—keeps alive the memory of the mass murder of our Jewish brethren. This massacre mustn't disappear from the memory of us Christian Germans for even a single second, since it belongs to the most heinous and abominable acts that the human mind has ever conceived and the human hand has ever carried out. . . .

Your poems could help in the work of raising awareness and—amid the desolation—of giving comfort, something that all of us so need, no less us Germans. . . .

Two years later, on June 5, 1948, Dr. Elemér Miklós, an exiled Hungarian writer living in Santiago, addressed a similar request to the Nobel Prize winner. Opening his letter by quoting three stanzas from the same poem, he describes how in the face of the unjust persecution and mass murder of the Jewish people he as a Christian found the verses especially moving and how, given the moral responsibility incumbent on writers, he would like her permission to publish it in a book he was preparing to advocate world peace and to condemn racial hatred, particularly its most vicious form, antisemitism. Could Mistral send him a statement to include in the book, together with the hymn (*himno*) "To the Hebrew People"? He made the same request to Thomas Mann, Hermann Hesse, Jacques Maritain, Benedetto Croce, and other prominent personalities. Mistral agreed to participate in the project; her remarks and the poem appeared in Miklós's volume *Paz en la tierra* (Peace on Earth), published in Santiago in 1949.[2]

About a decade later actress Berta Singerman, who had recited many of Mistral's poems in public, singled out "To the Hebrew People" when she spoke affectingly about Mistral's feeling the persecution of the Jews in the Hitler era so deeply that "it produced her great poem, 'Jewish race, flesh of sorrows'" ("[le] hicieron sentir tan profundamente la persecusión de los judíos en la era del hitlerismo, los que produjeron su gran poema "'Raza judía, carne de dolores'" (Singerman, 6).

Here is the "Holocaust poem" lauded by Grohmann, Miklós, and Singerman:

<table>
<tr><td>AL PUEBLO HEBREO
(Matanzas de Polonia)</td><td>TO THE HEBREW PEOPLE
(Massacres in Poland)</td></tr>
<tr><td>Raza judía, carne de dolores,
Raza judía, río de amargura:
como los cielos y la tierra dura
y crece aún tu selva de clamores.</td><td>Jewish race, flesh of sorrows.
Jewish race, river of bitter fate:
like heaven and earth, your snare of
cries still lasts and grows louder.</td></tr>
<tr><td>Nunca han dejado orearse tus heridas;
nunca han dejado que a sombrear te
tiendas,
para estrujar y renovar tu venda,
más que ninguna rosa enrojecida.</td><td>They have never allowed your wounds
to heal;
never let you rest weary in the shade,
to wring out and renew your bandages,
redder than a blood-red rose.</td></tr>
<tr><td>Con tus gemidos se ha arrullado el mundo,
y juega con las hebras de tu llanto.
Los surcos de tu rostro, que amo tanto,
son cual llagas de sierra de profundos.</td><td>The world has been lulled with your moans,
and it plays with the streaks of your tears.
The furrows of your face, which I so love,
are as deep as a mountain's cuts.</td></tr>
</table>

Temblando mecen su hijo las mujeres,
Temblando siega el hombre su gavilla.
En tu soñar se hincó la pesadilla,
y tu palabra es sólo el "¡Miserere!"

Trembling, women rock their babies,
Trembling, men stack their sheaves.
Nightmare is etched in your dreams,
and your only cry is *Miserere!*

Raza judía, y aún te resta pecho
y voz de miel, para alabar tus lares,
y decir el "Cantar de los Cantares"
con lengua, labio, y corazón deshechos.

Jewish race: yet you still have strength
and a honey voice to praise your homes
and hearths,
intoning the Song of Songs
with broken voice and lips and heart.

En tu mujer camina aún María.
Sobre tu rostro va el perfil de Cristo;
por las laderas de Sión le han visto
llamarte en vano, cuando muere el día . . .

Mary still walks in your women.
Christ's features shine in your face;
They have seen him on the slopes of Zion
calling you in vain, as day wanes . . .

Que tu dolor en Dimas le miraba
y El dijo a Dimas la palabra inmensa,
y para ungir sus pies busca la trenza
de Magdalena ¡y la halla ensangrentada!

He saw your pain in Dismas
and gave him his great word,
he seeks the Magdalene's tress
to anoint his feet—and finds it bloodied!

Raza judía, carne de dolores,
Raza judía, río de amargura:
Como los cielos y la tierra, dura
y crece tu ancha selva de clamores!

Jewish race, flesh of sorrows,
Jewish race, river of bitter fate:
like heaven and earth, your broad snare
of cries lasts and grows louder!

It isn't surprising in the least that Mistral's correspondents and friends saw the killing fields of Auschwitz or Majdanek and the guilt of the Jew-hating world, the Nazi system, and the German people as the prism through which to read "Al pueblo hebreo," especially with the pointed subtitle, "Matanzas de Polonia."

But the truth is that Mistral *did not* compose the lament and denunciation as a response to the Nazi death camps. She wrote it some twenty years before, while living in the far-southern Chilean city of Punta Arenas, in reaction to a previous outrage that, retrospectively, was an antecedent of the genocide: the anti-Jewish Polish pogroms of 1918–1919, a wave of plundering, machine-gunning, synagogue burning, raping, and murdering that spread throughout the newly independent Poland. The wanton violence, part of the chaos of the post–World War I years, with Poles fighting Ukrainians, turned into a cause célèbre widely covered in the world press and condemned by President Woodrow Wilson, who appointed a special commission to investigate the "excesses" (this was the official word), headed by

Henry Morgenthau Sr. (Morgenthau's son, Henry Jr., President Franklin Delano Roosevelt's treasury secretary, would be instrumental in trying to save Jews from the Holocaust, heading the War Refugee Board.)

On June 1, 1919, the *New York Times*, in a headline story titled "A Record of Pogroms in Poland," detailed excruciatingly the violence that had been verified, with the names of the 110 towns where Jews had been massacred (1;6). In Mistral's homeland, one eyewitness account came out the same June in the Santiago journal *Renacimiento* (Renaissance), entitled "Los judíos de Polonia" (The Jews of Poland); two months earlier the journal had reported on anti-Jewish mob violence in Ukraine and, closer to home, in Argentina, with its own antisemitic pogrom, the so-called Semana Trágica, or Tragic Week. In November of the same year *Renacimiento* published Gabriela Mistral's poem, subheaded there slightly differently, "A propósito de las matanzas de Polonia" (Regarding the Massacres in Poland), which signals a greater immediacy. Mistral collected the slightly variant canonical version three years later in her book *Desolación*. The eventually famous poem that could epitomize the expression of the Shoah in Spanish-language verse was originally published in a small "ethnic" journal just founded by Santiago's small Jewish community in repulsion at an earlier situation of antisemitic violence.

More on "Al pueblo hebreo"

Renacimiento looked like a strange editorial bird. Founded as a pioneering Spanish-language Chilean-Israelite review the same year as the pogroms, it picked up on the millenary persecution's contemporary manifestations, but even more vocally on the hoped-for renaissance after the 1917 Balfour Declaration—the British government's formal statement viewing with favor the establishment in Palestine of a national home for the Jewish people. *Renacimiento* wholeheartedly supported this cause, filling each monthly issue with articles on Balfour and Zionism, President Wilson's peace program including the rights of national minorities, and the place of Jews in the ancestral land.

At the same time, *Renacimiento* sought a rebirth of Jewish-Christian relations wherever Jews lived. The founding editorial explains that the journal wanted to spread Jewish thought and activities in Chile while popularizing Chilean culture in the Israelite community. (In the early twentieth century, Spanish-language Latin American Jewish publications strongly fostered "mutual understanding" as an acculturating stance.) Essays by prominent Latin American and Chilean intellectuals such as the Guatemalan Enrique Gómez Carrillo and verse by poets of the moment Juan Guzmán Cruchaga and Armando Blin sat side by side with translated selections from the Talmud and the Yiddish writer Isaac L. Peretz, lurid reports about the pogroms, and unceasing rallying for the *patria hebrea*. Most of the Chilean compositions had nothing to do with Judaism; a few tangentially did, even if they showed a Christological bent, a common strategy at the time.

Thanks to the good offices of Chile's National Library, I am able to reproduce Gabriela Mistral's poem as it appeared in *Renacimiento*, framed by an attractive Art Deco border. The experience of reading "To the Hebrew People" *in context, in its immediate textual milieu*—something that to my knowledge hasn't been done before—heightens the poem's historical-political import, its mimetic function, if you will. Appearing between an article on the Zionist movement and the Palestine homeland, and an item by Senator James A. Reed of Missouri, who had endorsed the idea, you see how the composition engages the multiple registers of the journal's ideology. The spiritualist, emotional, and melodramatic esthetics of the era, wedded to the inspiration of the Hebrew Bible and the New Testament that was so dear to Mistral, an inveterate Scripture reader, serve an *ideological* purpose rooted not only in the timeless "eternity" of biblical discourse but also in the here and now. It is a prescient instance of Mistral's increasing skill at manipulating the historical/poetic discourse, as well as a submissive/subversive rhetoric.

Chilean critic Grinor Rojo has described how this rhetoric functions in Mistral's poetry: first, there is a repetitive and submissive moment (patriarchy, tradition, Mother Tongue) and then a second moment of dissonance, crisis, and extrication from the normative. "To the Hebrew People" shows both moments, in tune with the "suffering Christ" motif of many of her early verses, scandalously romantic, dripping with sap, as she later laughed at them in a letter; and at the same time out of tune with a world complicit with the endless persecution (Letter to Fedor Ganz). Mary Magdalene's maternal and venerating gesture of purification, washing Jesus's feet and wiping them with her hair, turns into a bloody, hardly syrupy rite, in the poet's rendering. And the vituperated, seemly helpless folk (which hasn't answered Jesus's call, she reminds us) finds strength and a honey voice to praise its homes and hearths.

In a Zionist journal the suffering Jesus, embodied in the Jewish face, walks the slopes of Zion, and the mutilated Hebrew race still has the gumption to sing to the land flowing with milk and honey.

As she commonly did, Mistral worked and reworked "Al pueblo hebreo," looking for the mot juste. Her handwritten drafts of the poem show the

Al PUEBLO HEBREO

A propósito de las matanzas de Polonia.

Raza judía, carne de dolores,
raza judía, río de amarguras:
como los cielos y la tierra dura,
y crece aún tu selva de clamores.

Nunca han dejado orearse tus heridas;
nunca han dejado que a sombrear te tiendas,
para estrujar y renovar tu venda,
más que ninguna rosa enrojecida.

Con tus gemidos se ha arrullado el mundo
y juega con las hebras de tu llanto.
Los surcos de tu rostro, que amo tanto,
son cual llagas de sierras de profundos.

Temblando mecen su hijo las mujeres,
temblando siega el hombre su gavilla.
En tu soñar se hincó la pesadilla
y tu palabra es solo el «Miserere».

Raza judía, y aun te resta pecho
y voz de miel, para alabar tus lares
y decir el «Cantar de los Cantares»
con lengua, y labio, y corazón deshechos.

En tu mujer camina aún María.
Sobre tu rostro va el perfil de Cristo;
por las laderas de Sion le han visto
llamarte en vano, cuando muere el día.

Que tu dolor en Dimas le miraba
y El dijo a Dimas la palabra inmensa,
y para ungir sus pies busca aun la trenza
de Magdalena ¡y la halla ensangrentada!

Raza judía, carne de dolores,
raza judía, río de amargura,
que cual los cielos y la tierra, dura
y eleva su ancha selva de clamores.

Gabriela Mistral.

Courtesy Biblioteca Nacional in Chile.

effort, with lines crossed out and rejected verses marked with an *x*. The biblical flows into the historical-political even more sharply in the working versions, most forcefully in the lines "Con tus jemidos [*sic*] se ha arrullado el mundo / . . . desde Daniel a Dreiffus [*sic*] . . ." (The world has been lulled by your moans / . . . from Daniel to Dreyfus . . .). The bitterly fought Dreyfus case (1894–1906), which exposed the rabid antisemitism of the French home of liberty, fraternity, equality, stirred global passions just like the Polish pogroms Mistral was writing about, especially novelist Émile Zola's resounding "J'accuse," where he condemned as a crime "appealing to . . . odious anti-Semitism" (Gabriela Mistral Collection, Library of Congress; Co-Reel 20 H109–111).

Mistral didn't retain the Dreyfus line in the final version—perhaps at this stage it was too jarringly referential in a poem that achieved its effects through biblical allusion and nuanced diction. This reticence would evolve as Mistral matured under the pressure of personal and historical tragedy, and of her diplomatic experience in the hot spots of the Spanish Civil War and World War II Europe.

"Al pueblo hebreo" wasn't the only text Mistral wrote on the knotty subject of Jew-hatred. In October 1919 she penned a narrative equivalent to the poem in another literary journal, *Mireya*, published in Punta Arenas, a city filled with immigrants of all nationalities attracted by the economic opportunities of the Promised Land of Patagonia. In her column on "Revistas y escritores argentinos" (Argentine Journals and Writers) the future Nobel laureate picks apart the jealousies that had torpedoed her efforts and those of a group of like-minded Chilean intellectuals to found a *pluralistic* literary review in sync with contemporary times and *forward-looking politics*. She commends three new Argentine revues as exemplars of such openness. One was the large-circulation *Atlántida*, lauded for its cultural work and devotion to social issues. (Editorial Atlántida became a major force in Argentine publishing.) Another was the journal *Nosotros* (We), praised as Latin America's supreme intellectual publication, with "the courage to think and act in tune with the contemporary world, not some past era."

The third journal she mentions seems like an unexpected David after the two Goliaths. It is *Vida Nuestra* (Our Life), a monthly Chilean Jewish review akin to *Renacimiento*, where Latin American authors sat cheek by jowl with the best domestic and overseas Jewish literati. In just two years, says Mistral glowingly, *Vida Nuestra* has won the prestige of established reviews, "both for the quality of its contributors and for its difficult mission—the vindication of a people as great as it is hated, and as persecuted as it is rich in intellectual values, despite its millenary dispersion" ("Revistas y escritores argentinos," 284). Her own poem "Al pueblo hebreo" was reproduced in *Vida Nuestra*, and she contributed other verses later incorporated into her book *Desolación*, among them the poem "Ruth," printed under the rubric "Mujeres bíblicas" (Biblical Women).

More encomia coupled with historical commentary come in the book review section of the same issue of *Mireya*. Mistral again gives a jolt when she ends with a lengthy review of the story collection *Los cabalistas* (The Kabbalists), by Isaac L. Peretz, hardly a name that rolled off the tongue of Chilean literary circles, rendered into Spanish in Buenos Aires by Salomon Resnick, with an introduction by Alberto Gerchunoff; it was the first in a broader translation project spearheaded by Resnick, who saw the insertion of Eastern European Yiddish culture as a means to enrich Latin American culture without sacrificing Jewish modalities (Senkman, 452).

Confessing her familiarity with the Hebrew Bible and disconcerting unfamiliarity (her words) with the work of a master of the short story like Peretz, Mistral greets this translation of a representative of the intense modern Jewish literature, *la intensa literatura hebreo-moderna*, and reiterates the dual Jewish–Latin American agenda from her own perspective—"rehabilitating" the hated, supposedly brutally materialistic folk through knowledge of their superb literary talent and thereby enriching and enlarging Latin American culture. The consul-to-be doesn't see this new esthetic opening by an immigrant community as a threat but, in contrast to some of Mistral's interlocutors and adversaries, as an opportunity ("Libros nuevos," 286–88). These generous attitudes would be mightily tested during the Holocaust, when openness meant much more than cultural diversity but indeed the power of life and death that Lucila Godoy, using consul-speak and risky action, sometimes held in her hands.

For some contemporary commentators *Vida Nuestra* and its cohort publications were too anxious to curry favor with the local intelligentsia at any cost—look what good, loyal Argentines, or Chileans, we Jews are. From the perspective of the twenty-first century we could also poke holes in the poet-reviewer's own Christological bent (Jesus, Maria, Magdalene) and note the limits of pluralism as she understood it—for example, she advocated teaching about Jesus in public schools, and more than once mouthed stereotypes about the Jewish nose and Jewish gold and avarice. But at the turn of the twentieth century Mistral saw the legitimizing project in a positive light, part of the pluralism and forward-looking cultural and political project she sought to foment against xenophobes at a time of bare acceptance for Jews in the still-forming societies, where Hispanic-Catholic essentialism often reigned supreme.

I don't mean to be hagiographic, to construct a new political Saint Gabriela in place of the old holy Mother Gabriela. Yet there is no doubt about the thrust already revealed in this formative stage, a poetic and political trajectory later honed more sharply in the flames of an Old World gone mad. In view of this evidence I have to sharply disagree with Martin C. Taylor's book *Sensibilidad religiosa de Gabriela Mistral* (1975; English version 1968), where, after going out of his way to repeatedly downplay Mistral's special concern for the problems of Jews of her day, he singles out "Al pueblo hebreo" as proof of her disregard: "This homage shows a compassion that transcends any possible documentary value" (*Sensibilidad*, 64). Or: "It does not follow, however, that careful study of the Bible led Gabriela to a singular preoccupation with Jews" (1968 version, 19).

Where are *his* documentary sources for such an unequivocal judgment? It smacks of Carter Wheelock's analogous verdict at about the same years that Borges's "Deutsches Requiem" had nothing to do with Hitler or Nazi Germany gone mad but with ways of thinking. In Borges, during the 1970s, critics could only countenance imaginary planets or Kabbalah (religion as textual play); in Mistral they apparently could only allow transcendental mercies or Bible (religion as emotional outpouring). Were these readings less threatening to the image of the authors as fantasists or mother figures, less "tainting" with the mark of politics, especially involving Jews? Were they more in sync with the then reigning formalisms that disallowed context in a postwar world overwhelmed with contextual rot?

Taylor reproduces a lecture, now well known, that Mistral delivered on "Mi experiencia con la Biblia" (My Experiences with the Bible) in Buenos Aires on April 19, 1938, easily her major statement on the impact of the Hebrew Bible in her formation and on her forms of expression. Does the fact that she delivered this address at the Sociedad Hebraica Argentina (SHA), a leading Argentine-Jewish cultural center, and that it was first published in the society's respected journal in May–June 1938, the fateful year when Nazi anti-Jewish measures increased immeasurably, culminating in Germany's Kristallnacht pogrom of November 9–10, have no "documentary bearing"?

In point of fact, not only was the lecture published by the SHA, but the March 12 issue of *Mundo Israelita*, Buenos Aires's principal Spanish-Jewish newspaper, gave extensive coverage to her visit, and it reproduced both "Al pueblo hebreo" and her "Recado sobre los judíos" (1935), which I will deal with shortly, as indications of her particular attention to the problems of Jewry (*Mundo Israelita*, 1).

How about Mistral's closing paragraphs in the lecture, where she summons up Hebrew Scripture as a kind of sacred "lugar de convocación," a gathering place where Christians and Jews can meet, face-to-face, "vernos la cara," a gathering place that, she repeats three times as if in an incantation, is common, common, common to us, "que nos es común, común, común" (Taylor, 235)? Is this not an emphatic public political statement of significant "documentary bearing"? Mistral the diplomat was fully conscious of what she was saying and where she was saying it; the use of Hebrew Scripture is a sociopolitically intentional act. To talk about the Jewish personages who marked her childhood or about the spirit of the Hebrew language in 1938 was not innocent, anachronistic, or romantic.

Without any doubt (and her Jewish interlocutors knew it), Mistral's humanitarianism reached out to many groups; victims of the Spanish Civil War were a special, extensively documented concern of hers in the 1930s, but I wonder why Taylor makes such a concerted effort to almost "protect" Mistral from "contamination" and to ignore the documentary proof. To boot, he has an impressive *nihil obstat*, in the Spanish introduction to the book, when the Hispanist Juan Loveluck trips all over himself in concurring with Taylor: Mistral's antique biblicism is okay, and the possible Jewish ancestry through her maternal Villanueva grandmother that she played up and toyed with throughout her life might also be alright, but be careful with any contemporary Jewish connection.[3]

In contrast, Darrell Lockhart's fine discussion of the question of Mistral's possible "Jewish" forebears builds on the phrase "homosexual panic" when he speaks of "Jewish panic" as a parallel zealousness to burnish a certain image of Mistral that no longer holds (96). The Holocaust writings and actions serve to undo the carefully constructed Mother Mistral as does the more open approach to her sexuality.

After all is said and done, though, can we call "Al pueblo hebreo" "Holocaust literature"? Does the work of successive readers recreate a poem as "Holocaust literature" irrespective of when it was written? Mistral's precursory political-cultural involvement, *what* she wrote and *where* she wrote in the troubled year of 1919, prepared the ground for her engagement as an activist-author when fascist boots marched across Europe and threatened the Americas and, most aggressively, for her rescue efforts from the extermination in the making.

Grohmann, Miklós, and Singerman were aware of Mistral's opinions, even if their "objective" chronology was weak. Their awareness—and their world-historical situation—allowed old wine to be poured into new wineskins, so that their reading "created" Mistral's Holocaust poem, as Borges might have it, or as Singerman did: Mistral felt the persecution of the Jews so profoundly in the Hitler era that it "produced" the great poem. I think here of Umberto Eco's championing of the open work, *opera aperta*. Eco says, "*Every* work of art, even though it is produced by following an explicit or implicit poetics of necessity, is open to a virtually unlimited range of possible readings, each of which causes the work to acquire new vitality. . . ." These readings aren't "performed" sub specie aeternitatis but are in perpetual movement; even now, as I am writing these words (Eco, 63).

Why, then, shouldn't postwar readings of "Al pueblo hebreo" be considered part of its writing? And why shouldn't this fluid relationship between reading and performing lead to new categories of "Holocaust literature"?

"Recado sobre los judíos"

Nineteen thirty-five was a banner year for Nazi Germany. On September 15, at the rally of the party congress held in Nuremberg, one of Hitler's favorite cities, the faithful passed the Nuremberg Laws, or Nürnberger Gesetze—the Law for the Protection of German Blood and German Honor and the Reich Citizenship Law. The first, among other clauses, prohibited marriage and sexual intercourse between Jews and "racial" Germans. The second defined a Reich citizen as someone only of German blood, ready to faithfully serve the German people and the Reich. And just in case words could be misconstrued, color charts graphically indicated who was "pure" and who was a "half breed," *mischling*, and to what grade (recall Guimarães Rosa's "The Old Lady").

Exaltation of the image did other wonders for Nazi Germany in 1935. (See Mistral on the power of the image.) In March a motion picture premiered in Berlin that won Germany's National Film Prize, the Venice Film Festival's Gold Medal (*sic*!), and the epithet by many of "masterpiece" of world cinema—Leni Riefenstahl's *Triumph des Willens* (*Triumph of the Will*). Riefenstahl shot *Triumph of the Will* during 1934's Nuremberg Nazi Party Congress, transforming the tedious blah-blah of the National Socialist heresiarchs, who had just recently purged some of their own, into "innovative" cinema through editing, montage, lighting, and music.

As these dramas were enveloping Europe, *El Mercurio*, until today Chile's major newspaper, did not comment on the Nuremberg Laws or on the persecution of the Jews, although it did report on 1935's "El Día de Alemania,"

Germany's National Day (Wojak, 139). According to researcher Imtrud Wojak, a careful study of *El Mercurio* editions from 1933 to 1946 shows little inclination to critically cover any aspect of the Jews' dire fate, under the guise of so-called neutrality: Chile was "neutral" in World War II until 1943, when it broke relations with the Axis countries; it declared war on Japan in 1945. Even the atrocities of Kristallnacht, gingerly qualified as painful for "humanitarian" reasons, were neutralized away by the daily, noting that the reasons that led the Reich's authorities to adopt measures expelling members of that "race" from their territory couldn't be challenged, since every nation had the right to pass laws and defend its interests in the ways it considered most convenient (*El Mercurio*, November 11, 1938; Wojak, 139).[4]

Yet that's not all that happened in *El Mercurio* in 1935. On Sunday, June 16, the newspaper published its usual cultural supplement, with contributions by select intellectuals. The Spanish liberal diplomat and writer Salvador de Madariaga gushed on the honors bestowed by the Spanish Republic on the philosopher Miguel de Unamuno, and the Argentine poet Arturo Capdevila praised General José de San Martin, the country's nineteenth-century national hero and an object of cult veneration. Featured above Capdevila's "Ballad to the Death of General San Martin," an article stood out discordant with the paean below it and with *El Mercurio*'s "impartiality": Gabriela Mistral's "Recado sobre los judíos."

Neither gushing, venerating, nor agreeing, Mistral's "Recado sobre los judíos" dissected the etiology of antisemitism, reflected on the "Jewish question"—she does not use the problematic term—and proposed action from a *South American* perspective, from an antifascist diplomat-at-work witnessing the burgeoning *European* catastrophe. The message has never received the kind of sustained analysis it merits, nor has it been translated into English.

The *Recado*: A Baroque "Pony Express"

Mistral purposefully names her commentary *recado*, so some explanation on the form is in order. Starting in 1934, while consul in Madrid, Mistral began to write a series of short journalistic selections entitled "Recados quincenales" (biweekly messages). She also wrote longer selections in a similar vein called simply *recados*. Luis de Arrigoitia, who has studied the development of Mistral's prose, calls the *recado* "un género de amalgama," a composite genre, different from her clear-cut, informative previous journalism; a hybrid where the intimacy of personal conversation and letter writing tempers the seriousness of the essay, and the "baroque" colloquialism of popular speech unhinges classic European formulas. He sees the emergence of this literary bricolage as intimately related to the historical moment, to Mistral's need for a more flexible form adequate to its representation. He says of the *recados*, "Se inician en 1934 como grito de alarma ante la crisis política y cultural de Europa y se cierran con un llamamiento de comprensión, tolerancia y amor en los años de la llamada Guerra Fría" (They begin in 1934 as a warning cry about Europe's political and cultural crisis and they end with a call for understanding, tolerance, and love during the years of the so-called Cold War) (Arrigoitia, 283–84).

Mistral pours herself into these pages, capturing what matters most to her: "Only when a topic jells into a dense core of conviction does the *recado* emerge" ("Sólo cuando un tema cuaja en un núcleo denso de convicción nace el 'recado'") (Arrigoitia, 286). The future Nobel laureate beautifully defined it as a kind of "posta barroca," baroque pony express, tough in the impetus that drives it, tender in the hope it conveys. The "Recado sobre los judíos," among the first she authored, brought together all these strands.

Like the other writers in this book, Mistral adopted a new form of narration to "admit" Europe's descent into barbarism, the Shoah, and the postwar fallout.

When she wrote the *recado*, Mistral was about to become Chilean consul in Lisbon after a rude transfer from Naples, then an analogous kick in the pants in Madrid. Being a single, oddly dressed woman and an antifascist who expressed her opinions, who defied Mother Tongue and consul-speak, didn't help her in either posting. She was summarily shipped off to Salazar's pro-fascist Portugal, spied on, obstructed, and censored. (I have quoted some of her complaints.) The diplomatic exile of sorts had its advantages, however. It placed her in a good position to surreptitiously—and not so surreptitiously—help noncommunist supporters of the Spanish Republic, in opposition to the conservative, pro-Franco Chilean diplomats in Madrid and London (Horan, 402–3). She could help Jews too; Elizabeth Horan shrewdly remarks that the partial, hagiographic, and nationalistic readings of Mistral's figure usually fail to acknowledge her repeated decisions to live and work in or near war zones; when World War II broke out, she was consul in Nice.

Mistral, Curtius, and French Antisemitism

Horan, who has written authoritatively on Mistral's consular sojourns in Madrid and Lisbon, notes that Mistral composed "Recado sobre los judíos" after visiting Lisbon in late 1934 with a high-level delegation of intellectuals, among them Miguel de Unamuno, Maurice Maeterlinck, and the renowned German Romance philologist Ernst Robert Curtius, who with others wrote on her behalf to the Chilean government, asking that she receive better pay and more permanent placement (408). In Horan's opinion Mistral's approach to the topic of antisemitism reflects her friendship with Curtius, a University of Bonn grandee specializing in contemporary French literature, Franco-German cultural relations, and medieval writing; he published his magnum opus, *Europäische Literatur und Lateinisches Mittelalter* (*European Literature and the Latin Middle Ages*) in 1948 as a response to the German catastrophe and out of a concern for the preservation of Western culture.[5]

But the cultural-political imbroglios that Curtius addressed in the threatening 1930s, before chocolate and cigarettes became scarce, are more directly pertinent to "Recado sobre los judíos." One is French intellectual antisemitism—a witches' brew of Catholicism, integral nationalism leaking into fascism, and considerable literary venom simmered together with vehemence from the residue of the Dreyfus affair, which Mistral had denounced in her draft of "Al pueblo hebreo"; one of Dreyfus's chief antagonists was the writer Charles Maurras, through the journal *Action Française*. The other is the seething cauldron of Nazism, whose racial antisemitism Curtius had witnessed firsthand, and the danger it posed to the German spirit (*Deutscher Geist*). Both hatreds, French and German, coalesced in a crisis of exile, immigration, and rescue, with Portugal, at the watery edge of the continent, as a logical departure point.

How does Mistral's *recado* reflect her philologist friend's approach? Neatly divided into five subheadings, "Anti-Semitismo," "Envidia" (Envy), "Religión," "Decencia americana" (American Decency), and "Una lección nuestra" (Our Lesson), the "baroque pony express" opens with these paragraphs:

> ANTI-SEMITISMO.—Cuidado con no ver claro en esto: la persecución judía, especialmente la de los países sobrecultos, es sólo un departamento del odio del europeo hacia lo asiático. Henri Massis, lo mismo que Charles Maurras y los suyos, odian de odio cerrado las filtraciones orientales de que mana a regatos la cultura occidental. Los grandes talentosos y talentudos (Maurras es lo primero, Massis lo segundo), no quieren ponerse a pensar, o lo saben muy bien y se lo guardan, que si se aplican a raspar desde su primer arranque lo oriental en el pensamiento de Europa, la gran matrona se les queda en cueros. Europa mamó de la leona griega, llena de viscera asiática y después mamó de la loba romana, noble bestia híbrida

de la primera; y más tarde ha comido a carrillo ancho cristianismo, alimento oriental si los hay. . . .

Aborrecen al judío en cuanto miembro desgajado, pero íntegro del cuerpo germinal de Asia; detestan en él un orden opuesto y hasta podría decirse que un Adán diferente.

No vamos a seguirles en su aventura satánica. . . . (2).

. . . .

ANTISEMITISM.—Beware of not seeing this for what it is: the persecution of the Jews, especially in the highly cultured countries, is merely a department of Europe's hatred for the Asiatic. Henri Massis, just like Charles Maurras and his kind, hate the Oriental rivulets that abundantly nourish Western culture with a passion. These capable and cunning great ones (Maurras in first place, Massis, in the second), don't want to consider—or else they know it all too well and keep it to themselves—that if they start to scrape off the Oriental from the very beginnings of European thought, they will strip their Great Mother butt-naked. Europe first suckled from the Greek lioness, full of Asiatic entrails, then from the Roman she-wolf, a noble hybrid beast of the Hellenic; and later gorged itself on Christianity, an Oriental victual if there ever was one . . .

They hate the Jew as a broken off, but still integral part of Asia's germinal body; they hate in him an ethos opposite to theirs, and one could even say, an Adam different from their own.

Let us not follow them in their diabolic adventure. . . .

Horan sees Curtius's echoes in Mistral's access to the great loathing through the manias of its French branch, not the more expected German one. The assumption makes sense, but we likewise have to remember that Mistral lived in France at various points starting in the 1920s, that she knew French well and founded the project to translate Latin American literary classics into French as part of her work for UNESCO's forerunner, the International Institute of Intellectual Cooperation. While she worked for the institute (1927–1938), she read and befriended dozens of French intellectuals, from Henri Bergson to Paul Valéry to François Mauriac. Consul Lucila Godoy knew exactly what was going on, and her voluminous library contained many French books—some by the very authors who ended up being involved in the protofascist, fully fascist, ultranationalist, or collaborationist camp.[6] On the other hand, Mistral was not fluent in German and acceded to the Teutonic through other-language versions, often French.

The Hated "Asiatic" and the Role of *Mestizaje*

It is not amazing that the antisemitic/Asiatic connection irritated Mistral in the pointed and pungent *recado*. The "Oriental" stood for everything Maurras and Massis despised, "the culmination of the foreign—so dissimilar from Europe and its 'Greek' origins that it threatens . . . the French nation as a whole" (Carroll, 33). Maurras attributed all modern crises, economic, social, and cultural, to an "Oriental," Jewish cause that upset the order of the Occident, "an intellectual Hebrewism or Hebrew acts in flesh and blood" (Carroll, 89). During the Nazi occupation of France, when the collaborationist Vichy government realized to the nth degree Maurras's long-held dream of excising Jews with its antisemitic Statute on the Jews (October 3, 1940), the disappointed hatemonger complained that the measure was too moderate.

As for Massis, he was an ambassador of his fellow traveler's gospel not only at home but abroad, with his works particularly well known in the Spanish-speaking world. In 1927 he published his celebrated essay "Défense de l'Occident," in which he preached that danger inevitably comes from the East, which essentially meant anything not west of France, be it Bolshevik, Hindu, Buddhist, Taoist, Jewish, or any other sort of Asiatic "irrationalism"; Mistral knew all about Massis's hysterical book at the time of its publication, and her irritation at European blood-purity projects comes from her perspective as a Latin American—herself "impure," so to speak. She counters:

> No vamos a seguirles en su aventura satánica. Hay sobre la costra de nuestro Continente más carne asiática de lo que nos sabemos, y el mestizo americano, que lo ignora, tiene todo por aprender de su geología íntima. En cuanto a la porción blanca pura de nuestros países, española o italiana, aunque el aporte esté más sumergido, ella contiene orientalidad suficiente de sangre y cultura orientales, como para no manotee aventándola con asco o cólera. Muchos hacen comenzar Asia en Grecia, pero otros saben que empieza en . . . Sicilia, o en Venecia, o en Marruecos.
>
> Sería ocurrencia descabellada coger en nuestra América el cabo sucio de esta campaña anti-semita. Bastante tenemos que hacer en nuestros pueblos, donde todo está aún en su caldo químico, para que nos distraigamos en monerías francesas o en aventuras descabelladas de Berlín ("Recado sobre los judíos," 2).
>
> ....
>
> Let us not follow them in their diabolic adventure. Our continental crust has more Asiatic density than we care to admit, and the American mestizo, who

isn't aware of this, has a great deal to learn about his inner geology. As for the pure white, Italian or Spanish portion of our countries, it has enough Oriental blood and culture — although the contribution might be more submerged — so as not to slap it away in disgust, or drive it out in anger. Many see Asia as beginning in Greece, but others know that it begins in . . . Sicily, or in Venice, or in Morocco.

It would be a foolish decision for our America to grab hold of the filthy tail of this antisemitic campaign. We have enough to do in our countries, where everything is still in its chemical soup stage, for us to waste time on French idiocies or on ludicrous adventures from Berlin.

The passage is rich in its ideological suggestiveness as an outlook from "our America," in an Americanism that runs throughout the message. The term *nuestra América* gained currency through a classic essay of the same title published in 1891 by José Martí, the Cuban poet, political activist, and apostle of Cuban liberty. In "Our America" Marti conceives a cohesive Latin American identity that rejected with passionate vehemence any "pure-bloodedness" and defended *mestizaje*, a discourse of racial-ethnic coming together and pride in the "disparate factors" constituting the countries of the South. At the turn of the twentieth century he opposed this vision of *nuestra América* both to Greco-Roman superiority and to North American segregation.

Mistral, who venerated Marti, takes up the discourse of *mestizaje* at midcentury in opposition to Greco-Roman superiority and European fascism, with her poetic metaphors of a gestating continent, like biology's primordial soup a rich mixture that needs nurturing without the distractive, destructive madness of a Charles Maurras or Adolf Hitler.

A "Race Woman"

But there's a rub — in order to attack "purity" Mistral, like other supporters of *mestizaje*, falls back on the categories of thought formulated by those she assaults, such as when she uses the uncomfortable phrase *la porción blanca pura de nuestros países*. Mistral, as implied already, did not escape race-based reasoning — the sympathetic poem "Al pueblo hebreo" reiterates the "obdurate Jews" motif. And "Recado sobre los judíos" contains commonplace money-grubbing and Pharisaic stereotypes.[7] In her book *A Queer Mother for the Nation*, generally critical of Mistral, Licia Fiol-Matta berates the poet as a "race woman" whose defense of the Indian and the mestizo was a smokescreen for racism. Fiol-Matta says nothing about Jews or about Mistral's antifascist writing or consular activities during World War II, concluding that in the final analysis the writer-diplomat reproduced "the racist and homophobic state" with a paranoia "verging at times on fascistic nationalism" (36; see also 29).

Amy Kaminsky's discussion of Mistral's attitudes to *mestizaje* and related questions seems more productive, when she outlines the interaction of the normative and the nonnormative in the author's thinking and writing (especially the essays), concluding that the "critical factor" is the calling "into question" of the norm, the swerving from the conventional, the true concern for Indians, mestizos, and, I can add, persecuted Jews (Kaminsky, 113–30.)

Jew Envy

After demolishing the "hated Asiatic" canard, Mistral attacks the specifics of Europe's Jew-hatred:

> ENVIDIA.—Viene después el segundo manadero del anti-semitismo. Europa no quiere judíos, porque ese pueblo le resultó siempre, así en su franja española, como holandesa o germana, un competidor tremendo. Agudamente hábil en cuanto se pone a hacer, fuerte y fino, así en la industria joyera como en la tramoya bolsista; genio vertical en metafísica y capacidad cotidiana en letras, el judío, como la catapulta, tumba lo que le ponen delante como prueba o atajo. . . . Metal humano más probado a soplete de fuego y a martillo, no lo hay en este planeta ancho para el dolor. . . .
>
> Es como . . . si su metro cuadrado en suelo y luz no le correspondiese nunca, debiendo cederlo al mediocre, y hasta al necio de la otra orilla. . . . Parece que él sea realmente para nosotros un selenita o un saturnino, entidad de otro planeta que cayó al nuestro en inexplicables circunstancias, y que come contra natura nuestra harina, nuestro lechón, y nuestra fruta. La realidad se ve fantástica en su absurdo; nos parecería una fábula si la leyésemos por primera vez, pero es la verdad monda y oronda este acto universal de protesta sorda o timbalera ante la convivencia del judío con nosotros, los hijos regalones del Dios del cielo.
>
> ....
>
> ENVY—Then there is the second source of antisemitism. Europe doesn't want Jews because that people was always regarded, be it in its Spanish, Dutch or German branch, as a formidable competitor. Extremely able in any task he undertakes, strong and skilled, be it in the jewelry industry or in stock transactions; outstandingly brilliant in metaphysics and routinely gifted in literature, the Jew, like the catapult, knocks down whatever is put in his way as a

barrier or stumbling block. . . . There is no human metal on this planet forged more deeply by the hammer and anvil of pain. . . .

It's as . . . if his few feet of light and space can never rightly belong to him, and he is always forced to cede it to some second-rate nobody or idiot coming out of nowhere. . . . It seems as if he were really a Selenite or a Saturnite, a being from another planet who fell down to ours in unexplained circumstances, and who eats of our flour, our suckling pig, our fruit, violating nature's laws. The reality seems fantastic in its absurdity; we would consider it a fable if we were reading about it for the first time, but it's the plain and simple truth, this universal silent or shrill objection to the Jew's living alongside us, we the spoiled brats of God on high.

Three subthemes stand out within the "envy" section—mediocrity, homelessness, and absurdity—the "unreality" of the extreme persecution. Writing about a decade before Jean-Paul Sartre, the diplomat-author sees pedestrianism as a large component of antisemitism. Jews, no matter how accomplished, have to give in to what the French philosopher calls "a tradition and community of the mediocre" ("une tradition et . . . une communauté: celles des médiocres") (*Réflexions sur la Question Juive*, 27).

The wandering consul also connects the ordinariness of the antisemite to property rights, a theme Sartre, as a Marxist, develops extensively. Whatever Jews achieve or earn, whatever few feet of light and space they obtain, can be viciously snatched from them, simply because they are not of this planet Earth, they are so radically *unheimlich*, so un-at-home-ly, that they violate (human) nature's very laws. (Mistral owned Sartre's postwar essay in her personal library and underlined it extensively.)

Mistral was picking up on the same "unreal reality" of Nazism and its antisemitism as Lispector, Guimarães Rosa, and Borges had. The notion that Germany atrociously conspires to take over the globe seems like a deplorable fable, Borges wrote in 1941, but he added that, unhappily, reality lacks literary scruples. Both the Argentine and the Chilean convey the absurd, fantastic nature of the Nazi "truth" as if it were a sci-fi novel. For the record, Mistral was an enthusiastic reader of the nineteenth-century astronomer and popular writer Camille Flammarion, among the first to adhere to the idea of plural worlds; and Borges, in the same essay on Hitler and reality/unreality, references literary works of the implausible, including those of another Frenchman, Maurice Leblanc, who produced sci-fi about three-eyed Vesuvians.

The challenge that I have been tracing throughout the book is how to respond to the representational madness of this unbelievably "true," the Nazi shaping of "a book of delirious and obscene pictures" ("un libro de estampas delirantes y obscenas"), as Mistral terms it in the *recado* (2). So accustomed to double-maneuvering, dissonance, and extrication from the normative, in Mistral's work a movement toward plain speaking, the unvarnished truth, would become more acute as a means of re-placing representation in the face of obscene Nazi mendacity.

Religion

Religion, the supposed heart of Jew-hatred, ends the dissection of the beast of antisemitism. Mistral quickly dispatches as fraudulent any religious reasons for rejection of the sons of Shem. These were never valid to begin with, she argues, but now that Christian Europe has breathed its fetid materialistic breath on Jewish spirituality and succeeded in stamping most of it out, they make even less sense. Instead of disparagement, the Jewish heritage, part of the Asiatic anima, should be respected for any tinge of soulfulness that still remains in modernity. Mistral writes:

> Y sin embargo . . . mirar con cuidado en filosofía o letras . . . y nos hallaremos con un síntoma curioso: el hombre que aquí o allá sostiene en pie alguna viga espiritual en el pensamiento o en el arte, nos confiesa, si lo tocamos, la víscera judía: ese hombre se llama Henri Bergson, un empecinado del alma, o Stefan Zweig, un biógrafo lleno de unas vistas casi religiosas sobre la vida de los héroes, o se llama Romain Rolland, abogado del Asia en Europa. . . . (2).
>
> . . . .
>
> And yet . . . if we look carefully at philosophy or letters . . . we'll find a curious characteristic: the man who here and there still retains some spiritual grounding in thought or art will, if we touch him, reveal his Jewish innards: this man's name is Henri Bergson, a stubborn defender of the soul, or Stefan Zweig, a biographer imbued with an almost religious perspective on the life of heroes, or Romain Rolland, Asia's advocate in Europe. . . .

In Mistral's view, Europe's contemporary false Christians have less right than ever, Pharisee-style, *a lo fariseo*, to continue flinging medieval accusations. Is Mistral repeating the age-old antisemitic canard of Phariseeism, or trying to stand it on its head, since it is Christians who are sanctimonious hypocrites empty of spirituality and Jews (and those seen as Jews, like Romain Rolland) who are keepers of the flame of the intuitive and mystical?

American Decency: Our Lesson

The final paragraphs of the "Message on the Jews" deal with Latin America's response to Europe's feast of hatred:

> An American feels a supposedly feeble sense of moral rectitude doubly strengthened when she runs through the list of German or Ukrainian assaults against the Jews expelled from their national body. It's as if a book of horrid and obscene pictures were taking shape. . . .
>
> The German, Polish, or Lithuanian Jew has been deprived of the damn right of escape; it's a major accomplishment for him to get a passport, and if the clever individual does succeed in finding a way out, he falls into a special category of outcast that consulates and police forces have come to recognize: the man at the border without proper papers, the individual without a country who seems not to have been born anywhere on this planet, who, and as I've said earlier, seems to have dropped down to us from Saturn. . . . (2).

For centuries Latin Americans had been assigned the role of barbarians by the former colonial masters, but who were the barbarians now and who the transmitters of virtue? The burden of a diplomat who could decide life or death by granting an immigration visa threads a chill through Mistral's words, leading her to call for a partial opening of Latin America's doors. "Partial" needs to be understood against the background of a political reluctance—tinted with Latin America's own pockets of antisemitism—to open the doors at all, and of a concrete effort, launched exactly at the time of her message, to cast Latin America as a place of refuge. The poet-consul describes the existing landscape:

> Our America continues to seek, encourage, and at the very least accept European immigration. I am well aware that it prefers other races to Jews, sometimes looking for the greatest similarity to them, sometimes the greatest disparity . . . if we examine certain areas of Argentina or Chile. Let's not ask our countries to accept a mass immigration of unfortunate Jews. But let's ask of them, within reason, with a modicum of humanity, to accept a small, precise quota of those Jews that Europe is spitting out of her twisted Christian viscera. Argentina has decided on that number, rather generously, I believe. . . . If each one of our countries fulfills this great gesture of decency . . . we will have carried out an efficient, honest and generous enterprise. . . .

In late February 1935, just months before the *recado*, James G. McDonald, the League of Nations' high commissioner for refugees, had begun a mission to Latin America, accompanied by Dr. Samuel Guy Inman. In each of the countries visited, starting with Brazil, then Argentina, Uruguay, and Chile, they were, in McDonald's words, "to undertake to secure by direct negotiations with the governmental authorities permission for the admission of a limited number of Jewish and Christian refugees from Germany." These nations were chosen because—as Mistral echoes—they had followed benevolent immigration policies since the nineteenth century and their populations contained a significant proportion of European settlers. It seemed logical that Mistral's "Our America" would fulfill a "decisive role" in the campaign to save "unfortunate Jews" (Avni, 47).

The future Nobel winner's "Recado sobre los judíos," timed around the visit, and mirroring its purpose, itinerary, and language—humanitarian rescue of a small number of stateless refugees—was, it seems fair to say, her attempt to help persuade the Chilean powers that be to admit "unfortunate Jews" (Avni, 47). To my knowledge, no one has made the connection between the McDonald-Inman journey and this urgent piece of Mistralian writing, so volcanically rich in philosophical elements, literary allusions, and experiential components. The *recado* potently relates activism and writing and helps capture the "complex" Gabriela Mistral / Lucila Godoy.

Writing and Rescue: Letter to Victoria

The savvy diplomatic maneuverer who was one and the same with the adroit handler of rhyme and reason comes across dramatically in a cluster of documents that reinforce "Recado sobre los judíos." Largely personal letters and diplomatic messages, many have not been published, or have been tucked away. Finding them holds the revelatory wow of discovery, as they uncover the extent of Godoy/Mistral's refusal to bury herself in belles lettres, and her commitment to rescue even if it potentially put her in harm's way. To expand on Teresa Montero's words about Clarice Lispector: today we increasingly value the epistolary genre, an author's correspondence, because it reveals moments of personal and public lived experience; this "laying bare" couldn't be more pertinent in the time of the Shoah.

I'd like to cite two published letters in which she rejects elitist "art for art's sake" when more is at stake. The better known of the two is Mistral's response to the grand dame of Argentine intellectual life, Victoria Ocampo, publisher of *Sur*, where many of Borges's essays and stories first appeared. Victoria was a vocal anti-Nazi and enthusiastic Francophile: "La belle France" could do no wrong. The wealthy aristocrat and the poor mountain girl maintained a friendship and correspondence for decades; Ocampo underwrote Mistral's second major volume of poetry, *Tala* (1938), with the proceeds devoted to aid orphans of the Spanish Civil War. But Mistral did not hold back from telling Ocampo like it was, even about *la sublime patrie*.

On January 6, 1942, despite feeling in ill health, Gabriela writes sharply to Victoria, because "it matters that I clarify some things for you, short and to the point." She gives an eyewitness testimony of the horrid persecution in the south of France in 1939, even prior to the German occupation and the establishment of the puppet Vichy regime. "When I speak to you about 'rotten France,'" she tells her dear "Votoya,"

> . . . I don't hesitate to tell you that the France in which I lived a year, half of it in wartime, was a country in dissolution. Nor am I afraid to add *that the most vital viscera of the country are rotten*. . . . In Nice, I had the Chilean consulate in the building where your consulate was. . . . The offices of the refugees, Jews, Czechoslovaks, etc., were on the same premises.
>
> Beautiful France of the wide-open arms had begun to hunt Jews and emigrants in general. They took the men and brought them to live in a . . . powder magazine . . . located in Antibes, and every half hour they'd send the news over the radio, directed to the Germans, that a concentration of Germans had formed at such and such a place. Three Jewish families, friends of mine, knew that their men were sleeping in this secure place. All the refugees with money were doing business with the French officials. They were allowed to leave every fifteen days, thanks to medical certificates that the doctors offered and gave out, for hefty fees. . . . The rest of the families were periodically summoned . . . by the police, the unspeakable French police. . . .

There follows a bone-chilling Holocaust account that merits more than dust-gathering in a book of letters. A representative of a neutral government when many of her fellow Chilean foreign service officers were openly, actively antisemitic, Mistral had no need to get involved in the "hunts," but get involved she did, and diplomatic immunity notwithstanding she was approached by the unspeakable police, who were cooperating with the unspeakable Germans. Here are her words again, with their *Casablanca*-like turns: "I went to one of those summons," she begins,

> to accompany some unfortunate people, and I found myself among a kind of damned flock. The Chief of Police in Nice, or rather the official who is one civil grade below the Prefect, said something to them that I don't know how to describe to you, a peroration or some such thing. He was insulting, threatening, joking, in jailhouse language or gangster talk. Never in my life have I seen anything like it, in terms of outrage, mockery, and cynicism, in order to collect

> money. I left there with my head spinning, like someone about to collapse, and I went to see the bishop of Nice. . . . I told him that I couldn't stay calm and sleep at night after what I had seen and heard. He heard me attentively and courteously; he told me that he already knew all that, but he hadn't found anyone who'd be responsible for the reports in order to give them to his friend, the Prefect. . . . I told him that he could use my name, since I was going away. . . .

The payoff for going to a roundup of Jews and confronting a prince of the Catholic Church:

> At nightfall I stepped into the small hotel, the one I showed you, and I was surprised by a man in the dark, in the doorway. . . . It was the Chief of Police and he was . . . begging me, for his children's sake, not to reveal what I had seen, not to my government or to the Chilean Legation in France. . . . He promised that he would let . . . [the Jewish family Mistral had accompanied] leave for free, *in exchange for my silence*. He had the look of a Cheka agent [Russian secret police], but the same types existed in every department.

At the end of this terrible memory Mistral poses the post-Auschwitz question that would trouble Theodor Adorno and other heavyweights: how can you reify Culture (with a capital C) as a sphere divorced from reality, from the human animal's basest instincts? "You believe, Votoya, *with an absolutely literary criterion*," Gabriela chides, "that a country lives or dies through its elite. . . . And it isn't so." It simply isn't so that "by the fact of creating some more or less good books, the French have the right to send all decency to the devil, to persecute the Jew and the Spaniard just a little bit less than Hitler" (Horan and Meyer, 113–16). Literature, Culture, Poetry are fraudulent when torn from the "somatic," as Adorno would say, a posture that Mistral defends and deepens in her visceral, austere writing during the dark days, with the bankruptcy of grandiose and crass make-believe forms of representation.

Writing and Rescue: Elly León

The letter to Victoria isn't the only place Gabriela set aside belles lettres divorced from the somatic. On December 17, 1939, she wrote a letter from Nice to Adelaida Velasco Galdós, an Ecuadorian writer, close friend, and promoter of Mistral's blooming candidacy for the Nobel Prize in Literature. She begins by putting literature on hold: "Tengo que molestarla hoy por el asunto siguiente, que es todo mi interés." (I have to ask a favor of you today on the following matter, which is extremely important to me.) "La Srta. Elly León, judía turca de origen sefardita (es decir, español) necesita absolutamente salir de Alemania porque se agrava más en más la persecución." (Miss Elly León, a Turkish Jew of Sephardic [that is, Spanish] origin, must absolutely leave Germany because the persecution is growing greater and greater.) She continues:

> Las autoridades . . . alemanas . . . no pueden darle autorización para salir sino en el caso de que un país *neutro* la acepte como inmigrante. Los países neutros de Europa han cerrado completamente la inmigración. La Srta. Elly León tiene medios holgados de vida. Pertenece a una distinguida familia turca y me consta que tiene depositados a su nombre en el banco Barclay de El Cairo, cuyo gerente es su tío, la suma de 1200 libras esterlinas para sus gastos personales. (305)
>
> ....
>
> The German authorities . . . won't give her permission to leave unless a neutral country accepts her as an immigrant. The neutral countries in Europe have all completely closed off immigration. Miss Elly León is in a comfortable financial situation. She belongs to a distinguished Turkish family and I know that she has 1,200 pounds sterling deposited in her name in the Barclays bank in Cairo, whose manager is her uncle.

Why does Mistral want to help Elly León, when, for example, the Chilean consul in Prague, Gonzalo García Montt, not only agreed with extreme anti-Jewish measures in Bohemia and Moravia aimed at doing away with Jews completely—as he coolly describes—but proposed extending them to South America! (Farías 105). Mistral feels, as she hopes Velasco will, that this is an absolutely pure, righteous, and Christian act, and describing Elly León's situation in Berlin precisely, along with her address there, her financial resources, her noninvolvement in political agitation, and the caution with which she must be approached because of Nazi surveillance, Mistral asks Velasco to turn to their "mutual friend," the president of Ecuador, to grant Elly León an exit visa. "Yo no puedo, amiga mía, hacer nada por ella, pues Chile ha cerrado la inmigración después de haber recibido más o menos 3000 israelitas." (My dear friend, I can do nothing for her, since Chile has closed off immigration after having allowed some 3,000 Jews to enter.) To put it bluntly, Elly León was a real-life "emigrada judía" of Mistral's moving poem bearing the same title, caught like the poeticized escapee in the deadly web of German antisemitism. The poem "Emigrada judía" appeared in *Lagar*. It reads in part: "Home and habits and household gods / stayed behind in my village / with linden trees and banks of reed grass / on the Rhine that taught me to speak . . . I am erased from my own land and air / like a footprint in the sand" (see *Selected Poems*, 134–35).

I was so intrigued by Mistral's plea, which without equivocation documents her involvement in Jewish rescue, that I dug further into the fate of Elly León, whose mother in Nice had brought her daughter's situation to the future Nobel winner's attention. With the help of Nicholas Webb, an archivist at the Barclays Group Archives in Manchester, I established that one of the three top men at the Cairo branch in 1939 could well be the uncle mentioned in Mistral's letter, since he had the unmistakably Sephardic name Obadia Aboaba. The Central Database of Shoah Victims' Names at Yad Vashem contained the name Elly Sara León, born in Berlin, died in Macerata, Italy, in March 1944. Could this be the Elly León of Mistral's request, I wondered? With a shudder, tinged with immense sadness, I came to understand it was so. Gisèle Levy, the chief librarian at the Unione delle Comunità Ebraiche Italiane, helped me fill in the blanks: Elly Sara León, born in Berlin in 1905, whose final place of residence was in Macerata, Italy, was dragged through the network of Italian concentration camps, Pollenza, Tolentino, Fossoli (where Primo Levi was briefly held), then transported to Auschwitz in 1944. The existing documentation seems to indicate that Elly León did not make it to Ecuador, despite Mistral's efforts.

Other cases were equally heartrending. Unpublished letters gathered from the Chilean Foreign Ministry, the Library of Congress, the Center for Jewish History, and other sources flesh out a story that Mistral's missives begin to sketch. While consul in Lisbon, Godoy intervened on behalf of Israel Kowalksi Lipalowski, who had relocated to Portugal and whose Chilean visa was not ratified, despite his having lived and worked in the country since the 1920s. On May 15, 1937, she devotes a lengthy letter to the foreign minister asking him to ratify the visa granted to Kowalski in January, explaining that valid circumstances beyond his control had prevented this longtime Chilean resident from picking up his visa on time, and adding an intimate, and cultural-literary, note:

> Mi impresión personal de señor Kowalski es favorable: habla y escribe cabalmente nuestra lengua y es persona estimada en la sociedad portuguesa, y he observado su afecto por Chile en su biblioteca de libros chilenos, en una bonita colección de objetos de arte nuestros y en su conocimiento, bastante inteligente, de nuestro país.
>
> ·········
>
> My own impression of Mr. Kowalski is favorable: he speaks and writes our language fluently and he is well regarded in Portuguese society; I've seen his affection for Chile in his library of Chilean books, in his nice collection of Chilean works of art, and in his quite well-informed knowledge of our country.

Godoy knew that conditions were not on Kowalski's side: because of the Spanish Civil War, Chile had limited the number of immigration visas. Like a palimpsest, the various notations in the margins of her request, written in different hands, reveal what the Polish Jew, even if previously living in Chile, was up against, and they echo with specifics the general tone of the "Recado sobre los judíos": it is a major accomplishment to get a visa, and if the clever individual does succeed, he falls into a special category of outcast: the stateless man without proper papers. One marginal notation says that the petitioner is an old-time resident of Chile and is therefore not part of the immigration quota assigned to HICEM, the aid organization that enabled Jews to escape from Europe. A second rejects the argument "por tratarse de un israelita" (since it involves a Jew). A third comments with finality that the decision has been transmitted as indicated (Archivo Nacional de Chile, M. RR. EE. 38 98). Culture, Kowalski's collection of Chilean books, and nice objets d'art couldn't grant him lifesaving papers. As to his fate: I did not find his name in the Yad Vashem database of victims, or in the HICEM archives from the years 1937–1938.

Brasilien: Ein Land der Zukunft

On March 20, 1937, writing from Lisbon, Gabriela Mistral began a confidential report to her superior in Santiago, Carlos Errázuriz, chief of the Foreign Ministry's consular section. Most of it deals with the alarming situation in Europe. Gabriela, as she signs it, also repeatedly asks her chief to transfer her back to the Americas, to a livable land.

The question of art's role in this impossible situation comes up again. It would sadden Mistral to leave her work in the International Institute of Intellectual Cooperation, set up after World War I by the League of Nations to foster intellectual contacts toward mutual understanding and international "rapprochement." Henri Bergson, Albert Einstein, Marie Curie, Béla Bartók, Thomas Mann, Paul Valéry were among its members. But, she writes wistfully and significantly, perhaps I've been very naïve in wanting to continue this activity, if you look at the groundswell (*marejada*) about to wash over Europe. We know that Gabriela Mistral did not stop her poetic and prose writing, but the utopian dream of Culture as a bulwark against strife was fast waning, as Godoy/Mistral would see with even greater vengeance in Brazil, where she was next sent to be consul as she had requested, and where she would live through the suicide of one of her great friends, neighbors, and believers in a pan-European Kultur, the exiled Austrian-Jewish writer Stefan Zweig, only to be topped by the suicide (or murder) of her son, Yin-Yin, apparently caused by fascist-inspired youths.[8]

Consul Godoy was posted to Rio de Janeiro in 1939, setting up a combined household/office in Petrópolis, a nearby resort city, largely for climatic and health reasons. Her activism allied with penning continued unabated, although Godoy/Mistral was aware that here, too, the authoritarian Vargas regime kept a tight watch. But given awareness of her position on Nazism and the Jews, the pleas for help continued pouring in. Not every refugee found Brazil to be the Shangri-la depicted in Zweig's 1941 book, *Brasilien: Ein Land der Zukunft* (*Brazil: Land of the Future*).

The popular German-language master, who had found refuge there in 1941 and like Mistral had settled in Petrópolis, where the two developed an extraordinary literary and personal closeness, had so dubbed the South American republic in his rose-colored historical travelogue. After escaping from a racist world hell-bent on "destroying itself," the renowned humanist explains that he is writing this optimistic book because Brazil, despite its complex ethnic mix, has solved the central problem of each generation —how human beings can live peacefully together, despite all the differences of race, class, and creed, and so enviably that it demands not only the attention but the admiration of the whole world (Zweig, 7).

Zweig was much taken to task for his apparent gullibility and essentialism, for his exoticism and his elision of racial prejudice and antisemitism, for hiding his own liminality as a foreigner and the despair that ended in suicide. Yet if the book revealed a hopeful if simplistic (not to say censored) side, his letters betray the pain of belonging nowhere and the preoccupation to provide help and obtain visas for friends and family. Darien J. Davis and Oliver Marshall have published many of these emotional writings in *Stefan and Lotte Zweig's South American Letters: New York, Argentina and Brazil, 1940–42* (2010). When her friend died, Mistral published "Un recado de nuestro Stefan Zweig," her lament for the pacifist tired of horror, and for the language-smith deprived of his mother tongue.

Alongside Zweig's now-published correspondence, there are the unpublished letters that Gabriela Mistral / Lucila Godoy received from desperate Jews seeking her assistance in a more darkly colored Brazil, and who, while turning to her, also wrote considerably gloomier memoirs and poetry in a country that didn't always receive them with open arms. One was the world-class German-Jewish urologist Paul Rosenstein, a stalwart of the Jewish Hospital in Berlin. After the Nazi takeover Rosenstein selflessly treated Jewish patients in clinics not yet shuttered by the Gestapo, but after

Kristallnacht he left Germany, eventually reaching Brazil, hoping to find not only a safe haven but a more favorable climate for pursuing his practice. It was then that his contacts with Mistral started.

The Mistral archive in the Library of Congress contains several letters from the great doctor reduced to nothingness. Rosenstein dealt with Mistral both as a physician and a petitioner, and by his testimony Consul Godoy earnestly tried to help him and his family.[9]

In a December 1942 letter the émigré physician opens by commenting that he hasn't seen Mistral for a long time, and he hopes that her appendicitis troubles are behind her. Then comes the heart of the letter: He had been forced to leave his son behind in Amsterdam, now under Nazi occupation, and the son has sent him a coded message suggesting that he has a way of escaping Holland, but to leave he needs a visa from a neutral country (like Chile), which he would use only to exit, not to settle. Could the consul help him? His sisters, brother-in-law, sister-in-law, and their thirty-three-year-old daughter have all been sent to Poland, and you know, Rosenstein tells Mistral, about the barbarians' killing methods toward their victims. Isn't it my duty to do all I can to save my son, he asks? The son eventually did make it to Brazil, but neither Mistral nor Rosenstein gives details of how (December 8, 1942).

Two years later Rosenstein apologetically takes the liberty of writing again, since he knows of her kind feelings. He now painfully recounts his travails in obtaining permission to practice medicine, despite reaching President Vargas himself. Does she know of any way he could succeed in his frustrated quest?

The final letter, sent after Mistral had left Rio, expresses Rosenstein's distress at reading in the press of her hospitalization, and he underlines, "I will never forget your unparalleled willingness to help my relatives, threatened by the barbaric transports" ("Jamais j'oublierai votre incomparable attitude de secours aux parents, menacés par le barbare transport") (November 22, 1956). He never did receive the license to practice, but he continued to lecture on cancer surgery and cure.

Rosenstein's letters themselves constitute a form of Holocaust testimony, but the doctor also published a book-length memoir in German, under the title *Narben Bleiben Zurück* (1954; The Scars Remain).[10] This work deserves translation and a full analysis within broader considerations of the Holocaust memoir genre, such as how to make every phase of the Shoah, from persecution to extermination, "real," and what the borders are between fact and fiction in works where history and autobiography tussle; but my immediate interest here is how Rosenstein's memoir, or first-person dispossessed, engages Lucila Godoy / Gabriela Mistral in the hierarchy of helpful and unhelpful established by the scarred exile.

In this scenario, when Rosenstein is still without his family, and friend and foe are clearly delineated, Mistral makes her appearance among the saviors. He recalls:

> Im Hause Nabuco-Rio Branco lernte ich die Dichterin und Nobelpreisträgerin Gabriela Mistral kennen, die hier die amtliche Stellung eines Konsuls ihres Heimatlandes Chile innehatte. Sie ist eine ganz ungewöhnliche Frau. Da ich ihr Artz in Petropolis war, wo sie eine aufrichtige Freundschaft mit Stefan Zweig verband, trat ich ihr auch persönlich nahe and wurde immer wieder von neuem ergiffen von ihrer natürlichen Menschenfreundlichkeit und von ihrer aufrichtigen Ergriffenheit über die Abscheulichkeiten der Nazis gegen die Juden. Sie war selbstlos besorgt um das Schiksal meiner Geschwister, für die ich in keinem sicheren Land die Erlaubnis zur Einreise bekommen konnte. Sie brachte mich in Verbindung mit dem mexikanischen Botschafter, der ebenfalls ein anerkannter Dichter war. Alles wurde vobereitet, dass meine vier Schewestern, mein Schwager und sein Sohn nach Mexiko einwandern sollten. Da erklärte Mexiko Deutschland den Kreig, und auch diese Hoffenung musste begraben werden. Sie Kamen alle in den deutschen Vernichtungslagern um.
>
> ....
>
> In [Ambassador] Nabuco-Rio Branco's home I met the writer and Nobel Prize winner Gabriela Mistral, who held the official position here of consul of her homeland, Chile. She is a truly exceptional woman. Because I was her doctor in Petrópolis, where she formed a strong friendship with Stefan Zweig, I came in close touch with her personally and was again and again struck by her naturally philanthropic spirit and by her sincere feelings about the abominations of the Nazis against the Jews. She took a personal interest in the fate of my siblings, for whom I was unable to get permission to enter any safe country. She brought me into contact with the Mexican ambassador, also a well-known poet. Everything was arranged for my four sisters, brother-in-law and his son to immigrate to Mexico. Then Mexico declared war on Germany, and this hope too had to be buried. They were all sent to die in the German extermination camps.

There are others who receive praise, but the consul is among the highest, despite the fact that the war's progress had upended the promised aid. Mistral used this particular stratagem frequently: when she could not get visas because of Chilean restrictions, she sought cooperation from fellow Latin American diplomats.

A second German-origin refugee who turned to Consul Godoy and poet Mistral in both personal and belles lettres was the writer Fedor Ganz, who, born in Hamburg in 1910, was the quintessential *Heimatlos* Jew that she had described in her "Recado sobre los judíos." When Fedor/Federico sends her an unpublished curriculum vitae drafted at her request to help him find work, he tells his tale of woe and his intellectual history, and about his escape from Europe in 1938, first to Peru, then to Chile, to Argentina, finally to Brazil, where, he writes, he had hoped to visit his mother's and his friend Gabriela Mistral. He was a man without papers or identity (Fedor Ganz Archive).

Ganz and Mistral exchanged letters well into the 1950s; she was trying to aid him as late as 1952 (Letter from Ganz to Mistral, February 15, 1952). In January 1955, she sent him one of the last letters, later chosen for her *Antología Mayor*, a poignant valedictory about the roots, emotions, intuitions, and style shifts of her poetry, particularly her final, excruciating book, *Lagar*.

Thirteen years earlier, in the realm of belles lettres, Mistral had written Ganz a perceptive *carta-prólogo* (prologue-letter), used as the introduction to his bilingual French-Spanish poetry collection entitled *Entre ser y no ser* (Between Being and Non-Being), published in Rio de Janeiro in 1942, during the height of the war. His poems, with titles such as "Europa" and "Fuga" (Escape), radiate the heat of battle, Mistral comments in her prologue, as well as the infighting of the languages that want to win him over, and the countries he has lost. In style too, she says, his poetry emits bone-dry hardness—a quality she admires—without the frivolity of so-called "futurist" verse. But despite it all, judges the poet-diplomat whose own verse had turned bone dry, she wishes that the future will offer him some relief, allowing him to find, as she does, joy in cultivating her garden, her few meters of earth, and thinking of the children to be born, placing some hope in them (*Entre ser y no ser*, 5–9).

"Poema de los hebreos"

"Al pueblo hebreo" appeared in Gabriela Mistral's first book, *Desolación* (1922); "Poema de los hebreos" in her posthumously published volume *Lagar II* (1991).[11] The brief early poem reads easily in comparison with the opacity of the long, late work, which shares in the harsh complexness of Mistral's mature writing, and which, barely discussed, merits much more scholarly scrutiny. The world, the war, the Shoah, had been too much with her in the intervening years. She felt that those who had survived on the edge of the Holocaust—protected diplomats, for example—were still dying day by day, hurting from the scars that remained.

The troubled world continued to be with her in the post–World War II era, as she worked in the newly formed United Nations, alongside personalities such as Pearl Buck and Raphael Lemkin, to contribute to a new convention that would ban the kind of genocide that had befallen the Jewish people.[12] One urgent issue of the war's aftermath was the establishment of a Jewish homeland in British Mandatory Palestine to accept the *Heimatlos* Jews diplomat Mistral had come to know in her missions. Diplomat Mistral was also fully aware of the wheeling and dealing to establish such a state while satisfying Arab claims. In a letter written in 1948 to her soul mate and literary colleague, the Jewish-American author Waldo Frank, when she was stationed in Santa Barbara, California, she describes the machinations in Lake Success, New York, the UN's first seat: one by one, rather than take a firm stand, the major Latin American nations, including her own Chile, in cowardly manner abstained in the November 1947 vote to partition Palestine into Jewish and Arab states. Mistral, however, did take a stand, lobbying fellow diplomats without, she admits, much success. Still, she told Frank, she was willing to do what she could.

She writes to her dear Waldo: "Constantemente yo te pienso, pero en el mes de la tragedia hebrea te tengo cada día delante y casi te hablo con la crudeza que sale de la cólera." (I think of you constantly, but in this month of the Jewish tragedy I have you in front of me every day and I talk to you with the harshness that grows out of rage.) To judge by the date of her letter and of Frank's answer, the month of the Jewish tragedy to which Mistral alludes is likely May 1948, when the British Mandate ended, a Jewish state was declared, and the combined forces from Egypt, Jordan, and Syria immediately invaded the new entity. "Tú no puedes saber hasta qué punto la tragedia judía me remueve y agita" (You can't imagine to what extent the Jewish tragedy agitates and upsets me), Mistral reiterates. On June 4, Frank responds in kind: "Your having written to me when you did, dearest Gabriela, at this crisis of Israel, moves me greatly, proving as it does the bond between us."

How does "Poema de los hebreos" fit this picture? If "Al pueblo hebreo" grew out of the early twentieth-century Polish pogroms, and "Recado sobre los judíos" out of the midcentury Holocaust, I will venture that "Poema de los hebreos" emerged as the echo of the post-Holocaust struggle to found a state for the stateless. Mistral herself provided a clue, albeit not easy to find. Buried among Mistral's many handwritten notebooks housed in the Biblioteca Nacional de Chile is a draft of an incomplete letter with no date, addressed to an unidentified "Respetado y querido amigo" (dear and respected friend). The fragment thanks the mysterious recipient for his lovely invitation to visit his homeland ("vuestra Patria"). She has wished for this grace and this joy for many years, and her government had even approved a leave of absence for the trip. Then, alas, there was a regime change; the new president, who had dismissed her on another occasion, would probably do so again. It was very painful to give up the delight of this journey. Now, she continues, she is too ill with heart problems to undertake such long travel. She is extremely sad to have to let go of what has been her life's greatest aspiration.

After tendering her apologies, the diplomat-poet switches gears, and here is where the clue to the country she is talking about may lie.

> Hace poco tiempo yo he comenzado un poema largo sobre Israel. No está acabado aún porque necesito de muchos datos, precisamente yo iba a hacer en estos días una visita a V.E. para solicitar de su bondad que me indique una persona hebrea que pueda darme una información. . . .
>
> ....
>
> A short time ago I started a long poem about Israel. It isn't finished yet because I still need to collect many facts; I was just about to visit your Excellency in the near future in order to ask for your goodwill in recommending a Jewish person who could provide me with some information. . . .

"Poema de los hebreos" sounds a great deal like "un largo poema sobre Israel." And as for the trip that, in her own words, has been her life's great wish, could that be to the State of Israel? A possible additional hint is found in a letter from Benno Weiser, director of the Latin American Department of the Jewish Agency, dated July 6, 1955, inviting Mistral to come to Israel, knowing of her long-standing sympathy for the Jewish people (Gabriela Mistral Papers, Library of Congress, Reel 31). The letter is addressed from New York, where Weiser was stationed, to Roslyn Harbor, Mistral's last residence. Is it possible that Weiser, who was within commuting distance of the poet, is the anonymous "Respetado y querido amigo" to whom the letter is addressed? The signs seem strong.

To turn to the poem itself: read through its web of biblical allusions and historical suggestions, it recalls the martyrdoms of millennial exiles, as well as the renewed right to a few feet of light and space. Here is the poem:

POEMA DE LOS HEBREOS*

Ya asoma ya viene, ya arriba
la Madre que estuvo perdida.
Nunca creímos la fábula
de su muerte en noche o día
el sol y la luna nos vieron
cantar a la Madre nuestra,
e hija nuestra
año por año, día por día.

Ninguno te olvidó nunca.
Del nombre tuyo se vivía.
Caminabas nuestros caminos,
al primer sol aparecías
y en la noche que todo lo pierde
la cantábamos como en el día.

Caminabamos de noche
como por ruta sabida
nombrándola y apresurándola
Con gozo o con acedia.
Entera y hermosa y cauta
llegaba la nunca rendida
en los caminos y en las posadas
mentándonos de nuestro nombre,
sonriendo de su sonrisa
y en el silencio de la noche
su grito de madre venía
para decirnos: — No hay tiempo.
Sigue soñando lo que veías — .

En espera está el olivo
ríen los cañaverales
del día, del mes, del siglo
y cruzan mentando tu nombre
David y el Señor Jesucristo.
La tierra se llama Esperanza
y el cielo se llama lo mismo.

POEM OF THE HEBREWS

Here she appears she comes, she arrives
the Mother who was lost to us.
We never believed the fable
of her death by day or night,
the sun and the moon saw us
sing to our Mother,
and to our daughter,
year after year, day after day.

No one ever forgot you.
We lived uttering your name.
You walked our paths,
and appeared at first sun
and at dark when all is lost in shadows
we sang to you as in the day.

We walked at night
as on familiar routes,
naming you and hurrying you
in gladness or in travail.
Whole and beautiful and cautious
came the never-bowed
on the roads and in the inns,
reminding us of our name,
smiling her smile
and in the silence of the night
came her Mother's cry
telling us: "There is no time.
Dream your vision on."

The olive tree is waiting**
reed beds laugh
at the passing day, month, century
and David and the Lord Jesus
cross by pronouncing your name.
The land is called Hope
and the sky is called the same.

*Gabriela Mistral dio su aprobación al texto.
(Gabriela Mistral gave her approval to the text.)
**En espera está el olivo. En espera está la higuera.
(Waiting is the olive tree. Waiting is the fig tree.)

Nombre los otros la Muerte.	Let Death name others.
Nosotros nunca la vimos	We never saw her
en desiertos en huertas y en islas	in deserts in gardens and on islands
En ciudades ni en caminos.	in cities or on roadways.
Vivos, vivos nos hablamos	Alive, alive we talked to each another
en el desierto y en las montañas,	in the desert and in the mountains,
a la mañana y a la noche	in the morning and in the night,
como mareas que juegan	like tides at play
y la muerte no conocimos.	and death we never met.
Tuvimos un sueño largo	We had a long dream
Como de viejos o de niños.	like the old or the young.
En el sueño hablábamos lenguas ajenas	In the dream we spoke foreign tongues
Que a la mañana ya eran olvido.	forgotten by morning.
Pero el sueño fue nuestro padre	But the dream was our father
y nuestra madre y nuestro hijo.	and our mother and our son.
En toda mañana de gloria	In every morning of glory
y en la sangre del martirio	and in the blood of martyrdom
cantaremos para olvidarnos,	we'll sing to forget,
por recordar cantaremos.	to remember we'll sing.
Sobre la tierra, bajo los cielos,	On earth, under the heavens
Dormidos como despiertos.	asleep as awake.
	(*Lagar* II, 156–57)

The poem opens with a hint of expectation and mystery. Who is the lost and long-awaited Mother-Daughter, whose death was never believed and whose name was never forgotten, who was constantly spoken and sung by her people? Who was it who walked with her folk day and night, in good times and bad, urging, encouraging, and always hoping? Here, the people have the versifying and questioning word, not a narrator outside the community. This is the poem *of* the Hebrews, not a poem *to* the Hebrews. A different sense of agency dominates.

The initial verses begin to take on meaning with the Hebrew Bible as a guide. Mistral had not totally left behind the biblical shading of her youthful poetry. We hear the ring of Psalm 137: "By the rivers of Babylon, / there we sat and wept, / as we thought of Zion . . . Our captors asked us there for songs . . . / Sing us one of the songs of Zion . . . / If I forget you, O Jerusalem, let my right hand wither; . . . if I cease to think of you, / If I do not keep Jerusalem in memory / even at my happiest hour." Or the reverberation of the scriptural epithet "Daughter of Zion" (sometimes rendered as "fair Zion") that appears repeatedly in Psalms and the Prophets; or the wail of Mother Rachel, waiting for her children's homecoming from exile.

Mistral names geographic points and biblical species characteristic of the ancient (and modern) land, the olive and the fig trees, and the reed beds, likely of the Galilee. David, the sweet singer of old Israel, and Jesus, both of whom ascended to Zion, reappear in an image used decades before in "Al pueblo hebreo."

But the present makes its strong claim too: "La tierra se llama Esperanza / y el cielo se llama lo mismo." I'd like to suggest that Mistral is riffing on the national anthem of the State of Israel, entitled "Hatikvah" — "the hope" in Hebrew — composed at the end of the nineteenth century, then proclaimed as the national song when the state was established. "Hatikvah" (note that Mistral capitalizes *Esperanza*) places us in the here and now, rather than in some remote past. The hoary and contemporary meet, Realpolitik combines with age-long aspirations.

The Shoah rears its head in the closing stanzas, but it is at the same time refused, negated, as if in the latest, life-affirming chapter it only lingers like a ghoulish nightmare: "Nombre los otros la Muerte / Nosotros nunca la vimos . . . / Tuvimos un sueño largo / como de viejos o de niños." The verses have a split personality, possibly poetically recreating the vagaries of trauma — the people can and cannot name the horrors that befell them: "Vivos, vivos nos hablamos . . . / y la muerte no conocimos." Is this a declaration of joy at having pulled through toward a new beginning, or the expression of a suppressed hell in order to pass as "normal," a strategy common among survivors? Or is it both? The welter of unresolved opposites reaches a crescendo in the poem's closing lines. The people will sing to forget and sing to remember; sing asleep and sleep awake; in every morning of glory and in every blood-filled martyr time. The contradictions of trauma and of the not-yet-cohered future remain. There is no prettifying, no sweetness, no sap, just the unvarnished truth.

Mistral's final years were marked by disoriented roving, fruit of the war, by the Holocaust, by the suicide of loved ones. These tortuous events injured her physically and psychologically but, as always, spurred her to song and to deeds. Writing and doing again came to the fore — writing as visceral outpouring, not as vacuous high Culture, doing as activism to prevent another genocide. The "Jewish tragedy," as she called it, triggered action and a *summa poetica hebraica*, a concluding assertion of a lifelong concern.

Works Cited and Consulted

Agosín, Marjorie, ed. *Gabriela Mistral: The Audacious Traveler*. Athens, OH: Ohio University Research and International Studies, 2003.

Arrigoitia, Luis de. *Pensamiento y forma en la prosa de Gabriela Mistral*. Río Piedras, PR: Editorial de la Universidad de Puerto Rico, 1989.

Avni, Haim. "Latin America and the Jewish Refugees: Two Encounters, 1935 and 1938." In *The Jewish Presence in Latin America*, edited by Judith Laikin Elkin and Gilbert Merkx. Boston: Allen & Unwin, 1987. 45–68.

Bajohr, Frank. *"Aryanisation" in Hamburg*. Translated by George Wilkes. New York: Berghahn, 2002.

Carroll, David. *French Literary Fascism*. Princeton, NJ: Princeton University Press, 1995.

Catalog of the Gabriela Mistral Collection. New York: Barnard College, 1978.

"Crónica transatlántica de Hamburgo." *Revista Alemana* 5:20 (1937).

Cúneo, Ana María. *Para leer a Gabriela Mistral*. Santiago: UNAB–Cuarto Propio, 2000.

Curtius, Ernst Robert. *European Literature and the Latin Middle Ages*. Princeton, NJ: Princeton University Press, 1953.

———. Letter to Gabriela Mistral, October 11, 1947. Gabriela Mistral Papers, Library of Congress, Reel 34.

Dana, Doris, ed. and trans. *Selected Poems of Gabriela Mistral*. Baltimore: Library of Congress and Johns Hopkins University Press, 1971.

Davis, Darien J., and Oliver Marshall. *Stefan and Lotte Zweig's South American Letters: New York, Argentina and Brazil, 1940–42*. New York: Continuum, 2010.

Dines, Alberto. *Morte no Paraíso: A Tragedía de Stefan Zweig*. Rio de Janeiro: Nova Fronteira, 1981.

Eco, Umberto. *The Role of the Reader*. Bloomington: Indiana University Press, 1979.

Farías, Victor. *Los nazis en Chile*. Barcelona: Seix Barral, 2000.

Fiol-Matta, Licia. *A Queer Mother for the Nation*. Minneapolis: University of Minnesota Press, 2002.

Frank, Waldo. Letter to Gabriela Mistral, June 4, 1948. Waldo Frank Archive, University of Pennsylvania.

Galleguillos Rojo, Antenor. "Conversando con Gabriela Mistral en Hamburgo." *Revista Alemana* 5:20 (1937): 17–21.

———. *Die Entwicklung des chilenischen Höheren Schulwesens Ausländische und gegenwärtige Probleme* (The Development of Chilean Higher Education, Foreign Influences and Current Issues), PhD diss., 1941. Hamburg: Hans Gildenverlag, 1941.

Ganz, Fedor. CV and letter, February 15, 1952. Gabriela Mistral Papers. Library of Congress, Reel 35.

———. *Entre ser y no ser*. Rio de Janeiro, 1942.

Grohmann, Walter. Letter to Gabriela Mistral, March 25, 1946. Gabriela Mistral Papers. Library of Congress, Reel 32.

Horan, Elizabeth. "Cónsul Gabriela Mistral in Portugal, 1935–37." *Historia* 2:42 (2009): 401–34.

Horan, Elizabeth, and Doris Meyer, eds. *Esa América nuestra: Gabriela Mistral and Victoria Ocampo, Correspondencia, 1926–1956*. Buenos Aires: El cuenco de plata, 2007.

Kaminsky, Amy. "Essay, Gender, and *Mestizaje*: Victoria Ocampo and Gabriela Mistral." In *The Politics of the Essay: Feminist Perspectives*, edited by Ruth-Ellen Boetcher and Elizabeth Mittman. Bloomington: Indiana University Press, 1993. 113–30.

Lockhart, Darrell. "Jewish Issues in Gabriela Mistral." In Agosín, 95–112.

Miklós, Elemér. Letter to Gabriela Mistral, June 3, 1948. Gabriela Mistral Papers, Library of Congress, Reel 32.

———. *Paz en la tierra*. Santiago: N.p., 1949.

Mistral, Gabriela. "Al pueblo hebreo." *Renacimiento* 1:9 (1919): 156–57.

———. Draft of "Al pueblo hebreo." Gabriela Mistral Papers, Library of Congress, Co-Reel 20, H 109–11.

———. Draft of letter to "Respetado y querido amigo." Digital Mistral Archive, Biblioteca Nacional de Chile, Document AE0011319.

———. "Emigrada judía." *Selected Poems of Gabriela Mistral*. Translated and edited by Doris Dana. Baltimore: Library of Congress and Johns Hopkins University Press, 1971. 134–35.

———. "Imagen y palabra en la educación." *Magisterio y niño*. Santiago: Andrés Bello, 1979. 195–205.

———. *Lagar II*. Santiago: Biblioteca Nacional, 1991.

———. Letter on behalf of Israel Kowalski Lipalowski, May 15, 1937. Archivo Nacional de Chile. M. RR. EE. 3898.

———. Letter to Adelaida Velasco Galdós. *Antología Mayor*. Vol. 3, *Cartas*. Santiago: Editorial Lord Cochrane, 1992. 305–6.

———. Letter to Carlos Errázuriz. Ministerio de Relaciones Exteriores, Vol. 1571A, Carta II.

———. Letter to Fedor Ganz. *Antología Mayor*. Vol. 3. Cartas. Santiago: Editorial Lord Cochrane, 1992. 574.

———. Letter to Waldo Frank, May 31, 1948. Waldo Frank Papers, Kislak Center for Special Collections, Rare Books and Manuscripts.

———. "Mi experiencia con la Biblia." *Revista S.H.A.* May 1, 1938, 3, 4; May 15, 1938, 6, 7; June 1, 1938, 6. Reprinted in Taylor, 228–35.

———. "Navidad," *Antología Mayor*, Vol. 2: 301.

———. "Poema de los hebreos." *Lagar II*, 156–57.

———. "Recado sobre los judíos." *El Mercurio*, June 16, 1935. 2; *Mundo Israelita*, March 18, 1938. 1.

———. "Revistas y escritores argentinos." *Mireya*, October 1919. In Scarpa, Vol. 2: 281–83. "Libros nuevos." 284–88.

———. "Un recado de nuestro Stefan Zweig." *Gabriela Mistral en el "Repertorio americano."* San José: Editorial Universidad de Costa Rica, 1978. 275–79.

Moll, F. H., M. Krischel, P. Rathert, and H. Fangerau, "Urologie und Nationalsozialismus: Paul Rosenstein, 1875–1964—zerissene Biographie eines jüdischern [*sic*] Urologen. *Der Urologue* (2011): 1–11.

Mount, Graeme S. *Chile and the Nazis: From Hitler to Pinochet*. Montreal: Black Rose Books, 2004.

Quezada, Jaime. *Siete presidentes de Chile en la vida de Gabriela Mistral*. Santiago: Catalonia, 2009.

"A Record of Pogroms in Poland." *New York Times*, June 1, 1919. 1;6.

Rojo, Grinor. "Summa mistraliana." http://www.gabrielamistral.uchile.cl/estudios/nomadias/grojo.html.

Rosenstein, Paul. Letters to Gabriela Mistral: December 8, 1942; February 20, 1944; November 22, 1956. Gabriela Mistral Papers, Library of Congress, Reel 31.

———. *Narben bleiben zurück*. Bad Wörishofen: Kindler and Schiermeyer, 1954.

Sartre, Jean-Paul. *Anti-Semite and Jew*. Translated by George J. Becker. New York: Schocken, 1948.

———. *Réflexions sur la question juive*. Paris: Morihien, 1946.

Scarpa, Esteban Roque. *La desterrada en su patria*. Vol. 2. Santiago: Nacimiento, 1977.

Senkman, Leonardo. *La identidad judía en la literatura argentina*. Buenos Aires: Pardes, 1983.

Singerman, Berta. "Recuerdos de Gabriela Mistral." *Cuadernos israelíes* 4 (1960): 5–7.

Slaughter, Joseph R. "'A Wor[l]d Full of Xs and Ks': Parables of Human Rights in the Prose of Gabriela Mistral." In Agosín. 19–46.

Taylor, Martin C. *Gabriela Mistral's Struggle with God and Man*. Jefferson, NC: McFarland, 2012.

———. *Sensibilidad religiosa de Gabriela Mistral*. Madrid: Gredos, 1975.

Varon, Benno Weiser. *Professions of a Lucky Jew*. New York: Cornwall, 1992.

Webb, Nicholas. E-mail to author. February 6, 2013.

Wojak, Irmtrud. "Chile y la inmigración judeo-alemana." In *Entre la aceptación y el rechazo: América Latina y los refugiados judíos del nazismo*, edited by Avraham Milgram. Instituto Internacional de Investigación del Holocausto. Yad Vashem: Jerusalem, 2003. 128–73.

Zweig, Stefan. *Brazil: Land of the Future*. London: Cassell, 1942.

———. *The World of Yesterday*. New York: Viking, 1943.

Epilogue

The Anti-Nazis Were There Too

Hitler and his cohorts did not found a Fourth Reich in Latin America, nor develop a host of local supermen, as Borges and so many had feared. Yet the Shoah has a unique echo in Argentina, Chile, Uruguay, and other countries of the South because of the government violence unleashed there primarily during the 1970s under murderous right-wing armed-forces dictatorships. The ghosts of this state of terror live on till today. Military academies trained cadets with antisemitic, pro-Nazi books, graduating them from the bayoneting of animals to kidnapping, whipping, and maiming humans, then dropping their live, drugged bodies from low-flying helicopters.

Swastikas adorned police stations, and "special treatment" was reserved for Jewish detainees. (Even I, commenting about these happenings on the *New York Times* Op-Ed page, received antisemitic hate mail from former officers.) Clandestine interrogation centers sinisterly injured the urban landscape, for example, Buenos Aires's main torture and killing field, the ESMA, Escuela Mecánica de la Armada, Navy Mechanics School; or, in neighboring Chile, Santiago's Villa Grimaldi, another tile-floored hot spot for reducing human beings to nothingness. It seemed for a while that fascism had won a horribly reminiscent victory in the South. And even in the 1980s, when it appeared to be largely over, and democracy had returned, it wasn't so completely.

In 1994, what is assumed to be a deadly coalition of ex-military officers and Iranian operatives succeeded in blowing up the AMIA (Asociación Mutual Israelita Argentina)

Jewish Center in Buenos Aires, leaving eighty-five people dead. The suicide bombing was one of the worst antisemitic attacks since World War II, the "Never Again" conflict. In 2015, after decades of foot-dragging, as accusations about the present-day Argentine government's alleged collusion in allowing the explosion's perpetrators to go free were about to surface before a congressional committee, Alberto Nisman, the federal prosecutor leading the investigation, was found dead in his apartment under suspicious circumstances.

Some Argentines expressed the fear that this episode could be marking the return of the worst shadows of the 1970s, when arms and crime were the ways to resolve ideological conflicts; other hoped that the traffickers of death would be stopped before they went too far. The watchwords of the 1980s antifascist movements were heard again: "Justice, justice."

And to go back to the 1980s, just as the terror events of the military juntas were read through the Shoah (Latin America's "Holocaust"), so were the anguished commemorative gestures that immediately followed. For instance, the use of Auschwitz in Poland as a model for dealing with the buildings of the ESMA, often called "Argentina's Auschwitz" and now emptied. With the return of democracy, Latin American culture makers turned to the Shoah too as a precedent for understanding what had happened, for seeing who had resisted, and for finding antecedents in intellectuals such as Borges, whose "Deutsches Requiem" is probably the most important Latin American Holocaust fiction from the Shoah era itself; in Clarice Lispector, who tended to wounded Brazilian soldiers fighting with the Allies in Italy and skewered programs of purity in her *crônicas* and fiction; in Alberto Gerchunoff, who gave up his health and his imaginings to make the Shoah known in Argentina's press as the genocide was happening; in João Guimarães Rosa, a junior consul in Hamburg, who helped Jews escape, defying his superiors and creating a language countering Nazism; and in Lucila Godoy / Gabriela Mistral, a tough-as-nails diplomat in Europe, who assisted Jewish and other refugees, denounced Nazism in Chile and pro-Nazi Chilean diplomatic functionaries, and wrote naked poetry and prose about the war and the catastrophe.

It is no accident that Victor Farías, the Chilean scholar who stirred up the contemporary debate about Heidegger and Nazism, quotes Mistral repeatedly in his mammoth study *Los nazis en Chile* (2000), written after he fled his Augusto Pinochet dictatorship-controlled homeland; in it Farías meticulously documents the extent of Nazi penetration in the southern land, including in the diplomatic corps, mostly antisemitic and profascist. Mistral is cited as a strong countervoice and example for the present.

Nor is it a coincidence that another exiled Chilean, Roberto Bolaño, finds inspiration in Borges's "fantasies" for his much-acclaimed novel *La literatura nazi en América* (1996). The book takes the form of a fictitious encyclopedia of right-wing "luminaries," with each entry containing the biography of a prose maker or poet sympathetic to Nazism. In the manner of Borges the lines between fact and fiction are blurred, as Bolaño digs his sharp, satiric knife into the rotten belly of local fascism, then and today.

Neither is it happenstance that Argentine writer and philosopher José Pablo Feinmann, who meditates on the implications of the ESMA as his country's "Auschwitz" in books and essays, cites Borges in his thriller *La sombra de Heidegger* (In the Shadow of Heidegger; 2005), where the abominable occurrences of 1930s and 1940s Germany are connected, bridge-like, to the atrocious circumstances of 1970s Argentina in the form of a written father-son exchange. Dieter Müller, the father, a student of the Freiburg philosopher and a Nazi escaped to Argentina, pens an extended suicide note to his offspring, an apologia pro vita sua in the manner of Borges's Otto Dietrich zur Linde; the younger man, in turn, tells how he visits the Nazi sage in Germany in the late 1960s in order to try to understand his father's past, only to have to escape later from the Argentine "Reich," as Feinmann labels it, back to the Germany. Feinmann tries to exorcise the ghosts of fascism so as to build a democratic state.

Finally, it comes as no surprise that the prominent Argentine historian Andrés Bisso gives Alberto Gerchunoff and his fiery articles a place of honor in his mammoth study *El antifascismo argentino* (2007). Bisso, part of the twenty-first-century intellectual movement to resist the weight of fascism, real and imagined, counters the vision of a merely nazified Latin American continent, as I have tried to do throughout this book. With some two hundred documents from the *anti*fascist groups and writings, he evidences a permanent antifascist mobilization, quoting Gerchunoff: "El señor Hitler es una expresión del satanismo. Es Satán. Y Satán no triunfa" (Mr. Hitler is the embodiment of Satanism. He is Satan. And Satan doesn't win) (79).

The Nazis may have gone to Argentina, but the anti-Nazis were there, then and now.

Notes

Preface: Didn't All the Nazis Go to Argentina?

1. For instance, a front-page article in the *New York Times* about a major Nazi death doctor, Aribert Heim, hiding in Cairo, Egypt, still reaffirmed the trope: "While the secret lives of Nazis in countries like Argentina and Paraguay captured the popular imagination in books and films like *The Odessa File* and *The Boys from Brazil*, the Heim case casts light on the often overlooked history of their flight to the Middle East . . . ex-Nazis were welcomed in Egypt." Souad Mekhennet and Nicholas Kulish, "Uncovering Lost Path of the Most Wanted Nazi," *New York Times*, February 4, 2009.

2. One of the best-known modern studies of mimesis, understood as a form of realism, is Auerbach's *Mimesis: The Representation of Reality in Western Literature*, which opens with a famous comparison between the way the world is represented in Homer's *Odyssey* and the way it appears in the Bible. From these two seminal Western texts, Auerbach builds the foundation for a unified theory of representation that spans the entire history of Western literature.

1. "Deutsches Requiem": Jorge Luis Borges "Represents" the Shoah

1. Ocampo befriended Jewish intellectuals like the American Waldo Frank, a germinal figure in the *Sur* constellation; helped Jews escape from the Nazis (one was the German-Jewish photographer Gisèle Freund); witnessed and reported on the Nuremberg Trials; and, highlighting the plight of Spanish Republicans and European Jews, provided a supportive context for all stripe of antifascist writers, prominently Borges. (She still never could condemn her former lover, the later French Nazi collaborator Pierre Drieu La Rochelle.)

On pro-Jewish writings in *Sur*, see Aizenberg, *Aleph Weaver*, 32–34. Among these were Waldo Frank's "¿Por qué ha de sobrevivir el judío?" (Why Should the Jew Survive? May 1934) and "El judío en el futuro de América" (The Jew in America's Future; February 1941); reports on the suffering of German Jews in concentration camps (February 1939); and Giuliana Tedeschi's testimony on Auschwitz (June 1946).

2. Rosalie Sitman's astute study of the "grupo *Sur*" details how its pro-Spanish Republicanism and philosemitism was at once "a humanitarian response to the horrific crimes being committed in Europe" and a "rhetorical" leitmotif intended to position the journal within the intellectual and political domestic front as against everything

the right wing stood for (Sitman, 151; see also 134). In 1942, when first place for Argentina's National Literary Prize was predictably handed out to a second-rate nationalist novel of rural gaucho realism, with Borges's first story collection, *El jardin de senderos que se bifrucan* (*The Garden of Forking Paths*), relegated to second place, Ocampo—who had published the book—not only put together a protest issue but boldly continued opening the journal's pages to his essays and fiction, including "Deutsches Requiem."

3. The scathing story "Monsterfest" ("La fiesta del monstruo"), which Borges wrote jointly in a heightened version of Buenos Aires *lunfardo* slang with his frequent collaborator, Adolfo Bioy Casares, under the pseudonym H. Bustos Domecq, expressed this sentiment with a vengeance, portraying a bookish Jewish student murdered savagely by an animalistic Peronist mob. Such texts, which could only be published after Perón's demise in 1955, didn't endear Borges to a younger generation of "Third Worlders" for whom Perón and Evita meant hope for the underdogs, and even societal openings for minorities like Jews (Fló, 187; see also Rein, and chapter 3, on Gerchunoff, for more on Perón, fascism, and the Jews).

4. On Alazraki's own connection to the Holocaust and its consequences see his autobiographical "La escalera de Elías."

5. On the Book of Job as significant in post-Holocaust theology, relevant to the thinking of Richard Rubenstein, Emil Fackenheim, Elie Wiesel, and others, see Morgan, *Beyond Auschwitz*, and Friedlander, *Out of the Whirlwind*.

6. On the controversy surrounding the revelations see Lehman and Barish. My thanks to Professor De Graef for providing me further information.

7. For an important study on Eichmann's capture see Rein. See also Bettina Stangneth's *Eichmann before Jerusalem* for a contemporary take on Eichmann's Argentine years.

8. These questions began to gnaw at the Argentine body politic and infiltrated the intellectual arena. The process of coming to terms has been slow but steady, and it is still going on. For example: in 1997 the Argentine government at last created (was forced to create?) a Commission to Clarify Nazi Activities in Argentina (CEANA), whose final report included a long section on the Nazi impact on Argentine literature and the cultural field, seamlessly moving from what was written pro and contra during the Hitler era and up till the present day, with Borges's anti-Nazism figuring prominently (see Sosnowski and Senkman (2009).

9. "Ante la fácil condena por las primeras declaraciones de Borges sobre Videla, la condecoración que aceptara de Pinochet y opiniones que seguramente compartían el deseo de escandalizar, conviene recordar que firmó una solicitada de la Madres la Plaza de Mayo y condenó a la dictadura, como también lo hiciera frente a la guerra de la Malvinas en su poema 'Juan López y John Ward'" (Sosnowski, 80). See also Juan Gelman's comments: "A diferencia de otros intelectuales, que nunca supieron reconocer sus agachadas frente a la dictadura militar, Borges reconoció sus errores" (334).

10. Just a few among them: Griselda Gambaro's *Información para extranjeros* (Information for Foreigners; 1973), a "guided tour" of places of torture; Abel Posse's *El*

viajero de Agartha (The Agartha Traveler; 1989), based on the Nazi Tibet expeditions searching for the font of the "Aryan" race; Daniel Guebel's *Adiós Mein Führer* (Goodbye My Führer; 1999); Roberto di Marco's *El fantasma del Reich* (The Phantom of the Reich; 1994); Marcos Aguinis's *La martiz del infierno* (Hell's Womb; 1997), all about the Nazi Germany–Argentina associations; Tomás Eloy Martínez's *El cantor de tango* (The Tango Singer; 2004), with Borges's Buenos Aires geography of terror redux for the late twentieth century; José Pablo Feinmann's *La sombra de Heidegger* (Heidegger's Shadow; 2005); and Patricio Pron's *El comienzo de la primavera* (Spring Awakening; 2008), dealing with two Argentines' Borgesian search for the philosopher-sage of Freiburg, his controversial Nazism, and with philosophy as a *political act* and politics as a *philosophical act*.

11. Heidegger's thought was brought to Argentina in the 1930s. The fifth issue of *Sur*, published in summer 1932, contained a Spanish translation of Heidegger's influential essay "Was ist Metaphysik?" ("¿Qué es metafísica?" or "What Is Metaphysics?"), followed by a not entirely laudatory analysis, "Martin Heidegger ante la sombra de Dostoiewsky" (Martin Heidegger Confronts Dostoyevsky's Ghost), from the pen of the Romanian-French-Jewish poet-thinker Benjamin Fondane. Borges's essay "El arte narrativo y la magia" (Narrative Art and Magic) appeared in the same issue. The German phenomenologist's main Argentine spokesman was Carlos Astrada, who had studied with the "master" himself in Freiburg, was part of the original *Sur* group together with Borges, and wrote on Heidegger's ideas in *Sur*, again sharing pages with Borges (Astrada: "De Kierkegaard a Heidegger"; Borges: "Lawrence y la Odisea" —both in October 1936).

By the 1940s Astrada had adopted an increasingly nationalistic, antisemitic posture, and his adhesion to Heidegger earned him the same Nazi label locally. As his detractors headlined it in a 1942 article: "Heidegger, filósofo oficial nazi, y su alumno Carlos Astrada" (Heidegger, Official Philosopher of Nazism and His Student Carlos Astrada) (Flaumbaum and Rodríguez, quoted in Alemán). As for Borges, he expressed no love for Heidegger's nihilistic and immoral philosophy that plays with desperation and anguish, in comments published in 1951 (*OC*, 749).

Borges's "Guayaquil" (1970), a story about the vagaries of nationality, hero worship, and national memory, gives Heidegger a central role. Speaking of Eduardo Zimmermann, his fictional German-Jewish historian escaped to Argentina from the Third Reich, and the refugee scholar's argument against demagogic government and the cult of personality, Borges has the Freiburg thinker refute Zimmermann: Here is Borges on Zimmermann: "[His] argument was refuted by Martin Heidegger, who with the help of photocopied newspaper headlines decisively proved that the modern head of state, far from being anonymous, is rather the lead player, the choragos, the dancing David who enacts his people's drama, with all the paraphernalia of staged pageantry, and the unhesitating manipulation of hyperbolically exaggerated rhetoric. Heidegger likewise showed that Zimmermann was of Hebrew, not to say Jewish, extraction. The publication of this essay by the venerated existentialist was the direct cause of our guest's exodus and subsequent nomadic adventures" (*OC*, 1063; see also Farías 1987; and see Wolin and Faye, 8).

12. In his analysis of the tale Jason Wilson opines that Borges isn't a "proto-Holocaust writer, rather a propounder of lucidity." Alfonso de Toro, mimicking decades-old critiques of "Deutsches Requiem," with shades of Wheelock and Sturrock, asserts that its sister story, "El milagro secreto," isn't about the Nazi invasion of Prague, or the persecution of Jews, or the role of art in the face of annihilation, but about "existential problems" such as anguish, identity, and the psychological state and feelings on confronting imminent death (Wilson, 119; de Toro, 161).

De Toro, a respected critic of Latin American literature, demonstrates ignorance of the body of criticism on Holocaust representation, failing to even mention names such as Lang, Friedländer, and Langer. Other scholars, Louis, for instance, share the same gap.

13. I had the unsettling experience of reading an actual copy of the now-rare book at the Kupferberg Holocaust Resource Center and Archive in New York. The intensity of the red and black script spewing out the words, and the sharply colored graphics, was shivering: blond and muscled "Aryans" versus obese, dark, fez-wearing Jews (Borges pointed out the absurdity of this particular depiction), and happy little straw-haired children looking up to, giving flowers to, and "Heil Hitler" saluting a uniformed Julius Streicher. It was worsened by the calm, business-is-business normality of the final page: "Alle Rechte vorgehalten [all rights reserved], Copyright 1936 by Stürmer-Verlag Nürnberg. Printed in Germany."

2. Besieged in Berne: Clarice Lispector and the Murmur of Catastrophe

1. For full information on the diplomat's heroism during the war, see the website of the Sousa Mendes Foundation. It contains a list of those known to have received visas from the diplomat and his staff, among whom is a member of my family.

2. With the help of director Eliane Vasconcelos, I found an original in the Lispector Archive in Rio de Janeiro, without indication of where it was published, only the handwritten date.

3. See *Stefan and Lotte Zweig's South American Letters* (Davis and Marshall) for the couple's views on Brazil. An example from one of Zweig's letters: "The neighborhood is very primitive and therefore pitoresque [*sic*], the poor people are so nice here as you cannot imagine; our black housemaid is silent . . . diligent, clean . . . and it is the inborn civilization and humanity I admire so much here in this country. . . ." (March 10, 1941; 144).

4. Among the Latin Americans, Borges and Guimarães Rosa listened as well about the same years, hearing and simulating, Borges in "Deutsches Requiem," with the Nazi war criminal's manic embrace of Spengler's "essentially German [*kerndeutsch*] and military spirit," and Guimarães Rosa in "A Velha," where the Führer's raspy, rabid voice spews forth the venom of "racial purity" from the radio, *a voz de Hitler ao rádio —rouco, ravioso* (*Ave palabra*, 108; Borges, *Labyrinths*, 142).

5. Elisa Lispector's novel *No Exilio* (In Exile; 1948) addresses her Jewish roots openly. A thinly veiled autobiography, the novel tells of her family's travails on the way to Brazil, their difficult life on arrival, the Jewish tragedy in midcentury in Europe, and the creation of the State of Israel. The book is often used to fill the gaps in Clarice's "hidden" Jewish biography, but I have chosen not to use it in this way. Elisa Lispector published novels, short stories, and journalistic articles, but this is the only novel that deals directly with her Jewish background.

3. Good-bye Jewish Gaucho: Alberto Gerchunoff, Anti-Nazi

1. The Central Union of Polish Jewry published 175 books in Yiddish in Buenos Aires between 1946 and 1966. The collection was under the direction of Marc Turkow, a prominent journalist who wrote for the important Warsaw Yiddish daily *Der Moment*. After immigrating to Argentina in 1939, Turkow assumed significant communal and editorial positions. The book series he initiated, called Dos poylishe yidentum (Polish Jewry), was one of the most important editorial memorial projects undertaken by world Jewry in the Second World War's immediate aftermath. It fell under the category of what is known as Khurban Literatur, Literature of Destruction—memoirs, novels, diaries, and poetry that chronicle the history and demise of Europe's Jews.

The series contained works by experienced writers and by novices, both inside and outside Argentina. Many were by survivors, as was the case with Wiesel. The cover illustrations, themselves significant acts of memory, were largely by immigrant or survivor artists (see Chinski).

2. My initial study on the Jewish gauchos (1977) already began to focus on the contradiction between Gerchunoff's early celebration of the cowboy figure and his later denunciation of the pampas horseman. This shifting view was not generally recognized by critics. My research then was conducted under the guidance of the late Prof. Ana María Barrenechea. I dedicate this chapter to her memory.

3. During the period of the Spanish Civil War and World War II, Manuel Kantor's (1911–1983) political illustrations and cartoons appeared in Buenos Aires newspapers and were collected into a book, *De Munich a Nuremberg* (1946). Clément Moreau praised Kantor in introductory words to the book as a creator for whom art doesn't only imply questions of form but also responsibility toward humanity (10).

4. Antonio "Toño" Salazar (1897–1986) had a distinguished career as an illustrator-cartoonist. He worked with Diego Rivera in Mexico, participated in the Paris artistic bohemian scene, and spent the war years in Buenos Aires working for *Argentina Libre*. After years abroad he was named to El Salvador's diplomatic service. (For more details see Mixco.) Clément Moreau, born Carl Joseph Meffert (1903–1988), militated in favor of socialism and, after escaping from the Gestapo, was active in anti-Hitler German exile groups in Buenos Aires, as well as in Argentine antifascist circles. His cartoons appeared both in German- and Spanish-language publications. He drew two important anti-Nazi series (1937–1938), which were proto-graphic novels (*Mein Kampf*, an illustrated sarcastic life of Hitler, and *La comedia humana* or *Noche sobre*

Alemania [Night over Germany]). They were published in the *Argentinisches Tageblatt* and reproduced with minor variations in *Argentina Libre* (1940).

The artist ultimately settled in Zurich and in 1984 set up a foundation dedicated to preserving and exhibiting his works and to supporting artists who shared his vision of fighting for human rights with their pen.

4. Diplomacy, Literature, Rescue: João Guimarães Rosa, Consul in Hamburg

1. The coordinated attacks by SA and SS units shattered not only the synagogues and apartments but also the business quarter near Hamburg's city hall, crushing storefronts, plundering stocks, and filling the nearby Alster canal (the Alster is Hamburg's river) with ruined mannequins and merchandise. Such organized pillage and humiliation of respected fellow businesspeople shook even the non-Jewish Hamburger bourgeoisie's sense of property and propriety, and some dared to opine that it should trouble the entire citizenry. What unstoppable, virulent whirlwind has been unleashed over their country, with their acquiescence?

2. Luis Martins de Souza Dantes, who used every loophole to help Jews leave Vichy France, issuing doctored visas hiding their recipients' Jewishness, did so in the face of contrary instructions from the Foreign Ministry, at great personal cost. (In one of her letters Clarice Lispector, who had met Souza Dantes after the war, called him a wonderful person.)

3. My thanks to Professor Otte for sharing a copy of the diary with me.

4. Teresa Montero's comments about Clarice Lispector, comments that I cited in chapter 2, on the author of *The Besieged City*, apply in part to Guimarães Rosa as well: today we value an author's manuscripts, "incomplete" versions and perversions, along with "finished" literary creations, because as private documents they reveal stages of a creative process, and unlock moments of personal and public lived experience (*Minhas queridas*, 15).

5. "Greater Germany" (*Grossdeutschesreich*) was one of the key words of Hitlerism, as Klemperer explains, the religiously coded term harking back to the Teutonic Holy Roman Empire, and the euphemism that masked the occupation of country after country and the "most criminal of all wars" (109).

6. ". . . e se potessi racchiudere in una immagine tutto il male del nostro tempo, sceglierei questa immagine, che mi è familiare: un uomo scarno, dalla fronte china e dalle spalle curve, sul cui volto e nei cui occhi non si possa leggere traccia di pensiero . . ." (Levi 1987, 92).

5. Not Just Children's Poetry: Gabriela Mistral, Consul in Nice

1. See Galleguillos Rojo (1941). The thesis appeared in a series of scholarly monographs published by the University of Hamburg.

2. These letters are from the Gabriela Mistral Collection in the Library of Congress. I will be using this collection extensively in this chapter.

3. Taylor has published an updated edition of his book under the title *Gabriela*

Mistral's Struggle with God and Man (2012), in which he ably takes up much new bibliography, new information, and the controversial issues that have surfaced in Mistral criticism since the 1970s, including her private life. The analysis of "Al pueblo hebreo," however, remains about the same, and repeats the line on scant documentary value (119). (The whole approach to Judaism has an antiquarian flavor, with clichés about the Old Testament God of Wrath versus the New Testament God of Benevolence [136] and the immobility of Jewish belief vis-à-vis the liquidity of Christian faith.) The major *aggiornamento* can be found in the brief introduction to Mistral's Spanish-language lecture on the Bible that Taylor includes in his book (there is no English translation). Taylor notes that Mistral's speech, given in Argentina, a country—he simplifies somewhat—of "emigrant Jews and Christian Germans," can also be seen as her positing Scripture as a unifying thread in "combating fascism, since it is given when militarized Germany threatened Europe and persecuted Jews" (228). In the context of the long and considered revaluation in other areas of Mistral criticism, the failure to more fully rethink her powerful stance and in-your-face writing on *contemporary* Jews is disappointing.

4. Another word on Chilean "impartiality": in point of fact, many sectors in the southern republic, including the previously mentioned Partido Nacista, had an exceedingly chummy relationship with Nazi Germany, minutely dissected in books such as Victor Farías's *Los nazis in Chile* and Graeme S. Mount's *Chile and the Nazis: From Hitler to Pinochet*.

5. A letter from Curtius that I found in the Mistral archive at the Library of Congress says much the same thing, but with the epistolary pathos of personal petition: "Nous sommes sortis sains et saufs de la catastrophe, ma femme et moi. L'année 45 a eté dure. Mais depuis, je me suis repris et j'ai pu mener à bien un livre volumineaux que résume 15 ans d'étude. Il doit paraître en 48." (My wife and I survived the catastrophe safe and sound. Nineteen forty-five was hard. But since then I'm back to myself and I've been able to complete a huge book that sums up fifteen years of study. It should appear in 1948.) He then asks Mistral, who had offered any possible help after being cut off from the professor during the war, if she could get chocolates for his wife and cigarettes for him (October 11, 1948).

6. Among these are Charles Péguy's *Le mystere de Saints Innocents* (1912), Maurice Barrès's *Les diverses familles spirituelles de la France* (1940), and Robert Brasillach's *Anthologie de la poésie grecque* (1950); Mistral also owned Curtius's *Essai sur la France* (1932), the French translation of *Die Französische Kulture* (*Catalog of the Gabriela Mistral Collection*, 1978).

7. This isn't the only place in Mistral: an essay published in *El Mercurio* on Christmas Eve, 1949, bluntly says that Christ's feast exerts a fascination on believers and nonbelievers of every "sect" except the Jews, hardheaded as a horn and impermeable as slate ("excepto la judía, testaruda como un cuerno, y sin permeabilidad posible, como piedra-pizarra") (*Antología Mayor*, Vol. 2: 301).

8. In this sense I do not entirely agree with Joseph R. Slaughter's fine essay on

Mistral's conception of culture, human rights, and, later, genocide, when he says that her "faith in the capacity of culture . . . is too unproblematic given the history of the twentieth century" (Slaughter, 42). On the contrary, she "problematized" this faith exactly at one of the most stinking moments of the mid-1900s.

9. Rosenstein's life and work have been researched, with related documents available from the German Museum and Urology Archive in Cologne (see Moll, Krischel, Rathert, and Fangerau).

10. Rosenstein's very title identifies his book as a narrative of rupture, part of the nature of refugee memoirs, which are now receiving more attention alongside writings by former concentration camp inmates, long considered the "true" Holocaust survivors. In these exile testimonies, an old world has been lost and a new world frightfully approached, but—a surgeon would know this well—damage and disfigurement endure. After recounting his comfortable pre-Hitler life Rosenstein narrates the immense personal, professional, and material toll that becoming a hounded second-class citizen entails. After his wanderings to escape the brown beast, Brazil finally becomes the "neue Heimat," new home (land), as Rosenstein recounts the negative and positive aspects of his first days in Rio. Only a few pages earlier he had described the anomie, despite everything, of leaving the beloved "alten Heimat" (old homeland) and the bitter tears shed at a forced run for life into the unknown at the ripe age of sixty-three. (The German concept of "Heimat," love and attachment to the native soil, isn't quite conveyed by the English.)

11. In the typescript version of *Lagar II* the original title is "Poema de los judíos." Mistral crossed out "judíos" and replaced it with "hebreos" (Gabriela Mistral Papers, Library of Congress, Reel EE1).

12. Mistral was instrumental in fighting for the ratification by member states of the UN Convention on the Prevention and Punishment of the Crime of Genocide, adopted by the General Assembly in 1948.

Index

References to specific works will be found under the author.
Page numbers in *italics* indicate illustrations.

COVER ILLUSTRATION: Diego Rivera, *Nazi Kultur*, from the mural series Portrait of America, New Workers' School, New York, 1933.

Rivera pointedly arranged his painting around the words "Nazi Kultur" at the center, immediately above Adolf Hitler, who is portrayed ranting on the radio. On the bottom left the white-haired head of Albert Einstein shows through, symbol of the Nazi drive against science and critical thought; next to him is the tortured body of a Jew and the shaved top of a Christian woman punished for sleeping with a "non-Aryan." Right near her glares the ominous Hermann Goering, Hitler's deputy and a heresiarch of the Holocaust. Scenes of torture, beatings, book burnings, Nazi marches, and hands raised in the Nazi salute fill the rest of the tightly worked space.

Rivera painted the frescoes of Portrait of America on movable panels in the run-down quarters of the New Workers' School, a training center of the Communist Party USA. A lifelong Communist, he undertook the project after the murals he had been commissioned to paint at Rockefeller Center in 1932 were destroyed, among other reasons, for including a portrait of the Communist revolutionary Vladimir Lenin.